P9-BYH-468

The
Home Run
Heard 'Round
the World

Also by Ray Robinson

IRON HORSE: LOU GEHRIG IN HIS TIME
OH, BABY, I LOVE IT! with Tim McCarver

The Home Run Heard 'Round the World

THE DRAMATIC STORY OF THE 1951 GIANTS–DODGERS PENNANT RACE

RAY ROBINSON

HarperCollins*Publishers*

Excerpt from "You Can't Get There from Here," by Ogden Nash. Copyright 1955 by Ogden Nash. Copyright © renewed in 1983 by Frances Nash, Isabel Nash Eberstadt and Linnell Nash Smith. By permission of Little, Brown & Company.

THE HOME RUN HEARD 'ROUND THE WORLD. Copyright © 1991 by Ray Robinson. All rights reserved. Printed in the United States of America. No part of this book may be used or reproduced in any manner whatsoever without written permission except in the case of brief quotations embodied in critical articles and reviews. For information address HarperCollins Publishers, 10 East 53rd Street, New York, NY 10022.

FIRST EDITION

Designed by Alma Orenstein

Library of Congress Cataloging-in-Publication Data

Robinson, Ray
   The home run heard 'round the world / Ray Robinson.—1st ed.
     p.   cm.
   Includes bibliographical references.
   ISBN 0-06-016477-8
   1. New York Giants (Baseball team)—History. 2. Brooklyn Dodgers (Baseball team)—History. I. Title.
   GV875.N42R63 1991
   796.357'64'097471—dc20   90-55551

91 92 93 94 95 AC/HC 10 9 8 7 6 5 4 3 2 1

For NANCY, born in 1951,
and a Willie Mays fan from the start

Contents

Illustrations follow page 84

Acknowledgments

IN AN EFFORT to recapture the drama of the 1951 baseball season, I spoke to many of the most important participants, primary and peripheral. In that gracious and cooperative group were Wes Westrum, Andy Pafko, Al Dark, Bobby Thomson, Don Mueller, Sal Yvars, Willie Mays, George Spencer, Carl Erskine, Roy Campanella, Bill Rigney, Larry Jansen, Jim Hearn, Clyde Sukeforth, Rocky Bridges, Sheldon Jones, Wayne Terwilliger, Rachel Robinson, Red Barber, Ernie Harwell, Vin Scully, Rube Walker, Pee Wee Reese, Clem Labine, Barney Stein, Monte Irvin, Herman Franks, Frank Slocum, Irving Rudd, Charles Einstein, Warren Cowan, Dr. David L. Wu, Harold Rosenthal, and the late Bill Terry.

The library of the New York *Daily News*, made available to me through the kindness of Faigi Rosenthal, was invaluable, as were the bound copies of the *New York Times*. *Sports Illustrated*'s library, presided over by Peter Miller and Linda Levine, was a repository of 1951 arcanum. The columns of such journalists as Red Smith of the New York *Herald Tribune*, Larry Merchant of the New York *Post*, Dan Parker of the New York *Daily Mirror*, and Arthur Daley of the *New York Times* were a helpful delight.

Many books provided an excellent overview of the events of the 1951 season:

The Baseball Encyclopedia by Joseph Reichler
Willie's Time by Charles Einstein
Baseball's 25 Greatest Pennant Races by Lowell Reidenbaugh
The Incredible Giants by Tom Meany
Baseball's Great Experiment by Jules Tygiel
I Never Had It Made by Jackie Robinson, with Al Duckett
The Miracle of Coogan's Bluff by Thomas Kiernan
Voices of the Game by Curt Smith
Bums by Peter Golenbock
My Giants by Russ Hodges, with Al Hirshberg
Tuned to Baseball by Ernie Harwell
The Giants and the Dodgers by Lee Allen
New York City Baseball by Harvey Frommer
Esquire's Great Men and Moments in Sports
Farewell to Heroes by Frank Graham, Jr.
Born to Play Ball by Charles Einstein
Baseball Has Done It by Jackie Robinson, with Charles Dexter
The New York Giants by Frank Graham
Baseball in the 1950's by Donald Honig
Mays, Mantle and Snider by Donald Honig
Day with the Giants by Laraine Day
Nice Guys Finish Last by Leo Durocher, with Ed Linn
Wait 'Til Next Year by Christopher Jennison
The Ball Parks by Bill Shannon and George Kalinsky
Red—a Biography of Red Smith by Ira Berkow
When Brooklyn Was the World by Elliot Willensky
The Greatest Dodgers of Them All by Steve Gelman
The Boys of Summer by Roger Kahn
The Ball Players, edited by Mike Shatzkin

I owe special thanks to Buz Wyeth, a kind and insightful editor, and to my agent, Jay Acton, a true baseball aficionado, who gave enthusiastic support for this project.

The final lap in the life of any book is the Xerox machine. For the unstinting use of Bob Witten's Xerox, handled by Marianna Sorshek, I am very grateful.

Ray Robinson
June 1990

Now it is done. Now the story ends . . . the art of
fiction is dead. Reality has strangled invention . . .

Red Smith, reporting from the
scene on October 3, 1951

How the muscles bulge
in his sweatshirt,
How his heart with hope
is full.
When the manager beckons the bullpen
to send him another bull!
How he mutters a silent prayer,
Lord, let me be that bull . . .

Ogden Nash, in "You Can't Get
There from Here," 1953

1951

IT WAS THE SUMMER OF 1951, a half dozen years after America's four-time President, Franklin D. Roosevelt, had slept the night away in Warm Springs, Georgia, and a nuclear device had devastated Hiroshima, hastening the end of World War II. The hero of that war, General Dwight D. Eisenhower, had, as a young cadet, roamed the outfield for West Point's baseball team, but in 1951 he hadn't yet made clear whether he was a Democrat or Republican, frustrating those who wanted him to run some place other than on a diamond.

It was a time when President Harry S Truman (to his detractors the middle initial stood for nothing, which is exactly how little they thought of him) hunkered down in the White House, encircled by fierce enemies, led by the whiskey-belting, dyspeptic Joe McCarthy, who hissed that most of Truman's cronies were Communists, near Communists, or traitors.

"I have here in my hand a list," Senator McCarthy darkly hinted, as he waved sheets of paper in front of the camera that had nothing more on them than shopping-reminder doodles from his girlfriend. A confused country quailed and buckled under his insinuations, for he had virtually made it un-American to dye your hair red, cheer for the despicably named Cincinnati Reds, or garnish a salad with Russian dressing.

In such a paranoid environment, Julius and Ethel Rosenberg, dreary and vulnerable targets, were sentenced to death for espionage against the United States. When they appeared as benumbed black-and-white figures in the newsreels, there was a bloodthirsty reaction in the movie theaters, for the country's marrow had been chilled by the cold war. In polls taken that year a clear majority of Americans said they backed prosecutions of Communist party members, even if by that time the party was composed of a tiny number of pathetic dissidents.

"I guess that we'll always remember the fifties as the time when the cold war overshadowed everything," Harry Truman said in his clipped Missouri voice.

Only days before the 1951 baseball season began, and while the much-argued Korean War still raged, Truman nervelessly removed the seventy-one-year-old five-star general Douglas MacArthur from his Far East command. As a result, cries to impeach the president fouled the air. Midst such rancor and public distemper, General MacArthur came marching home, to be met by adults and little children in the streets waving American flags in tumultuous receptions that dwarfed even the grandiose productions of Hollywood's Cecil B. DeMille. General MacArthur was a man "of great professional ability," Secretary of Defense James Forrestal had said earlier, "but mortgaged to his sensitivity and vanity."

In New York, the site of one of these MacArthur galas, the once ubiquitous mayor Fiorello LaGuardia had been gone from the corridors of City Hall since 1945. His current successor was Vincent Impellitteri, a name the newspapermen happily shortened to Impy, a memorable nickname for an unmemorable man. When MacArthur came to town it appeared as if all of the city's 8 million people (2,738,900 from Brooklyn, 1,960,000 from Manhattan) were massed in the streets, hailing their defiance of Truman.

In 1951 James Jones's gritty war novel *From Here to Eternity* was on the best-seller list. So was Herman Wouk's absorbing celebration of navy rectitude, *The Caine Mutiny*. J. D. Salinger's *The Catcher in the Rye*, which had absolutely nothing to do with either baseball or booze, was also on the list. Two autobiographies, *His Eye Is on the Sparrow*, relating the life of the black American singer and actress Ethel Waters, and *A King's Story*, concerning the life of a white British king, the Duke of Windsor, appeared in the nation's bookstores. *South Pacific* was in its second year on Broadway, with Mary Martin, while *Guys and Dolls* was making columnist Damon Runyon popular again. Male baldness was becoming popular, too, thanks to Yul Brynner, who was starring nightly in *The King and I.*

Advertisers for Lucky Strike cigarettes weren't required to warn folks that they'd get heart disease or cancer if they smoked, and celebrities such as Edgar Bergen, Jack Benny, Fred Waring, Dave Garroway, and Bob Hope trotted out the superlatives for General Electric's Black Daylite Television (prices ranging from $249.95 to $775). Royal was the number-one portable typewriter, Philly cigars were a nickel, and color TV was introduced for the first time, causing movie producer Sam Goldwyn to remark that "I'll believe it when I see it in black and white."

Rexall Drugs laughed along with Amos 'n' Andy in its ads, using two white men to play blacks, an atavistic reminder of Al Jolson, who painted on a black face to sing "Swanee" in the twenties. June Allyson ebulliently praised Jergens Lotion because it kept her hands soft, certainly to the liking of her husband, crooner-actor Dick Powell.

France's World War II Nazi puppet, Henri Pétain, died of old age, and Juan Perón remained the hero of Argentina's *descamisados*, winning reelection as the country's President.

In that summer of 1951 many big-league baseball players still maintained that they would play for the sheer joy of it, much as fabled old-timers such as Walter Johnson, Wahoo Sam Crawford, and Rabbit Maranville once claimed that they did.

Only ten years earlier a tiny shortstop from the New York area, Phil Rizzuto, was signed by the Yankees for little more than a bologna sandwich and a glass of milk, for which Phil expressed his humble gratitude. Baseball fans continued to recall that Babe Ruth, dead only since 1948, had often wondered out loud why anyone would actually "pay me to play ball," the implication being that he would have swung his oversized bat for damn near nothing. It would be more realistic to point out, however, that not all players of those years, including Ruth, were simpleminded altruists. After all, immediately following World War II, when Jorge Pasquel, a Mexican multimillionaire, dangled mucho dinero in the faces of disaffected players, more than a few of them were lured south of the border to the Mexican League. One of these disgruntled mercenaries was a Giants pitcher, Sal Maglie.

"They offered to double my salary of eight thousand dollars to sixteen thousand," Maglie recalled. "I was not sorry I went. I not only made good money for two years, but I learned how to pitch."

Players in 1951 did, indeed, still play on green mattresses of grass. They would run, throw, hit and spit on playing fields that were *really* fields. Who ever heard of players in those days lifting weights to build their muscles and their home run totals? And did anyone ever hear then of mysterious split-fingered fastballs or intimidating agents unafraid to throw legalistic spitballs at owners! The designated hitter was also a debasing invention whose time had not yet come.

Forty years ago there were only 16 million television sets in America and candy bars and ice cream cones could be bought for a nickel. Ballplayers incubated for the majors at any one of 450 minor league sites, and nonpareil Ted Williams showed the world how to hit for a bit more than $100,000, a week's pay for the .240 hitters and nine-game winners of today. Ralph Kiner, the National League home run champion, made only $65,000, certainly enough to chaperone Elizabeth Taylor on dates but pocket money compared to the income of baseball's millionaires of 1991. A total of $4.5 million in bonuses was paid out to the wunderkinder of the 1950s, that sum equaling the salaries paid to players on sixteen teams. In all of major league baseball the gross income was 65 million dollars, hardly enough today to purchase the game's most enfeebled franchise.

2

The Feud

IN 1951 NEW YORK BASEBALLDOM was divided into three parts.

There were the lordly grand seigneur Yankees, at Yankee Stadium in the Bronx, born to win and to win again. Soaring into primacy in the Roaring Twenties via Babe's and Lou's higher-than-heaven homers, they were now presided over by that weathered mangler of the English language, Casey Stengel.

In the borough of Manhattan were the traditionalist, haughty Giants, descendants of churlish John McGraw, the sainted Christy Mathewson, and Master Melvin Ott and at present led by that kinetic transplant from Flatbush, Leo Durocher.

In Brooklyn were the snappish, klutzy, sometimes tragicomic Bums, whose owner, Walter O'Malley, knew, as any Irishman would, that life is ultimately going to break your heart. "Remember," O'Malley once said, "that half the lies they tell about the Dodgers aren't true."

The Yankees played in the triple-tiered Yankee Stadium, with its ineffable façade and cornices. When it opened in April 1923, the Stadium was appropriately christened with a mighty Ruthian home run, in the first game ever played there. Once over 80,000 people, violating every fire law of the city of New York, jammed into the cavernous place for a double header. That never happened again. But crowds of 50,000 or more became commonplace as the years went by. A short right-field fence in the Stadium, some 295 feet down the line, was custom-made for such left-handed sluggers as Ruth and Gehrig. But center field was an endless pasture, where only flawless defensive performers, possibly a Combs, DiMaggio, or Mantle, could be expected to perform minor miracles in hauling down fly balls.

The Giants, who played at the horseshoe-shaped Polo Grounds starting in 1891, were still at home there in 1951. It was at the Polo Grounds that John McGraw's cocky teams succeeded in turning "Harlem into heaven."

The oldest of the three metropolitan teams, the New York Mutuals were charter members of the National League in 1876. They were thrown out for a year, only to return in 1883. In 1885 the club's president, Jim Mutrie, dubbed his team the Giants for the first time, and the label stuck.

During the long reign of McGraw (1902–1932), a one-time ringleader of the famous Baltimore Orioles who jumped from the Orioles to the Giants in 1902, the Giants became more than hyperbole, for they won ten pennants and three world titles. Known as "The Little Napoleon," McGraw was a testy, demanding man who developed much of the useful strategy of the game, including the hit-and-run, bunting, and relief pitching. There were times when he'd call almost every pitch from his perch on the bench, and he used signals the way admirals do on the high seas. With a personality bordering on the paranoid, McGraw was one of the first managers to hire private detectives and house spies to trace the nocturnal adventures of his players. He would even fine a player for hitting a home run! The culprit, Red Murray, had been ordered to bunt by McGraw.

"When I saw that fat pitch coming at me," said Murray, "I just knew I had to belt it."

"Well, I just have to fine you one hundred bucks for disobeying orders," snapped McGraw. Murray was not the first or last player to be exposed to McGraw's astonishing tyranny.

Before 1880 the Polo Grounds actually had been used for the game of polo, mainly by the social clubs of the New York *Herald*'s multimillionaire publisher, James Gordon Bennett. While the horses romped, rich, proud gentlemen in striped trousers gazed at the exotic activity from under their silk hats.

The Polo Grounds was situated in the lee of Coogan's Bluff—once called Coogan's Hollow—a craggy cliff that was named for James Coogan, a prominent merchant and Manhattan's first borough president in 1899. It was located on the fringe of Manhattan Island, bordering on the Harlem River at 157th Street and Eighth Avenue, and was probably the only ballpark a fan entered by walking downhill.

Over the years many notable and controversial events were staged at the Polo Grounds. In 1923 four world championship fights were held there, chief among which was the hectic Jack Dempsey–Luis Angel Firpo heavyweight brawl before 82,000 people on the night of September 14. In 1924 Army battled Notre Dame at the Polo Grounds, the only time these college gladiators ever used the premises. Out of that 13–7 Irish victory emerged sports columnist Grantland Rice's famous lyrical lead to his next day's story—"Outlined against a blue-gray October sky the Four Horsemen rode again . . ."

From 1913 through 1922 the Giants played landlord at the Polo Grounds to the Yankees, as Babe Ruth took aim at the inviting right-field porch before Yankee Stadium was built to celebrate his specialty.

But perhaps the most riotous and confounding incident took place there on the afternoon of September 23, 1908, when the Giants' Fred Merkle failed to touch second base and headed for the dugout after what was thought to be a game-winning hit by Al Bridwell. The contest was then declared a 1–1 tie between the Cubs and the Giants. When the Giants ultimately lost the pennant that year by one game to the Cubs, Merkle forever was stigmatized by his technical indiscretion. He had a long, honorable career as an adept first baseman, but Merkle's "boner" became engrained in Giant history.

An eight-story ballpark, with green, wood, concrete and steel grandstands, the Polo Grounds had 55,000 seats, some of which were close enough to the field to enable fans to tune in on the chirpy repartee of the athletes. Some of the park's main features were box seats patterned after the royal pews of Rome's Colosseum and a decorative frieze on the façade, which disappeared soon after the Polo Grounds was renovated.

Standing at home plate in the Polo Grounds a batter could stare straight out, some 500 feet away, to the center-field clubhouse, where owner Horace Stoneham, who had a strong affection for his players, could watch the progress of each game through his binoculars. At the base of the wall in center was a five-foot-high memorial to Eddie Grant, a Harvard graduate and former Giant third baseman who was killed in action in World War I.

When the Giants won, a blue pennant was raised from the clubhouse roof for all passersby to relish. When they lost, a red and white pennant, signifying defeat, was hoisted up the pole.

There were tiny bleachers on the left and right side of the center-field area—and looming above it all in more recent times was a large Chesterfield sign. About 4,000 plank-dwellers could be accommodated in the bleachers, but there was no individual seating there for these most fervent of all Giant fans. It was first come, first served. Those who couldn't come up with the price of a bleacher ticket could climb to the top of Coogan's Bluff, where it was possible to see second base, and not much else, while perched on rocks, grass, and dirt.

The Polo Grounds' center field was a cruel expanse, mischievously designed to foil the efforts of those hitters not inclined to pull balls toward the beckoning right-field stands (257 feet; 10 feet 7⅝ inches high) or left field (279 feet; 16 feet, 10 inches high). The asymmetrical dimensions, an absurdity to some, glorious to others, had frustrated even the finest of batsmen, with the exception of McGraw's protégé, Mel Ott, who gleefully deposited many of his "Chinese" home runs down the right-field line.

The upper left-field deck hung over the lower deck by some twenty-three feet, an unusual circumstance and one destined to play a singular role as events transpired in the season of 1951. From the air the Polo Grounds, on the left bank of the Harlem, had more the appearance of an enormous outdoor bathtub than a ball field. Certainly it looked a good deal less like a ballpark than Yankee Stadium, its rival on the right bank of the Harlem in the Bronx.

In Brooklyn, from the Dutch Old World name of Breuckelen, a borough crammed with impossibly boisterous baseball fans, a record number of churches, and a polyglot population of Italians, Irish, Jews, Germans, and blacks, there was another religious institution called Ebbets Field. This bandbox of a baseball playground, named after Charles Ebbets, a peanut peddler who became the owner of the team, and disastrously designed by C. A. Buskirk, opened its gates in 1913. Built at a cost of less than a million dollars, it was shoehorned into several acres of filled-in marshland in a slum area known as Pigtown, midway between the Flatbush and Bedford Avenue sections of Brooklyn. The main residents of Pigtown were Italian immigrants.

Perhaps no more intimate ballpark than Ebbets Field was ever built. If you were in a box seat you thought you were playing in the infield, said Red Barber, the Brooklyn broadcaster. An eccentric Dodger pitcher chimed in that hurling in Ebbets Field "was just like pitching in a phone booth."

There were few comfortable rest rooms, poor parking facilities, and overcrowded concessions. But such imperfections didn't discourage fans from coming to the park.

If there were only 32,000 seats in Ebbets Field, there seemed to be a joke to go along with each seat. With the Dodgers as the butt, jokes never stopped coming. Every fan who paid to get into the sanctum of Ebbets Field thought he owned a piece of the club. But that didn't stop them from joking about the flaws of the home team.

However, if the barbs came from the lips of "foreigners," which was often the case, any Brooklyn fan worth his weight in Nathan's Famous Hot Dogs would be ready to stand up and fight. Or at least yell. After all, that's what World War II was all about, wasn't it? Nuts to that Mom and apple pie stuff! The war was fought for the inalienable right to root for the Brooklyn Dodgers! For millions of rabid Dodger fans Ebbets Field and its club represented a passport to America. (Before World War II a Society for the Prevention of Disparaging Remarks about Brooklyn was formed. By 1946 it claimed over 40,000 members, who kept careful count of media libels.)

The loudest rooter for the Dodgers for over thirty years was a plump woman named Hilda Chester, who attended every game at Ebbets Field, armed with a frying pan and iron ladle. Later she added brass cowbells to her cacophonous equipment. She specialized in advice to her beloved Dodgers, most of whom she referred to by first names. But she had only insults for the rest of a hostile world.

"Eatcha heart out, ya bums, ya," she'd screech at her hated enemies when things went swimmingly for the Dodgers, which wasn't too often in those days.

Adding to the din was a discordant musical combine known as

the "Dodger Symph-phoney." Consisting of players on bass drum, cymbals, snare drums, and trumpet, the Symph-phoney performed at night and on weekends, making enough noise to raise Charlie Ebbets himself from the dead. Calls made by umpires against the Dodgers were met by a needling "Three Blind Mice," and a dirge-like "Worm Crawls In" accompanied enemy players as they shuffled back to the dugout after making an out.

The Musicians' Union was convinced that Walter O'Malley had paid this ragtag group and threatened to call a strike. O'Malley shrewdly set up a Music Appreciation Day, when anyone carting a musical instrument was admitted free to the park.

Eddie the Milkman (he had no other name) also attended all Dodger home games. Protected by a sun helmet, the Milkman released balloons into the air whenever his hero, Cookie Lavagetto, performed a deed that warranted such a display.

Of the many harsh jokes about the Dodgers, one dealt with a budding ninth-inning rally by the locals when they were three runs down. Sitting high in the grandstand, an aggrieved fan noted that many people were leaving the ballpark.

"Hey, come back, ya jerks," the fan shouted down at the faint-hearted, as they disappeared into Flatbush via McKeever Place. "The Dodgers got three guys on base and Phelps is coming up." (Babe Phelps was a Dodger catcher from 1935 to 1941 and was known occasionally to belt a home run.)

"Oh, yeah," a disgruntled fan shot back, hardly breaking his stride. "Which base?" After all, any Dodger fan could recall, with pain, how the legendary tangle-footed outfielder Floyd Caves Herman, Babe for short, had miraculously doubled into a double play in a game against the Braves in 1926. Things like that people didn't ever forget.

A yarn often circulated about the corpulent manager, Wilbert Robinson, who was so lovable that the Dodgers were dubbed the Robins in his honor. (The club constantly experienced alterations of its name: They had been the Bridegrooms and then the Superbas, a name taken from a popular novel. Then, in the 1890s, they inherited the sobriquet "Trolley Dodgers," after the newfangled maroon- and cream-colored vehicles that carried people around Brooklyn.)

In Robinson's tenure the club had operated in a catch-as-catch-can manner in the business of putting together a lineup out of its bouillabaisse roster. Notoriously fuzzy at recollecting players' names, Robinson had equal difficulty in spelling them. One day Robinson brought up a new outfielder named Oscar Roettger, with the intention of immediately installing him in the Dodger lineup. When a reporter inquired how Roettger's name was spelled, Robinson was stumped.

"Oh, hell," he finally blurted out, "let Carey stay in right!"

Certainly these jokes about past Dodger malefactions couldn't have been directed at the 1951 Dodgers, who were talented, classy, and hardly the clowns of legend. But Willard Mullin, a cartoonist for New York's *World-Telegram*, almost made a living depicting the inimitable Brooklyn bum bearing patches on his scruffy pants and murder in his heart for the hateful Giants.

The most serendipitous architectural feature of Ebbets Field was its ornate rotunda, more befitting a twentieth-century movie palace than the entrance to an untidy ballpark. Inside, too many pillars obstructed a clear view of the field, although some grumpy fans said that it was better not to see what was going on.

The park's unforgettable adornment was Brooklyn clothier Abe Stark's four-foot-high sign at the base of the scoreboard. HIT SIGN, WIN SUIT, it dared. But with Carl Furillo stationed as a trusty Cerberus in right field, few ever visited Mr. Stark's Pitkin Avenue store to pick up their reward. Stark became so celebrated that he was elected Brooklyn's borough president.

Ebbets Field's clubhouses, for both friend and foe, were ill lit, dingy, and badly ventilated. They were singularly egalitarian in their lack of privacy and cramped locker space and were built at street level, went the story, to prevent depressed managers from jumping out of windows. Today, Little Leaguers probably have it better. Shortstop Pee Wee Reese, the Dodger captain, managed to scavenge an antique swivel chair in which he would often spread out before and after games. The other oppressed Brooklyn players had to settle for rickety three-legged stools.

When Dodger players once pressed owner Walter O'Malley, who originally grew up in the Bronx and became a Giant fan, about installing a water cooler in their dugout, he expressed astonishment. "I never realized," he said, "that they had to carry a jug down there in order to get a drink." Many of those who worked for O'Malley, who had a considerable educational background at Penn, Columbia Law School, and Fordham, enjoyed his conviviality. They acknowledged he was among the wiliest of men—but, they added, he was also among the cheapest.

"Ebbets Field was where one learned to duck a punch and get along with a lot of different people," remarked Tony LoBianco, an actor who claimed Bay Ridge in Brooklyn as his home. "Being born in Brooklyn is as American as you can get. You get the culture of the streets which prepares you for life."

During World War II, an American soldier tried to describe a Japanese banzai charge, which he managed to survive. "They make the weirdest sound, as they come at you screaming. It sounds like Ladies Day at Ebbets Field," he said.

Everett "Rocky" Bridges, who arrived with the Dodgers by way of Refugio, Texas, and Long Beach, California, in order to play part-time infielder in 1951, said, "Nobody who ever played in Ebbets Field will forget the experience. I would rather have sat on the bench there, as a young donkey, than have been anyplace else. The fans got more emotional and tense than the players did, but it was catching. For any player from west of the Mississippi, Ebbets Field and Brooklyn was like a foreign environment when we first got there. But all of us got to love it."

The Dodgers had also blazed the way on the crucial issue of integration. In 1945, in a revolutionary move engineered by Branch Rickey, they hired the gifted and fiery Jackie Robinson, a former all-around athlete from UCLA. At the time the rest of baseball was hardly welcome territory to Robinson's black brethren. For that matter, most of America scarcely hung out the welcome sign for people of color. (The Giants, however, took on several black players soon after the Dodgers signed Robinson.)

An irrepressible Dodger publicist of that era, Irving Rudd, proclaimed that Robinson would have been the ideal guy to pro-tect a buddy's back in a dark alley. "He couldda done it better even than Bummy Davis," said Rudd, referring to a notorious fighter who had come out of Brownsville in Brooklyn, where Murder Inc. had been spawned in a neighborhood candy store.

Was there anyone in those years in the Western world who didn't know who the Brooklyn Dodgers were? Ironically, there was one such person. She was Utah-born actress Laraine Day, a genteel Mormon who had been raised strictly by her parents. She had appeared in several Doctor Kildare movies with Lew Ayres and in Alfred Hitchcock's *Foreign Correspondent* opposite Joel McCrea.

Before she met Leo Durocher, and before she was courted and wooed by him, she paraded her innocence for all to see. She hadn't a clue about Durocher's rowdy, scoundrelly past as pool-hall hustler and player, and she didn't seem to know much about his current work.

"He's the manager of the Brooklyn Dodgers," said a friend to her by way of explanation.

Laraine Day wondered what that could be. Was a Brooklyn Dodger a street urchin out of the novels of Charles Dickens? Was it a colorful bird? Or an automobile?

No, she was informed, it wasn't any of those things. Who told her? Durocher did.

It was someone, Durocher said, patiently, who played big-league baseball in a midget ballpark named Ebbets Field. The Dodgers, he continued, were Brooklyn's home team, as much a part of that embattled, historic borough as its old churches, brownstones, row houses, storefronts, punchball players, delicatessens, synagogues, and tight-knit ethnic neighborhoods.

Brooklyn fans, Durocher told Laraine, were the best damn fans in the world, even if they sometimes made umpires and players targets for Coke bottles, mustard-splattered hot dogs, and rolled-up newspapers. They came, he continued, from such noble cultural stews as Canarsie, Flatbush, Coney Island, Brownsville, Bay Ridge, Bensonhurst, Greenpoint, Prospect Park, and Brighton Beach.

"They go to Ebbets Field to root and they never give up," said Durocher.

A celebrated instance of Dodger fans' behavior occurred back in the 1920s. Naturally, it had to do with a Dodger-Giant game. All the seats in Ebbets Field had been sold, causing disappointed fans to ramrod their way past the center-field gate with a telegraph pole. Thousands of these miscreants then took their places in the outfield, as sympathetic police permitted them to remain there and watch the game.

When a Giant hitter lofted a fly ball to center, the crowd opened a path for Zack Wheat as he ran back to catch the ball. Later in the game, when a Dodger hit a fly in the same area, the Giants' Hack Wilson was cruelly hemmed in by the fans. Disappearing into the crowd, Wilson lost his cap, shoes, and, of course, the ball.

It was constantly said that Brooklyn fans were the most supportive in the world. They had "a chicken soup kind of love for their team," said Irving Rudd, "that brought about a mutual warmth that hasn't since been equaled in the baseball world."

After her marriage to Durocher, Laraine Day came to appreciate all of these qualities of Dodger fans. She also learned what a New York Giant was. Put the combustible chemistry of Dodger and Giant together, she discovered, and you got heat, fierce rivalry, duels to the death, and the arousal of partisan feelings that made the Civil War look like a garden party.

"It was like pulling teeth whenever they got to play," Laraine said. "When Leo left home for each game against the Dodgers, he could have been a man taking off for the Crusades."

The ancient, grudging competition dated back to New York's misty past, when the old Polo Grounds, at 110th Street and Fifth Avenue in Manhattan, was the scene of the first game of the World Series, on October 18, 1889. In that game the Giants faced the Brooklyn Bridegrooms, so called because four of their players had gotten married in quick succession.

The Bridegrooms represented the American Association, while the Giants had just won the National League title. The Giants won in nine games, and each player took home $200 out of a pool of some $4,000.

It has been suggested that Brooklyn's annual hot-stove league cry of "Wait 'til next year" began that winter. Those early Series games initiated a rivalry between the Giants and Dodgers that didn't cool off at all, as the years went by, and reached its apogee in 1951, over six decades later.

Even in the off season the sniping between the Dodgers and Giants went on, encouraged by the provocations of the New York baseball writers, ever on the prowl for snippets of gossip.

After Bill Terry's Giants won the World Series in 1933, the same year in which manager Max Carey failed to move the Dodgers any higher than sixth place, the writers met with Terry one winter day at the Giant offices in Manhattan. The first inspired question posed by the journalists was "How would the Giants do in 1934? Would they repeat?"

Terry said he thought his club would win again. "But if we don't," he added, "we won't finish any lower than third. I think the Cubs, Pirates, and Cardinals will give us some trouble."

"What about Brooklyn?" asked the writer from the *New York Times*.

"Brooklyn," Terry mused. "Gee, I haven't heard a peep out of them. Is Brooklyn still in the league?"

It's not clear whether Terry was being ingenuous or just nasty. Many thought the latter was the case, for Memphis Bill was generally judged to have a built-in mean streak. Whatever Terry's intentions were, the remark set off a hornet's nest in Brooklyn. The fans howled their protests as angry letters poured into the Dodgers' home office. Terry's insult won more linage in the newspapers than Hitler's bloodbath purge of his army in Germany, since the tabloids always managed to keep things in proper perspective.

One Brooklyn writer, Tommy Holmes, expressed his facetious thanks to Terry, looking upon it as a wake-up call. "I feel obliged to Mr. Terry," wrote Holmes. "Other news from the Brooklyn club has been as drab as a heap of sand. If I know my Brooklyn fans they'll get to the ball park if they have to hammer down the gate."

A month after Terry's bon mots, Casey Stengel was hired to manage the Brooks. Stengel, a gargoyle-featured past master at public relations even years before he managed so many home runs out of Mickey Mantle and Roger Maris, assured the world that Brooklyn was still in the league.

During the season, though, Stengel couldn't do much to substantiate that assertion. On Memorial Day of 1934 over 41,000 people crammed into Ebbets Field, an all-time record, for a doubleheader with the Giants. But the Dodgers got creamed badly in both games. The first six times the teams met in 1934, the Dodgers lost. Was Bill Terry right, after all?

On August 8, Wilbert Robinson, a jolly old soul to the end and still beloved in Brooklyn, keeled over in an Atlanta hotel lobby. His death, at seventy-one, coming the same year as John McGraw's death, deprived the New York baseball world of two of its most compelling personalities. But the rivalry between the clubs crackled as before, with Terry's remarks still causing heartburn in Flatbush.

As the season dwindled down, with two days to go, the Giants found themselves tied for the lead with the Cards. In first place since June, Terry's team, overtaken by the Dean brothers, as they fast-talked and fastballed the rest of the league, had two games left—both with the Dodgers. The Dodgers were in sixth place, going nowhere. The Cards had two games remaining with Cincinnati.

While thousands of Dodger fans stormed the enemy Polo Grounds for Saturday's game, many carrying banners informing the universe that the Dodgers were still in the league, the Giants proceeded to lose to Van Lingle Mungo, 5–1. Since the Cards beat the Reds behind Daffy Dean the same day, St. Louis advanced to first place.

With a Sunday game yet to be played against the Dodgers, the Giants could still tie for first, if they won—and if the Cards lost. But it didn't happen that way.

The Giants scored four runs in the first inning, then rolled over dead, as the Dodgers came roaring back to tie the score. In the tenth, with the score deadlocked at 5–5, the Dodgers pounded Hal Schumacher and Carl Hubbell for three runs. That brought the curtain down on the Giants, as the Cards put icing on the cake by beating the Reds again, as Dizzy Dean did the honors.

The humiliated Terry and his Giants were in mourning. Though the citizens of Brooklyn couldn't celebrate a World Series, they had achieved the next best thing—they could spend the winter needling the Giants.

This all may have happened in 1934, but the melody always lingered on. It was a fact of baseball life in New York and Brooklyn—spicy, raucous, and never-ending.

Baseball's fiercest feud requires little explanation from sociologists or psychologists. Ball clubs invariably duplicate the temperament of the cities in which they play. This blood vendetta was spawned primarily from geography—two ball clubs vying for the same market and for the same space on the sports pages inevitably must become hostile. Such animosity was nurtured by the presence of the truculent McGraw, who transferred his hatred of the Yankees to the Dodgers as the years went by. When McGraw's old pal and former teammate Wilbert Robinson committed the heresy of joining up with the opposition in Brooklyn, McGraw's outrage couldn't be contained.

With Durocher's shocking change of allegiance from Brooklyn to the Giants in 1948, more fuel was added to the flames. Out of the heat and hostility emerged the seething animosities between Durocher and Robinson, Robinson and Maglie, Carl Furillo and Durocher, and Alvin Dark and Robinson, all of which were headline fodder.

The score of the game between the two clubs sometimes was only incidental to the number of beanballs thrown. "I told my pitchers to get two of them for every one of our guys they knock down," said manager Charlie Dressen of his Dodger hurlers.

It became the imperious Giants, reared under McGraw's stern brand of baseball fundamentalism, and the long-time pets of carpetbagging high society, the gamblers, politicians, and Broadway's show-business elite, versus the underdog, recidivist Dodgers, from a land of people with hard-to-pronounce names.

Dixie Walker, the unreconstructed Southern hero of Flatbush, who beat the Giants so many times with clutch hits in the 1940s, was canonized in Brooklynese as "The Peepul's Cherce," while Carl Erskine, the nice-guy right-hander, was always "Oisk" to the natives.

When it was pointed out to Giant-lovers that as many young men from Brooklyn served in the U.S. armed forces in World War II as from almost three fourths of the country combined, this still failed to justify in their minds why Brooklyn belonged either in the Union or the National League.

So the Giants and Dodgers were sworn enemies, much as a stand-up comic's audience is always a natural enemy to him. "Good evening, opponents," Jackie Leonard used to say, in his greeting to the faceless nightclub crowd in front of him.

As the turnstiles clicked merrily at Ebbets Field and the Polo Grounds, the antagonists rarely missed a chance to harass the other. It was a mutual history replete with "rhubarbs," a term that Brooklyn children themselves invented to describe confusion-filled controversies.

"Every game between these rivals was a fierce blood-letting that froze the city's heart-beat until the final score was in," wrote baseball historian Donald Honig. The World Series was "nothing compared to the tension of Giant-Dodger games," insisted Monte Irvin, who played for the Giants in the 1950s.

Duke Snider, the Dodgers' center fielder, joked that "we Dodgers even disliked Halloween because its colors were orange and black"—those being, of course, the colors of the Giants.

"Dodger-Giant games always put butterflies in your belly," remarked Don Mueller, the Giants' right fielder. "I didn't always look forward to those games, either—because it hurt to get beat by them."

Erskine, normally a mild-mannered man with civilized instincts, admitted, "Your manhood seemed to be on the line when you played the Giants. There was electricity in the air, and if the Dodgers won they lifted the spirit of an entire borough."

Out of these no-holds-barred interborough quarrels flowed love and curses from the fans and the deadline-fighting, sports page poetry of such celebrated journalists as Red Smith, Bill Corum, Jimmy Cannon, Frank Graham, and others. The Giants and Dodgers were, indeed, good copy, but they were first and foremost flesh-and-blood foes, considerably more than the invention of the fevered imagination of sportswriters.

In the early days of the 1951 season the Giants played as shabbily as the Dodgers played brilliantly. Almost everyone had automatically awarded first place to Brooklyn before the season began. Now the Dodgers were fulfilling all those expectations. For once, it looked as if the seers were correct.

The first five games between the two teams, played in the usual white heat, ended in victory for the Dodgers. At this stage, Dodger players showed more concern about whether they'd be anointed to appear on Happy Felton's popular postgame show in Ebbets Field (on which they could pick up $150 for an appearance) than with their arch-rival Giants.

His own words coming back to haunt him, Durocher's "kind of Giant team," minus many of its most robust hitters, was drawing sneers around the National League. There were even reports that a considerable number of disenchanted Giant fans were seeking to cash in their season tickets.

Inexorably, however, the Giants started to win ball games. The unsettled look, with outfielders playing first base and first basemen playing outfield, disappeared. Then along came the nineteen-year-old Willie Howard Mays, with his easy, graceful skills and a bat that moved as quickly as any in baseball history. As Branch Rickey described Mays, he had "frivolity in his bloodstream." No single man brought the Giants back into the 1951 race, but it probably couldn't have happened without the presence of this black youngster.

"We felt the team moving," recalled Bill Rigney, an invaluable utility infielder on that club, known to his teammates as "The Cricket." "Even if some guys may have thought it was a joke and that we were nuts thinking we could still win, with the Dodgers so far ahead, Leo never lost interest. Neither did the rest of us."

Becoming increasingly confident, after they had been 13½ games behind the Dodgers in mid-August the Giants played remarkable ball for seven weeks. They kept inching up on the Dodgers, who reacted to the Giants' unwillingness to quit with a mixture of braggadocio and bewilderment. By degrees, everything seemed to be falling in on the Dodgers, except the Brooklyn Bridge.

By the year's end it was fitting, if incredible, that the Giants and Dodgers had battled ferociously to a flat-footed tie after 154 games, in a race full of more twists and turns than an Agatha Christie whodunit.

"I don't know if they put us in a state of shock," said Andy Pafko, the Dodgers' left fielder, "but we did start to get anxious as it came down to the end. I guess we were even lucky to wind up in a tie."

After what may have been the most riveting of all baseball seasons, the Giants and Dodgers, without a moment's rest, or a single day off, engaged in a play-off. The winner of two out of three games would advance to the 1951 World Series against the Yankees.

It was the second National League play-off in history—the other was in 1946 between the Dodgers and the Cardinals—and the Dodgers again were in the dogfight of postseason play. This time they would confront their former manager, Durocher.

The 1951 play-off would go the limit, as the Dodgers and Giants split the first two games, thus setting up a third, decisive encounter.

The last of these games would evolve into an unforgettable event, with an impact that succeeded in touching the lives of millions of people. Before that day many of those millions may have honestly thought Coogan's Bluff was some kind of simple children's game instead of the backdrop for baseball's most dramatic episode.

A true measure of the rippling effect of such a happening on the American community is that years later people can recall what they were doing and how they reacted when the moment of truth occurred. They can remember with precision where they were when the Japanese bombed an out-of-the way place called Pearl Harbor. They know where they were when Franklin D. Roosevelt died or they can tell you who they were with when John F. Kennedy was assassinated in Dallas in 1963. They remember where they were when World War II ended or when America landed a man on the moon.

This is how it turned out to be for millions, when Bobby Thomson's last-gasp home run was hit on Wednesday, October 3, 1951, at 3:58 P.M., at the Polo Grounds.

3

Durocher and His Giants

IN 1948, after Leo Durocher's uniform switch to the Giants had caused all of Brooklyn to regard him as a reincarnation of Benedict Arnold, the Giants ended up in fifth place. In 1949 they were again fifth, even winning five fewer games. Any way you looked at them— and Leo looked plenty—the Giants comported themselves like humpty-dumpties.

On the morning of July 20, 1950, Durocher saw by the papers, which he tried to read only when the Giants were playing well, that his team was in sixth place, hardly a recommendation to make him manager of the year.

Then things suddenly began to happen. The unlikely and superb pitching efforts of two right-handers, Sal Maglie and Jim Hearn, were, without doubt, the cause of the turnaround.

Maglie, a refugee from the Mexican League, had an unshaven, threatening mien that could have won him featured roles in the popular gangster movies of the 1930s. He looked like a natural partner of James Cagney and Edward G. Robinson. Instead, he got Durocher. Although, when you looked at it closely, that wasn't too far removed from those tough-guy movie stars, for Durocher could play every bit as rough as those fellows—and he was for real! After all, Leo had once admitted that if he were playing third base and his mother rounded the bag with the winning run, he'd trip her up.

Each time Maglie threw a pitch to a batter it looked like he hurt somewhere. There was a knot behind his right shoulder that didn't usually ease up until he'd pitched an inning or two. In the beginning of 1950, when Sal was thirty-three, he was working out of the bullpen, waiting impatiently for Durocher to discover him in one of his rescue stints.

"I knew I had a couple good years left," said Sal, "if only Durocher could give me a chance."

But Durocher ignored the fact that Maglie, performing under the tutelage of Dolf Luque, a wily Cuban who had been pitching since 1914, including four years in the 1930s with the Giants, had been the top pitcher in the Mexican League. "I learned plenty from Luque, enough to pitch well in the National League," insisted Maglie.

To some baseball people, however, the Mexican League was a euphemism for Siberia, so the fact that Maglie appeared to have picked up valuable pointers didn't convince everybody that he would be useful in New York. Sal kept telling his manager that he now knew how to pace himself and how to use his curveball to the best advantage. He also never hesitated to let the hitter know who was boss, a jurisdictional point that he'd also absorbed from Luque. If a batter had to be loosened up at the plate, Maglie did not hesitate to fire at him, or darn close to him.

In time these tactics won Maglie the nickname of "The Barber." One couldn't be certain that Jim McCulley, the *Daily News* sportswriter who gave Sal his nickname, was implying that Maglie shaved batters' heads too close or was simply saying that he was a master at picking up the corners of the plate with his pitches.

"I guess he meant I shave 'em like an Italian barber," said Sal. "That's better, any way you look at it, than someone calling you a shoeshine boy."

One afternoon in midseason of 1950 Durocher finally decided to give Maglie a start, but only because he had little choice.

"If a guy has ten suits and somebody steals nine of them, and the guy has to go out that night, well, he's got to wear that one remaining suit. There we were in a lousy losing streak and I had to have a pitcher. I had Maglie and nobody else, so Maglie was it," summed up the street-smart Durocher.

Bolstered by this roaring vote of confidence, Maglie went out and won his game against St. Louis, a grueling eleven-inning affair in which he hung on gamely until the end. Such competitiveness had to impress his manager. Before the season ended, Sal had won eighteen games, against only four losses. In one stretch Maglie put together a streak of 46⅓ consecutive scoreless innings. Only a freakish home run by the Pirates' Gus Bell, a blow that barely dented the right-field screen, brought the streak to an end.

Among his accomplishments during that season, Maglie learned how to demoralize the Dodgers. He beat them four times without a defeat and had the Brooklyn batters talking to themselves. Jackie Robinson, who never hit Maglie well, once growled at him: "I don't know how the hell you get by with that shit you're throwing." But Sal did—much to the discomfort of the Dodgers.

"This guy Maglie may even get better," said Carl Hubbell, once the meal ticket of the Giants' pitching corps and then their scouting chief. "Age isn't against him, either, because he doesn't tax his arm and he stays nice and lean."

Hearn was as different from Maglie as Durocher was from Ott. A tall (6'4"), soft-spoken, handsome Southerner from Atlanta who favored sports clothes such as porkpie hats and corduroy jackets, Jim had had a brief dalliance with higher education at Georgia Tech. When he went into the army during World War II, he got to play baseball with a talented service team in the Philippines that included such players as Early Wynn, who could have taught Hearn a few things about knocking people down at home plate, Max Macon, Joe Ginsberg, and Joe Garagiola. Both Ginsberg and Garagiola were a few years away from the big leagues.

"We played to entertain the troops," says Hearn. "But, of course, it was wonderful experience for me."

When he joined the St. Louis Cardinals organization after the war, Jim was slated to be a third baseman or outfielder. But when a pitching shortage popped up with the Columbus, Georgia, farm club, Jim volunteered to try his hand at pitching. Thereafter, that became his job, though times were not always easy.

In 1947 and 1948 Jim had winning seasons with the Cards— but rumors circulated around the clubhouses that Hearn preferred golf to hard-nosed pitching. The dastardly scuttlebutt went on to imply that Jim choked up in tight ball games. Hearn's own view was strikingly at variance with these theories.

"I had strained my shoulder pitching in cold weather," he explained. "When I tried to get my arm back in shape at Rochester,

I did pretty well, but there were times that I couldn't throw the ball thirty feet without some pain. Eddie Dyer, the Cards manager, wanted to send me to Houston, where it was warm. He thought that would help me come around."

But when the Cardinals asked for waivers on Hearn they seemed to be subscribing to the negative stories about him. The Giants were willing to take a chance on Jim, and it paid off beyond their wildest dreams. Under Durocher's goading, and aided by pitching coach Frank Shellenback, who taught his pupil how to throw a sinker, Hearn exhibited a combativeness he hadn't displayed with the Cards.

Hearn had won one game for the Cards in 1949 and none in 1950. But after joining the Giants after the midseason All-Star Game in 1950, Hearn won eleven games, lost only three, and posted the lowest earned run average of all National League pitchers. It was a remarkable transformation, and in short order he was referred to as "The Bargain Basement Beauty."

The turnaround in Hearn's condition and attitude was so complete that he couldn't wait to pitch every fourth day in a Giant rotation that was to use Larry Jansen, Maglie, Dave Koslo, and himself. "I felt strong and at the peak of my efficiency," recalls Hearn. "Funny thing, in the past I'd preferred starting every fifth day, giving me four days off. With the way Leo used me I got only three days off. But I liked it, and it worked out well for all of us."

Hearn admired Durocher, whom he felt handled the men under his command, including himself, well. "They used to say," he said, "that Casey Stengel was at his most difficult and nastiest when things were going good for his team. But with Durocher when the club was going good and winning, he was easy to get along with, at least for me. I know other guys don't agree on this—try to figure it out."

Durocher's other starting pitcher, actually his number-one moundsman, was the 6′2″, 190-pound right-hander Larry Jansen. Jansen was born in 1920 in Forest Grove, Oregon, a small hunting and salmon fishing mecca near Portland that he was reluctant ever to leave, with the exception of his excursions back east each year to play in the Polo Grounds.

When the Giants tried to get Jansen on the phone it was necessary for him to come into town to take the call at the local druggist. Usually, Larry was too busy shooting ducks on a little lake near his home to bother much with phone calls from the big-city folks.

Jansen possessed impeccable control of his curveball and of himself, a strong recommendation on a team led by such strident, overt egotists as the fiery Durocher and his disciple, Eddie Stanky. But it was Jansen's seven children (five girls, two boys) that made the most impression on the pragmatic Leo.

"A man with a family that size," said Durocher, "has got to realize he has big responsibilities. Every time he goes out to the mound he knows he's pitching to feed a lot of mouths. It's either him or the guy with the bat—and I don't think he's going to let it be the guy with the bat."

(Ultimately, Jansen fathered ten children. By 1990, when it was his fiftieth wedding anniversary, all of his children were happily alive, ages twenty-six to fifty. Jansen also had twenty grandchildren and five great-grandchildren, perhaps the largest conglomerate ever accumulated by a pitcher, at least a Giant pitcher.)

If Leo implied that Jansen would not be averse to thumping an opposing batter on the head or the shoulders with an occasional stray pitch, he may have been talking about the wrong man, for, in addition to being a talented pitcher, Jansen had a widespread reputation as a nice guy—the kind that Durocher himself had said don't win pennants.

Even National League president Warren Giles, who, as one of his weighty chores, imposed fines on pitchers for wayward behavior, once ruled that Jansen had "an excellent conduct record." Giles had refused to assess Jansen with a heavy fine after a Jansen toss one afternoon had plunked an enemy batter.

Jansen's estimate of his character profile was that he was aware other players thought he was "a good guy."

"In a way, I guess, that probably helped me," he said, "when I did pitch close to batters, as I did, sometimes. A pitcher must do that to win in this league. Maglie would brush them back with that inside curveball of his. Maybe mine didn't come quite that far inside."

Jansen emerged from the Pacific Coast League, where, in 1946, he won thirty games for the San Francisco Seals while losing only six. His earned run average of 1.57 would have been attractive even in the Three-Eye League.

Hank DeBerry, an astute Giant scout who caught for eleven years, mostly with Brooklyn, swore on a stack of old catchers' mitts that Jansen was as prepared for the majors as anyone he'd ever seen. Encouraged by such hyperbole, Horace Stoneham quickly bought up Jansen's contract.

Within one year DeBerry was proven correct. In his rookie season of 1947, Jansen won twenty-one and lost five. He appeared to be much in the tradition of such stalwart Giant pitchers of old, such as, well, not Matty, but perhaps Hubbell and certainly Prince Hal Schumacher. He took good care of his body, making certain to run every day in the outfield and then to play pepper for a half hour or so. Only on pitching days did he desist from this regimen, or when it just got too hot for a sane man to exert himself.

Including his freshman year, Jansen compiled seventy-three victories through the 1950 season, when he was 19–13. In what was assuredly his most satisfying performance to that date, Larry pitched five shutout middle innings of the 1950 All-Star Game at Chicago's Comiskey Park.

Eventually the National League won that exciting spectacle in the fourteenth inning on Red Schoendienst's home run. Although Larry did not get credit for the win, he struck out six and gave up only a solitary hit to Larry Doby. The next day tongues wagged in baseball circles; Jansen seemingly had come out of nowhere to impress the cognoscenti.

"I imagine I looked so sharp that day," said Jansen, with his usual modesty, "because the hitters just didn't know me very well. I'd love to have a tape of those five innings!"

What added to the irony of his performance was that earlier in the year the Giants had tried to trade Jansen to the Dodgers for pitchers Ralph Branca and Erv Palica. Branca was more than a journeyman, having won twenty-one games for the Dodgers in 1947, when he was only twenty-one. But Palica was a better than .500 pitcher in only one year—1950. The Dodgers nixed the trade.

After the 1950 season Jansen became the highest-paid pitcher on the Giants, working for an estimated $32,000. With Maglie and Hearn, Jansen gave the Giants perhaps the best one-two-three pitching punch in the National League, that is, if one chose to exclude the Boston Braves' entry of "Spahn, Sain and pray for rain."

In the off season, before the 1951 season got underway, Jansen went into the hospital for an appendicitis operation. But Leo didn't anticipate that this would cause any major disruption of his pitching plans for 1951.

At the end of 1950, it had been Jansen, Maglie, and Hearn who had roused their once slumbering team, which had been declared D.O.A. as late as June of that year. But there were a few other pitchers who also chipped in. There was Sheldon Jones, who had been dubbed "Available" in a perverse assessment of his skill, and the lefty Dave Koslo, brilliant one day, mediocre the next. And there was right-hander George Spencer, who had been to Ohio State for two quarters, one for football and another for baseball. Spencer, like so many other Giants, had great respect for Durocher as a baseball man—but when you asked him about the man's character he'd always add: "I wouldn't want my son to be like him."

Spencer pointed out that Durocher was a gambler, "who'd call for a hit-and-run when you should be waiting for a pitch, or he'd bunt when you should be hitting away. But sometimes he wouldn't talk to you for weeks and you couldn't figure out why."

So the Giants of 1950 started to move up in the standings. They went to fifth in July and August, then to fourth at the beginning of September. At the finish they were in third place, only five games back of the "Whiz Kid" Phillies. They had vaulted there by winning a torrid fifty games out of their last seventy-two.

Challenged determinedly by the Dodgers, the Phillies managed to squeak by on the last day of the season to capture their first National League pennant in thirty-five years. Dick Sisler's tenth-inning home run off Don Newcombe on the final Sunday at Ebbets Field sunk the Dodgers—and also did in their bespectacled manager, Burt Shotton, who had always been a loyal disciple of Branch Rickey. The fact that Cal Abrams failed to score from second base on Duke Snider's sharp (as it turned out, *too* sharp) single in the bottom of the ninth for Brooklyn, depriving the Dodgers of a first-place tie with the Phillies, added to the bitter pill that Dodger fans were forced to swallow. Within two months Shotton was replaced by Chuck Dressen, whom the wise guys said only differed from Durocher because of his tailor.

For Durocher, however, it was a decidedly sweet ending. How could he be morose over such a denouement, for his rabbit ears (it was said that Leo could *hear* somebody behind him giving him the finger) never failed to pick up the taunts of unforgiving Brooklyn fans whenever he dared to stick his balding, well-perfumed head out of the dugout in Ebbets Field.

"Hey, Da-ROACH-a, ya friggin bum ya," was the most innocuous insult that fans would fling at him in their harsh Brooklynese. He was a traitor to them, they charged, he'd sold out to the goddamn Giants. If that's the way they regarded him, Leo could hardly be expected to sympathize with them now. He was a guy, after all, who liked to get even—and usually did.

Now, in the early spring of 1951, Durocher could also enthuse over the apparent resurgence of his team in the last months of 1950. He wasn't reluctant to advertise that fact, adding that he thought he had the makings of a winner. With such a club he was willing to attempt an alteration of his often troublesome persona. At one time Durocher had even inspired sweet-natured people like the great Stan Musial to froth at the mouth. Watching Leo prance back and forth in the dugout, gleeful at things going his way on the field, Musial, totally out of character, said out loud: "Wait, Durocher, we'll get you, you prick!"

The umpire baiter, the rowdy, the incessant user of needling as a game tactic, and a manager who had been suspended from baseball for a year in 1947 by Commissioner Happy Chandler for "conduct detrimental to baseball," Durocher purportedly had "converted." At least, so it was hinted. Columnist Jimmy Cannon snorted that Durocher was "Milton Berle's version of Hamlet," and Red Smith wrote that he was nothing but an "actor with chutzpah."

But other observers were inclined to see changes. They said he was now more diplomatic, more understanding, perhaps more agile. He would coax, wheedle, flatter, and cajole in place of using strident, crude verbal attack. His players, said his supporters, were now being treated with consideration and, forgive the word, charm.

"I've mellowed and matured," Leo would insist. "Laraine did the most for me. Then came Horace Stoneham. Now I think more of the other guy."

This was a truly balanced team, he said—and not in a whisper. It had strength up the middle, tight pitching, batters who could make contact and knew how to run the bases and, he hoped, could think. "When I flash the bunt sign," he'd growl from his third-base coach's box, where he could put his machismo where his mouth was, "I don't want any wheels turning in their heads second-guessing me." He had gotten rid of all those heavy-footed, lumbering home run hitters, including "The Big Cat," Johnny Mize, and catcher Walker Cooper, who broke a lot of windows at an alarming pace, but didn't do much winning. When Cooper had been thrown on the dung heap by Durocher in 1949 he didn't take it very graciously, either. "I've always felt Durocher could ruin any ball club," he charged. "He doesn't know how to handle men and he pops off."

Durocher shrugged off such sniping. "Give the guy a crying towel," he said—and went about his business putting together the kind of talent that he was convinced would be more successful in the Polo Grounds. Others were convinced, too. Arthur Daley, a columnist for the *New York Times*, wrote that "for the first time since the days of 1936 and 1937 the Giants toe the mark a definite pennant contender . . . the Polo Grounders do look primed for a quick getaway this spring."

It was the kind of team some said John McGraw himself would have dearly loved. Certainly Leo's tastes in ballplayers were reputed to echo that of the archstrategist who had been part of the Polo Grounds scenery for over thirty years.

When you looked down the lineup, starting with Eddie Stanky at second base, there had to be reason for such red-hot optimism. Stanky was a small, pugnacious fellow, who, the saying went, couldn't run, hit, or throw but possessed all of "the intangibles." The only thing Eddie Stanky could do, continued the ironic refrain, was beat you.

The Yankees' Phil Rizzuto, a player even tinier than Stanky, and a good deal less bellicose, confessed that he wished he could do the same things Stanky did and get away with it. "He plays a snarling, dog-eat-dog kind of baseball," said Rizzuto, who had in mind that Stanky was a past master at purposely getting in the way of pitched balls and disconcerting opposing players and umpires in crucial situations. Stanky had discovered that if he moved around at second base, flailing his arms in the air just as the pitcher was preparing to release the ball, it could distract the batter. He was warned about the tactic by National League president Ford Frick, but he persisted in the practice. On a couple of occasions he set off near riots.

Although Stanky had accused Durocher in no uncertain terms of stabbing him in the back during a salary brouhaha he'd had with Branch Rickey when both men were with Brooklyn (the incident ended with Stanky being sold to the Boston Braves, opening the way for Jackie Robinson to take over second base), Eddie made peace quickly with Leo. "I'm glad to be back with you, Skip," said Stanky, who was dubbed "The Brat" by everyone in the National League.

Durocher had lobbied strenuously with Horace Stoneham, the Giants' owner and stout drinking pal of his ballplayers, to trade for Stanky. Finally, the trade was made in December 1949 for Eddie and his shortstop sidekick, Alvin Dark, for what seemed to be half of the Giant roster, including outfielder Willard Marshall, outfielder-infielder Sid Gordon, shortstop Buddy Kerr, and pitcher Sam Webb. The deal didn't go down too well with Giant fans. It was inevitable, as well, that as soon as Stanky showed his head in Ebbets Field he was "Stinky" to all of those fans who felt they'd been betrayed.

"The one guy I didn't want to give up was Gordon," said Durocher, "but unless I did, I couldn't have made the deal. I wanted to get a good second-base combination and that's what we got."

Too rarely had Jewish ballplayers performed with distinction in New York uniforms, going back to Andy Cohen's novalike experience with the Giants in the 1920s. (For two weeks Cohen hit the cover off the ball, then became the journeyman he was.) Hank Greenberg evolved into a Hall of Famer, but his home runs were hit for Detroit and Pittsburgh, while Sandy Koufax, in 1951, was still a sixteen-year-old basketball player at Lafayette High School in Brooklyn. Hank Danning was an able catcher for the Giants for ten years, but he never became a full-fledged star. By trading Sid Gordon the Giants had said good-bye to a Jewish player with more potential than any they'd ever had.

Stanky's infield partner, Al Dark, physically reminded some sportswriters of a Confederate cavalry officer. He was a born-again Christian with a penchant for sermonizing and had been a rugged three-sport athlete at Louisiana State University, where he was captain of every team he played on. He was LSU's quarterback before Steve Van Buren came along but was built along strange lines—high-hipped and wide-waisted.

With the Braves, who won the pennant with him at shortstop in 1948, Dark was known as someone who "got the job done," which could have meant he was little more than an average player. But that was far from the truth. He was an expert bat manipulator, with a good deal of finesse at hitting behind the runner (who was usually Stanky, batting ahead of him in the order). Durocher loved the hit-and-run play, and Dark, a right-handed batter, could go to right field better than most men hitting from that side. He was never an Ozzie Smith or Mark Belanger at shortstop, but he had enough range to get in the way of most ground balls.

What Durocher liked most about Dark was that Alvin was a fire-in-the-gut competitor, albeit a normally courteous and soft-spoken man. Because of these perceived traits Durocher named him team captain. Leo looked at Dark's curriculum vitae in college and in the Marine Corps and concluded that he had always been willing to take on responsibility.

"I think Leo thought he could draw more things out of me if he made me captain," said Dark. "He also knew that I had just turned down one hundred dollars to do a Chesterfield cigarette commercial, so he gave it back to me when I became captain."

In a short time, Dark became a fervent admirer of his manager. "He knew who to get for his team and how to get them to play as hard as they could. He was at his best in getting on certain guys and not getting on others," said Dark. "He always planned ahead of time with his pitchers, both starters and bullpen, and was helped a lot by Freddy Fitzsimmons, his pitching coach. Leo knew when to put a pitcher in and when to take him out, but he also knew the opposition pitchers and batters like the back of his hand. He knew how to handle men and encouraged all of his players to think about the strategy and inner game of baseball. He made all of us think about all aspects of the game."

If there existed one striking weakness in the arsenal of Al Dark it was his misfortune in being burdened by the wrong-headed racial shibboleths of his home region of Oklahoma, where he'd been born. Later in his career, when Dark managed the San Francisco Giants, he suffered damage to his reputation for fairness and judgment as a result of an interview he gave to Stan Isaacs, a New York newspaperman. In that exchange he expressed an opinion, which he later denied, that black and Latin ballplayers were not as "mentally alert" as white players.

When Dark came to New York he joined several black players, including Monte Irvin, Henry Thompson, and Artie Wilson. Ultimately, Willie Mays also became his teammate, in May 1951.

Nobody ever would have considered Durocher a civil rights activist. But there was a side of his surly personality that rejected bias based on a man's color, birthplace, or social standing. He didn't like to be told what to do or what not to do. He had been one of the first to urge Branch Rickey to bring up Jackie Robinson from Montreal to the parent Dodger team in 1947, and it didn't come from any humanitarian impulse. It stemmed from the irrefutable fact that Leo quickly accepted the thesis that a black man had as much right to play big league ball as anyone else, provided, of course, he was competent enough to do it.

Despite the mixed feelings some black players may have had about Leo's personality, almost to a man they later commended him for his willingness to deal with them as human beings. One suspects that Leo's own roots as a poor boy of French-Canadian heritage, growing up with few privileges and little money, may have had much to do with his cooperative attitude toward the emergence of the black man in baseball.

"I don't give a damn about the color of a man's skin," Durocher would say, when he was forced to utter his own sociological beliefs. "I'm only interested in how well or how badly he plays this game."

Robinson himself, who later had heated exchanges with Durocher, as a Dodger foe of the Giant manager, never accused Leo of prejudice. He did insist that Durocher lacked "some of the moral strength needed to handle young men." But he added that Leo was a good manager and a "great uplifter."

Bill White, who became the first black president of the National League in 1989, played briefly under Durocher on the Giants. "Durocher played people, not colors," White said, succinctly.

When Branch Rickey approached Durocher about Robinson, he knew his man. He knew Leo cared more about base hits and winning than anything else. Wisely, too, Rickey stressed that the final decision on when and where Robinson would play would be left solely to Durocher. Rickey had handled Durocher well—and Durocher, in return, handled Robinson well.

*   *   *

It is hard to imagine any man, including Durocher, having difficulty getting along in the same world with Irvin, who finally arrived with the Giants in 1949, at the advanced baseball age of thirty. Monte was a man of consummate dignity, gentleness, and composure. If he boiled from within about injustice—as well he might—he managed to keep it to himself. A number of people in baseball, even including Rickey, thought Irvin might have been the superior choice to be baseball's pioneer black player, for Monte's temperament was less explosive than Jackie's. "It was Irvin's way to avoid confrontation," Roger Kahn wrote. Cool Papa Bell, a great outfielder who played in the black leagues with Monte, said that "most black players thought Monte should have been the first black in the big leagues . . . he could do everything."

But all-around infield utility man Bill Rigney had a slightly different view of Irvin's general demeanor.

"Whenever there was an embroilment on the field that involved a fellow Giant," recalled Rigney, "Monte would come right out of that dugout. Sure, he was even-tempered, but he didn't hesitate for a moment to join in when the fur started to fly."

Stoneham had wanted to sign Irvin as far back as 1936, when Monte was a teenage all-around athlete in Orange, New Jersey, where his family had settled after leaving Alabama. But Stoneham was not ready at that time to help break the color line in baseball.

"There's only one problem with this kid," said the scout who had gone to New Jersey to look at Irvin. "He's colored."

In those years Monte, up around 200 pounds, was also a superb track-and-field performer, who was urged by some local admirers to seek his fortune as a heavyweight fighter. But Monte admitted having little stomach for that kind of work. Before his baseball career materialized he was forced to turn down a football scholarship to the University of Michigan because his family couldn't afford to pay his transportation expenses. Had Irvin attended Michigan he would have joined Tommy Harmon and Forest Evashevski in the Wolverine backfield, which might have given the team three likely all-American players.

When Monte played for one of the fine black baseball teams of that period, the Newark Eagles of the Negro National League, the club's black owner told him that he should feel privileged to be able to suit up with them, even if he was only getting paid small wages. Previously, at one point in his high school athletic career he developed an almost fatal case of blood poisoning from a seemingly insignificant scratch that he incurred on a basketball court. Desperately ill, Monte managed to pull out of it with the help of blood donations that came pouring in from people in Orange who admired him.

It is clear Monte had known how to put up with adversity. But had he not lost so many precious playing years, in his midtwenties, as a result of prejudice, he might well have become one of the most productive hitters of his time. Irvin could hit balls on a line to all fields, with scorching power. For a big man he was surprisingly quick on the base paths; in the outfield he was more than acceptable, with a strong throwing arm.

In seventy-six times at bat in 1949, after he was brought up from Jersey City, where he was blasting the cover off the ball, Irvin failed to connect for a single home run. But Durocher was confident that Monte would hit big-league pitching. In 1950, he did, hitting fifteen home runs while batting .299. Leo was indecisive, however, at where to play Monte in 1950, so he used him at ten more games at first base than in the outfield. Irvin, who didn't particularly like to play first base, was uncertain at the bag. But he didn't smolder at Leo's choice for him.

"He's no Boy Scout, but he understands people," said Monte about Durocher. "You'll get no special favors from him, but neither will anybody else."

(Limited to only eight years of big league play, and handicapped by an ankle injury that he suffered in spring training of 1952, Irvin quit baseball in 1956, after a final season with the Chicago Cubs. In 1973 he was voted into Baseball's Hall of Fame as a Negro League star.)

Henry Curtis "Hank" Thompson, only 5'9" and 170 pounds, was the third black to come to the majors. He made his debut with the St. Louis Browns in July 1947, batted .256, and played nineteen games at second base. The Browns were one of the worst teams in baseball and probably would have benefitted by keeping Hank around, but late in August manager Muddy Ruel released Thompson, with a statement suggesting that Hank "had failed to play up to major league standards." There was a suspicion that Hank had been hired to boost flagging attendance. Thompson acknowledged that he hadn't performed very well, but neither had most of the other players on that inferior Brownie roster.

On July 5, 1949, the same day that Irvin was also brought up from Jersey City, Thompson went along with him. He'd been banging the ball at a good clip for the farm team and Durocher put in the call for him. Now twenty-four years old and more experienced as a hitter, Thompson posted a .280 average in 1949 with the Giants, where Durocher used him mostly at second base.

Hank was a man with a troubled background. He had been arrested when he was only eleven years old for truancy. He was drinking heavily when he was fifteen, and his father had whipped him across his bare buttocks with a belt when he'd been in his teens. After he left the Browns he played for the Kansas City Monarchs, where he started to carry a gun. In Dallas one night, when he was with his sister, he got into an argument in a bar, pulled out his .32 automatic, and started firing. The man who had gone for him, someone named Buddy Crow who had played sandlot ball with Hank years before, died.

Thompson was arrested on a murder charge and released on a $5,000 bond. Thompson claimed that Crow had come at him with a knife. His lawyer argued that it was justifiable homicide. Thompson got out on bond and joined the Monarchs for spring training. Two years later, with the help of the Giants, the case against Thompson was dismissed. The Giants knew about this killing, of course, but what they didn't know was that Thompson had an alcohol problem.

In 1950 Thompson got into the record books in several ways. He was already the first black man to play with the Browns, the first black to play in both leagues, and, when he batted against the Dodgers' Don Newcombe, was the first black hitter ever to face a black pitcher. Aside from the trivia records, Thompson participated in forty-three double plays in 1950 at third base, also a record at the time.

There were five blacks in the National League when Hank joined Irvin with the Giants. Robinson, Roy Campanella, and Newcombe were the others, all with the Dodgers. All of them spent an inordinate amount of time on their backs, for pitchers were constantly throwing at them. One time when Hank hit a home run, the pitcher screamed at him as he rounded the bases: "I'll get you the next time, you black bastard!" If such indelicate words were still in common usage—and probably were even used by some men on Durocher's club—they stung deeply. Playing for Durocher, however, made life a bit easier for blacks like Thompson.

Another black youngster, Artie Wilson, a speedster from Springfield, Alabama, who was twenty-one years old, instantly caught Durocher's eye. Leo liked men who could move on the bases, and Wilson, who had hit well the year before in the Pacific Coast League, looked as if he might make it as an infielder. Wilson also had some potential as an interpreter for Ray Noble, the black Cuban catcher, whom Durocher hoped could spell Wes Westrum behind the plate during the 1951 season. Artie had learned to speak Spanish in Cuba and thus could help Noble, who had never mastered English during his employment at Jersey City, to order something other than chicken. Perhaps, too, Noble could learn enough words to comprehend the barked commands of Durocher.

Good pitching, in Leo's eyes, needed good quarterbacking. Catchers like Wes Westrum, a thick-muscled man of 198 pounds, with rosy cheeks, who was brought up to the Giants in 1947 from Minneapolis, was still there in 1951. Westrum was a dependable athlete who knew how to handle pitchers and showed sporadic power. In 1950 he hit twenty-three home runs, and much of the late-season pitching heroics from Maglie and Hearn could have been credited to his competence behind the plate.

"I'd notice little things about pitchers, whether they were coming in high or low, or out of the strike zone," said Westrum, "or whether hitters were knocking out line drives or pop-ups. I'd tell Leo what I was seeing and he relied on what I told him to make his decisions whether to yank a guy or keep him in."

Westrum was the type of durable player who could catch doubleheaders. "If Leo asked me to do it, I would. He'd just put my name on the lineup card, and that's the way it was," said Westrum, with more than a touch of pride.

Durocher was not the kind of person who could be intimidated, for *he* did the intimidating. But Westrum always remembered one instance when one of his relief pitchers got away with it. The reliever came in and, on Durocher's orders, was supposed to pitch a certain way. He shook Westrum off, however, threw his own pitch, and the batter got a game-winning double.

"You can imagine how hopping mad Leo was," Westrum said. "He got on me, real bad. He never minded hollering at guys in front of everybody and could be very profane. The good thing about him was that he'd forget the whole business the next day."

While Westrum was taking his tongue-lashing from his manager, the relief pitcher listened. When Durocher was finished, the pitcher looked right at him and said: "Wes didn't throw that ball, *I* did."

"That was one time Leo kept quiet. He gazed at the pitcher, shrugged, and walked away," recalled Westrum.

Westrum was born in Clearbrook, Minnesota, in 1922. During the Depression his father, a creamery man and extract salesman, ran into hard times. In thirty-below weather, his father chopped his own wood. The family had to go on relief.

"It was a hard, rugged life, but we always had enough to eat," Westrum remembered. "Maybe it was the best training in the world for catching those hot doubleheaders later on with the Giants."

A pleasant man, who always took his baseball work seriously, Wes occasionally stumbled into malaprops. He was known as the manager (in later years with the New York Mets) who referred to close ball games as "those one-run cliff dwellers." The Giants, under Durocher, Wes once said, were a team that really played together—"they were unionized," meaning that they were unified. In 1951 ballplayers had no unions. Durocher could send a man back to the minors in an instant, and often did.

4

The Outfielders

THE OUTFIELD has traditionally been the main roosting place for baseball's heaviest hitters. Around New York, in the years of the Yankee dominance, it was always the outfielders who led the way and were the most prolific group of sluggers. In the 1920s Babe Ruth, Earle Combs, and Bob Meusel formed for the Yankees as explosive an outfield as you could find then or at any future time.

In the first fifty years of the twentieth century there were some National League outfields that featured exceptional hitters. On the Chicago Cubs Hack Wilson, the human fireplug who hit an all-time National League high of fifty-six home runs in 1930, had two belting brethren in the outfield with him. One was Riggs "Old Hoss" Stephenson, one of the most underrated and sadly forgotten of all ballplayers. He played fourteen years, batted .336 in his lifetime, and only twice missed batting .300. Kiki Cuyler, the third Cub outfield, was a .321 lifetime hitter who justifiably made the Hall of Fame.

Some years after Wilson-Cuyler-Stephenson disappeared from the scene, the Cardinals put together an outfield triumvirate of Stan Musial, Country Slaughter, and Terry Moore, which collectively was a constant threat to all pitchers. Moore, however, was no Earle Combs when it came to hitting.

The Giants never managed to put together such similarly formidable outfields in the twenties, thirties, or forties. From time to time they developed individual stars such as Ross Youngs, Lefty O'Doul, and Edd Roush, who handled bats with skill. But they never presented a triple-threat outfield.

O'Doul had a lifetime batting average of .349, but he did his most productive hitting elsewhere, including, of all places, Brooklyn. The tragic Youngs, always a favorite of McGraw, batted .355 in 1924, but three years later he was dead of Bright's disease. Roush, a hardheaded negotiator at contract time, who once enraged McGraw by holding out for an entire year, was a better hitter with Cincinnati than he ever was with the Giants.

But in the mythogenic Melvin Thomas Ott, the Shetland Pony outfielder, the Giants came up with their chief competition against the Yanks' outfield hegemony. Unfortunately for the Giants, Ott was never surrounded, as Ruth was, by superior hitters such as Combs and Meusel. In the person of Joe Moore, the "Gause Ghost," who played a steady center field alongside Ott in right field, they had an able batsman. But where was the other big hitter in that trio?

Ott first sprouted on the Giant scene in early September 1925, when he reported to McGraw at the Polo Grounds. He was a fresh-faced, unsophisticated little kid from out of the Louisiana bayou country, where his father had been an oil refinery laborer. The young man stayed around for more than a quarter of a century, becoming, perhaps, the most popular of all Giants. In fact, Mel was often thought of as the first child ever born in a Polo Grounds dugout!

"Have you ever played the outfield?" McGraw asked his protégé, who had been a schoolboy catcher.

"Not since I was a kid," Master Melvin, not quite seventeen at the time, answered, according to legend.

Ott soon developed an inimitable, unorthodox southpaw batting style that was perfect for the Polo Grounds, with its inviting right-field sector. Before each mighty swing, Ott's right leg would lift crazily in the air, in a simulated goose step. In the next twenty-two years this stance produced 511 home runs.

No Giant outfielder before Ott ever came close to this 5'9", 170-pound slugger. No outfielder ever came close after he left, until 1951. But that's getting a little ahead of the story.

The Giants began the 1951 season with an outfield that, on

paper, was not meant to cause any tremors among the rival pitching fraternity. They had Carroll "Whitey" Lockman in left field, Bobby Thomson in center field, and Don Mueller in right field. Theoretically, the most curious member of Durocher's cast, Clint Hartung, played the role of pretender to either the left- or right-field jobs, in case of emergency or power failure on the part of Lockman or Mueller.

Lockman had to be rated the most consistent hitter in the outfield. He hit .295 in 1950, not much different from his finish in either 1948 or 1949. He got more than his share of doubles, but nobody ever considered him a home run slugger. Thomson, down at .252 in 1950, had a deserved reputation as a long-ball hitter, having accumulated twenty-five home runs that year. But there had been a lingering suspicion about him, often circulated by the press (despite Bobby's basic decency and modesty), that he was destined to be one of those ballplayers who would never quite come up to people's expectations. In 1949 he had hit .309, the only year he had ever reached that particular arbitrary standard of baseball excellence. In other years his average remained ordinary, supporting a common belief that he might be just an ordinary center fielder.

Prior to 1951, Thomson's chief claim to fame—a totally unfair assessment, by the way—was that he'd been born in Glasgow, Scotland. That made him unique; no other ballplayer could give that as his birth venue. Also, continued his critics, Thomson played as shallow a center field as that most wondrous of all defensive geniuses, Tris Speaker, but without the skill to wrap himself around balls the way Speaker did. Was it a knock on a man to say he wasn't as good as Speaker?

The other player in the Giants' outfield trio, Don Mueller, had hit .291 in 1950, with limited explosions of power. Don's seven home runs that year was a respectable figure for him, as, over a twelve-year career that ended in 1959 due to painful arthritis in his legs, it represented a shade more than his average home run output.

Mueller's father, Walter, a small man at 5'8", had been a part-time player with a good Pittsburgh team from 1922 to 1926. With Pittsburgh Walter played as an extra outfielder, behind Max Carey, Clyde Barnhart, and Carson Bigbee. The one year the Pirates made it to the World Series Walter was out of baseball in order to help out with a brick-building company that he and an older brother had formed.

Don, born in 1927 and raised on a fruit farm and tree nursery west of St. Louis, had never seen his father play. But around the Mueller household in rural Missouri there had always been talk about baseball.

When Don got to be a teenager and was playing ball for Christian Brothers High School, Walter said to him one day that "although I was a pretty good hitter, I expect that you'll be a much better one."

Walter Mueller "cracked the whip," remembers Don. "I always liked to go fishing on Sundays, but to my Dad Sundays only meant two things—church and baseball."

Don's brother, Leroy, was regarded as a better prospect for baseball, but three years in the Pacific during World War II, where he developed a jungle fever, took its toll. Leroy never got past Class C baseball in the Red Sox system. That left it up to Don to carry on the family tradition.

Not only did Don ultimately surpass his dad as a hitter, but by the time he'd reached his late teens he was taller, slightly over six feet.

By 1944, when Mueller was seventeen, he had achieved some renown in his home area as a smart hitter. His one perceived drawback was that he ran as if his spikes had been dipped in molasses. Nevertheless, the scouts were impressed by his play, at first base and in the outfield, in American Legion competition.

A Giants scout, Jack McGuire, wasted little time recommending Don to the Giants and Ott, who was then managing the team. (At the age of thirty-two, in 1941, five days before the Japanese ignited World War II with their attack on Pearl Harbor, Ott had been named to succeed Bill Terry as the Giants' manager.)

Ott took a busman's holiday to St. Louis, where he watched Don play at Sportsman's Park. He liked what he saw and got Stoneham to sign Mueller to a contract with the Giants' farm club in Jersey City.

First Don put in some time with the Merchant Marine. When he gained his discharge, he went to Jersey City, where a little fellow named Bruno Betzel (his full name was Christian Frederick Albert John Henry David Betzel) took him under his wing. In 1946

Don hit .359 in a half season. Then he went to Jacksonville and finally to Minneapolis, where he played under Tommy Heath.

In 1948, when he was just twenty-one, Don reached the Polo Grounds, where he encountered an entirely different type of manager than he had ever played for previously. Durocher could be intimidating for a vulnerable youngster like Mueller.

"Durocher really scared me at first," admitted Mueller. "But soon we started to get along just fine. Once he even made a friendly bet on me at spring training with Al Rosen of the Indians. Leo bet that I'd outhit Dale Mitchell, a teammate of Rosen's, over the season. I was ahead of Mitchell for a while, but near the end of the season I went into an awful slump and Mitchell finished ahead of me. Leo lost his bet, but he never took it out on me, even if he never forgot it. He was a butt-chewer of a manager, but I'd have to say he was the most astute guy I ever played for, and that includes Betzel, Heath, Bill Rigney, Gabby Hartnett, and Al Lopez. Durocher wasn't very lovable, but he got results."

In 1948 and 1949 Don played in fewer than 100 games for the Giants, hitting only a single home run in 137 at-bats. Even if he promised to be a clone of Wee Willie Keeler—hittin' 'em where they ain't and between the infielders and just short of the outfielders—some still insisted that he would have to generate more power to remain in the majors.

A Virginian named Willard Marshall was the regular right fielder in those two years—and he *could* hit home runs. In 1947 Marshall connected for 36 homers and drove in 107 runs. The next year Marshall hit a personal high of .307. Yet Durocher had made up his mind to make Marshall part of the controversial package that was sent off to the Boston Braves for Al Dark and Eddie Stanky. With the consummation of that trade Mueller advanced to the post of starting right fielder.

After the 1950 season, in which Mueller played 132 games but amassed only 28 extra-base hits out of 153 hits, Durocher still remained convinced that he had himself one of the genuine hitters of his era. The last of the .400 hitters, Ted Williams, who knew something about the art of hitting and spent countless hours talking about it, volunteered to Durocher, after watching Mueller in spring training, that he thought Don was the best hitter on the Giants.

"That's an opinion from a pretty good source," said Durocher, when he was informed about what Williams had said. "For my dough, I never saw a hitter with the alertness that Don has at the plate."

Such remarks raised the level of Mueller's confidence. "When I go up there to hit," he explained, "I see the way all the infielders are stationed. I pride myself in being able to hit just where the biggest hole is."

That might have sounded like utter nonsense coming from some players, but it made sense coming from Mueller. In due course, the newspapers elected to call him Mandrake, in honor of his magical performance with a bat. "Mueller approached the game, especially his hitting," wrote Thomas Kiernan, "with the guile of a street-wise pickpocket . . . but he was certainly not a city slicker."

Playing right field in the Polo Grounds was no simple saunter in the sun, either, for balls could ricochet at mean, crazy angles off the wall. After a while, despite his lack of speed, Don managed the position almost as skillfully as Ott had for so many years. Some even insisted he was better at it then Ross Youngs.

In the left-field spot in 1951 was the southpaw-swinging Lockman, who, at twenty-five, was in his sixth season with the club. That made him something of an elder statesman. Born in Lowell, North Carolina, in 1926, Lockman was only eight months old when his father died. He grew up as a loose, genial guy and in time was called "Whitey" in celebration of his cotton-top, which was visible anywhere on the field. Some of his boyhood pals preferred to call him "Pickle." Finally, when he landed in a big league clubhouse, he was referred to as "Lock." But whatever he was called by his peers, Lockman got along well with all of them.

Later in his career with the Giants, after an unknown character had phoned in a warning to the police that he was going to kill Lockman if he showed up for an exhibition game in Las Vegas, Whitey reacted in typical fashion. "I can't think of a soul who'd want to take my life," he said, mildly. "As a matter of fact, I have no relatives in southern Nevada."

Like so many other players on the Giants, Lockman viewed the coming of Durocher to the New York locker room in 1948 with more than casual dread. Leo's reputation as a hard-driving, foul-mouthed guy had preceded him.

"Hell, he sure scared some of us to death," recalled Lockman. "But once we got used to him and the way he operated, he didn't frighten me or anybody else anymore."

When Lockman was little more than ten years old he was already playing on a company team in Homestead, North Carolina. A fireman living in Charlotte tipped off the Giants about Whitey, when he was sixteen, and in short order he was signed for $1,000, plus $250 a month.

By 1945 he was with the Giants, still under Ott, and got in thirty-two games before joining the military service. The first time he batted in the majors Whitey hit a home run, putting him with an elite group that is suitably listed in the record books.

As a technical sergeant aboard a navy transport doing ferrying in the Pacific, Lockman lost the baseball year of 1946. Looking forward eagerly to his first postwar season in 1947, Whitey wound up on the sidelines after fracturing his right leg and dislocating his ankle on a slide into second base in an April exhibition game in Sheffield, Alabama, against Cleveland. He came to bat only two times that entire season.

Soon he realized that the injuries he had sustained had dramatically diminished the force and accuracy of his right-handed throws back to the infield from left field. It was hard for him to get a firm footing on the ground as he reared back to throw.

Remarkably, Lockman became a superb drag bunter, one of the most adept in his league. The next season, in an early game against the Dodgers, he proved to himself and others that he would be in left field to stay when he batted in all four Giant runs in a 4–4 tie at Ebbets Field, in a game that was halted when both teams had to catch trains.

"I felt I was back to where I'd been before getting hurt," said Whitey.

Of the three starting outfielders in 1951, twenty-seven-year-old Robert Brown Thomson was by far the most potent slugger. Bobby Thomson was a tall (6'2"), 180-pound, dark-haired man with a prominent nose and constantly wide eyes that encouraged you to think he was surprised at something you just said. His manner was pleasant, wry, often self-deprecating, and decidedly low-key. When he walked he plodded, and when he ran he had a loping, somewhat clumsy gait that could be spotted quickly from a distant bleacher seat. But his ambulatory style was deceptive, for he could move with good speed on the base paths.

Thomson's high, sloping shoulders surrounding a long, muscular neck and lean body caused him to be nicknamed "The Hawk" when he wasn't being good-naturedly referred to, due to his Scotch antecedents, as "Hoot Mon."

The Thomson family moved to America when Bobby was still a little boy. They settled in Staten Island, at 411 Flagg Place, New Dorp. By far the most sparse, isolated, and blue collar of New York's boroughs, Staten Island traditionally has been the home of many policemen and firemen who worked in the other boroughs.

To get to Manhattan from Staten Island, one took a ferry ride for a nickel for a trip that consumed less than twenty-five minutes. But Staten Island remained light-years away from the rusting old girders, metallic green seats, and noisy turmoil of the Polo Grounds.

Bobby was quite close to his father, James, and to his one brother and four sisters. Though life was generally a constant struggle for the elder Thomson, who made a sparse living as a cabinetmaker, that didn't deter him from having a warm relationship with Bobby. James, a soccer player who never played baseball, had been gassed in the First World War, when he had been a member of the Scots Guards in the British army.

Due to Bobby's involvement with baseball as a youngster, James also developed an interest in the game. He became a fervent rooter for the Brooklyn Dodgers and a special fan of Dolf Camilli, who came to the Dodgers in 1938 and helped lead them to a National League flag in 1941, after two decades of famine. It was often remarked in those years that Camilli, a slugging first baseman, bore a strong physical resemblance to Durocher, who was then Dolf's manager.

On many Sundays Bobby and his dad would walk two or three miles to watch ball games being played on Staten Island, and when Bobby played with local teams his father was on hand to cheer him in a sport that became less strange to him all the time.

"Dad chose the Dodgers as his team because they were known to be underdogs," remembered Bobby. "Unfortunately, he never got to see me play in the big leagues."

When Bobby's father went to the hospital before he died, a

friend said to him, kiddingly, of course, that Bobby would probably wind up playing some day with the Giants.

"Darn right, he will," said James Thomson.

"My father wanted me to play in the big leagues, even if it
wasn't going to be with his Dodgers," recalled Bobby.

By the time Bobby was seventeen, and a star at Curtis High
School in Staten Island, the Giants signed him for $100, which
must rank as one of baseball's most astonishing bargains. In 1942,
when he was still in his teens, Bobby played third base for Rocky
Mount in the Bi-State League. The next year he was sent to Bristol
in the Appalachian League. When his country put in a call for him,
he spent three years in the air corps, where he graduated from a
bombardier school in Victorville, California. He never went over-
seas. Following military service, he attended St. Lawrence University in upstate New York. But the educational exposure lasted only
several months. Urged by his family to continue his schooling,
Bobby informed them he hadn't any desire to remain there. It
didn't surprise anyone when he threw St. Lawrence up for baseball.

In 1946 he played for Jersey City, where he got into 151
games, in the outfield and at third base. He was swatting away at
.290, when Ott looked fondly at his output of twenty-six home
runs and put in a call for him. In eighteen games with the Giants,
all at third base, Thomson hit .315 and connected for his first two
major league home runs. Despite Bobby's efforts, the Giants
ended in the National League's basement. In retrospect, the season might have been notable if only for Bobby's indoctrination as
a Giant. But what is memorable at all, if you put it that way, was
that the most enduring Durocher legend was born that year on
July 5.

During a doubleheader on July 4 at the Polo Grounds against
the Dodgers, the Giants exploded for five home runs, a matter that
didn't sit well at all with Durocher, then the Dodgers' manager.

In the Dodger dugout the next night, prior to the game, Red
Barber, the lay preacher who had become Brooklyn's favorite baseball broadcaster, despite his roots in the Deep South, was engaging
in a bit of soft needling of Durocher.

"Those were quite some home runs," said Barber, quietly.

"Oh, hell, they were nothing but pop flies," barked Durocher.
"On a bigger field they would have been nothing but outs."

"Come on, Leo," continued Barber, "why don't you admit they were real home runs. Be a nice guy for a change."

Durocher leaped to his feet, almost striking his head on the dugout roof. "Nice guy? Who wants to be a nice guy," he exclaimed. "Look over there in that Giant dugout. Look at Ott. He's a nice guy. Why, those Giants are the nicest guys in the world. But where the hell are they? In last place!"

The gruff exchange with Barber has since been recrafted, and twisted into what was purportedly Durocher's trademarked gut philosophy of life. It won Leo a sort of reverse immortality. Maybe only Yogi Berra's "It's never over until it's over" can be rated on the same level of durability in baseball's market of familiar quotations as "Nice guys don't win pennants." No wonder nobody recalled that Bobby Thomson came up to the Giants that same year.

In 1947, Bobby's first full year with New York, he hit .283 and batted in eighty-five runs, with the help of twenty-nine home runs. The next year he sank to sixteen homers and a .248 average, indulging himself in the unpopular pastime called the "sophomore jinx."

But in 1949 Bobby had a satisfying year, as he played the entire schedule of games, batting .309 and smacking 27 home runs. While knocking in 109 runs in his 641 at-bats, Thomson struck out only 45 times, which makes today's sluggers look like Braille students. Only Ralph Kiner and Stan Musial finished ahead of Bobby in slugging average.

Just when everything looked like it was coming up roses for Bobby, he slipped back to .252 in 1950, after suffering a disastrous first four months of the year. Toward the end of the season he picked up, but there was little to write home about to the fans back in Staten Island.

It was, in some respects, a different and turbulent baseball world that Thomson was playing in in those few years—and a warm and understanding family background helped prepare him for it.

"We didn't have two nickels to rub together when I grew up," recalls Thomson. "But that didn't stop my dad from putting together a generous basket of food on Christmas Day and then personally delivering it to a poor black family living on Staten Island. Parents play an important role, it seems to me, in how kids are raised. So when black guys like Irvin and others came to the Giants, I don't think I gave it a second thought. To me, the way a guy conducted himself was the only thing that really mattered. That's how I judged a man. I can't speak for the other guys on the Giants, but I never was disturbed by the fact that we had black guys playing with us. Maybe I was too naive even to appreciate that some guys didn't like blacks or that some people treated them badly. But it wasn't in my thinking, and I guess my parents should get credit for that."

During the winter before the 1951 season got underway Bobby took long hikes at six-thirty almost every morning, with his boxer dog at his side. He was determined to restore his team's confidence in him and to continue the late-season surge he had experienced in 1950.

After some discussion about an alteration of his batting stance, Thomson decided to do something about it. He had previously had a posture at home plate that resembled the wide-open, picture-book stance of Joe DiMaggio, his Yankee neighbor across the Harlem River. Joe was envied and copied, but not too successfully, by many players. Bobby had something of a similar stance, but sometimes in swinging early, off his front foot, he could appear awkward in attacking the pitch.

"Even if I looked like him occasionally," said Thomson, "I never really copied DiMag's approach. I was actually a big Mel Ott fan. But I never would have thought to copy Mel's stance. Who could have? Nobody else could hit that way, could they?"

Durocher thought that Bobby might fare better with a closed stance, in a slight crouch, along the lines of a right-handed version of the southpaw hitter Stan Musial. It was often said about Musial that when he batted he looked like "a burglar peeking around the corner at the pitcher." If Thomson could inherit only a modest portion of Stan's success with a Musial-like stance, insisted Durocher, he'd be the hitter the Giants would like him to be. Bobby gave an ear to all these opinions and waited for the season to start.

With Thomson, Lockman, and Mueller presumably set as Durocher's first-line outfield, Clint Hartung was the spare—and a strange one, at that. He was tall (6′5″), floppy-eared, toothy, and hailed from Hondo, Texas, a small mining and ranching town that most metropolitan New York writers would have had difficulty locating on a map. Clint came to the Giants, right after World War II, as the widely heralded rebirth of every natural ballplayer that ever lived. He was "half-Feller, half-Foxx," the clairvoyants predicted. The Giants' veteran press agent Garry Schumacher could have put all the forests in the tundra out of business with his avalanche of press releases about this young Texan.

The straight truth about the poor fellow was that the Giants' abysmal performance in 1946 made it urgent that Schumacher spread such hype around. The New York press hungered for good news, and the fans yearned for a new, postwar era. When Schumacher boasted that "Hartung should head straight for Cooperstown"—a venue many long miles from Hondo—the writers cooperated and the fans bit eagerly at the bait. They had no idea that Hartung could play several positions—most of them poorly.

There had, of course, been other highly touted phenoms in baseball before Hartung ambled along. He wasn't even the first to be canonized, then flop with the Giants. There had been Cohen in 1928. Then, in the early forties, "The Crabapple Comet," Johnny Rucker, came and went, without so much as a dent in the record books. Elsewhere, Paul Strand was bought for the staggering sum of $100,000 by the Athletics in 1924, yet failed to last the season. Benny McCoy was another American League wunderkind in the 1940s, and the moon-faced "Mad Russian," Lou Novikoff, came to the Cubs in 1941 as a fence-buster. But the Cubs overlooked a minor point: he couldn't field much, even if he could sing "When Irish Eyes Are Smiling" more than adequately.

Hartung played some minor-league ball with Eau Claire in the Class C Northern League in Wisconsin in 1942 before entering the army. It was while Clint was in the service that his Bunyanesque legend was augmented considerably. In one season in Hawaii he hit a meager .567, or so it was reported, with a mess of prodigious home runs that floated through the warm air at Hickam Field. During the same season he won twenty-five games as a right-handed pitcher. Thereupon, he was signed to a Minneapolis pact, and by 1945 the Giants paid $25,000 plus four players to buy up the Hondo Hurricane's contract. When Hartung tried to reenlist almost simultaneously with his purchase by the Giants, the New York front office was flabbergasted.

"Doesn't this guy know that the war is over?" a Giant executive asked. He should have been forewarned. It was army pitching only that Clint could hit into the next county—and maybe Clint appreciated that.

In the Giants' spring training camp of 1947 Hartung connected for a long home run his first time up. But wise guys took note that he played ground balls in the outfield the way bettors bet on horses—on speculation. He started in right field on opening day, amidst much fanfare, but after a month of muffed fly balls, bobbled grounders, and hits that didn't fall, manager Ott, always the nice guy, requested that Clint return to the mound. As a pitcher, Clint had a reasonable facsimile of a fastball, but his curve didn't curve.

From 1947 through 1950 Hartung won twenty-nine games and lost twenty-nine games, which gave him pretty good balance. But his earned run average was never lower than 4.57.

When Bill Roeder of the *World-Telegram* wrote a wry article devoted to "The Legend of Hartung," Clint asked Durocher's permission "to punch out" the sportswriter. "I'm gonna kill him," announced Hondo, "if he writes that story one more time!"

Despite these misadventures, Hartung still was on Durocher's roster in 1951. He was a man who had had more chances than a good shortstop in a doubleheader. It remained to be seen just how much action Clint would get since Durocher was inclined to regard him as an outfielder, if he regarded him as anything, in the pennant drive of 1951.

5

In This Corner—
Charlie Dressen

NOBODY EVER had to order a cow to give milk or to command an orchid to release its wondrous fragrance. So it would have been equally ludicrous to teach Charles Walter Dressen the ropes about advanced solipsism. Dressen spent most of an insecure lifetime as a confirmed first-person-pronoun man, albeit a rather harmless one. Nothing pleased him more than to talk endlessly and ungrammatically about himself and his achievements. He simply refused to be topped by anyone.

Invariably, after teams he managed had won ball games, reporters could tune in—or out—on his shameless boasting about how "I did this" or how "I did that" to win the game. One famous afternoon when Dressen's team lagged behind in an early inning, he loudly promised his players that "if you stay close to these fellas, I'll think of something!" This brash pronouncement became a byword in every dugout that Dressen ever inhabited—but it also became a mock incantation from the benches of his rivals.

Dodgers pitcher Clem Labine said of Dressen that as much as he admired the manager's "guts and spirit" he always found that Dressen's suggestion that he was more important than his players "was an outright absurdity."

Nevertheless, say what you will about his bloated ego, Dressen was a hardworking, hard-thinking little man who had many admirers. Pee Wee Reese, the Dodgers' long-time shortstop and captain, said Charlie "must know more about baseball than any man alive" and Jackie Robinson added that "even if Dressen might get to guys a little with his way of expressing himself, those who know him well know he means well, and that he's for his players one hundred percent."

Dressen was born in Decatur, Illinois, in September 1898, the year the United States went to war with Spain over Cuba. Gene Tunney, who became heavyweight champ of the world, and Paul Robeson, who became champion of the world's singers, were born the same year. Dressen had a scant educational background, putting in only a single year at Assumption High School. This accounted in no small part for his difficulties with verbs and syntax, but it didn't stop him from being a compulsive talker and gabber all his life.

"He wanted to be known as a smart baseball man," wrote Frank Graham, Jr., "and he worked at it 24 hours a day, dreaming up clever moves, as an adolescent creates fantasies, eager to talk to anybody if it might help his ball club . . . he was a born loser, who sometimes won."

One day Dressen spotted a young sportswriter lugging around a copy of Dostoevsky's *Crime and Punishment*. Charlie's curiosity got the better of him.

"What's that you've got there?" he asked.

"That's a book," answered the writer.

"I know—but what kind of a book?"

"A novel, a tragic novel," explained the writer.

"You know," said Dressen, sadly, "I've never read a book in my life."

"You ought to. It might help you make pep speeches and things like that," the reporter said, kindly.

"Nah," said Dressen, shaking his head. "I've got by pretty good so far without books. I ain't makin' no changes now."

While Dressen's father ran a neighborhood saloon (Babe Ruth's dad did the same thing on Baltimore's waterfront), Charlie was out at an early age selling newspapers and magazines, an enterprise that yielded him about ten dollars a week. For a while Charlie dabbled in semipro football, despite his small size (never more than 145 pounds and 5'5" tall). He played a pretty good quarterback for the Decatur Staleys, a hometown team, for sixty-seven dollars a week. By the time the Staleys became the Chicago Bears, Dressen was a minor-league infielder with St. Paul, where he hit .347 in 1924 and batted in enough runs to attract the attention of the Cincinnati Reds, then managed by Jack Hendricks. After the Reds bought up Charlie's contract, he became a third baseman, second baseman, shortstop, and even occasional outfielder for them, from 1925 to 1931. One of those years the Reds ended up in second place; the rest of the time they played less than .500 ball. If Dressen could do precious little to improve the Reds' performance, he brightened things up with his guile.

In a game in 1929 against the Cubs, Charlie pulled off a bit of mischief that became memorable. After Hack Wilson of the Cubs singled, the Reds' bench, particularly Ray Kolp, a Cincinnati pitcher, got on Hack so bad with his insults that Wilson bolted from first base and plunged into the Reds' dugout. After Hack unloaded a punch on Kolp's jaw, Dressen quietly produced a ball. Tagging Wilson for the out, Charlie informed the baffled umpires that Hack had failed to call time out. The Cubs protested that the bench jockeying was sufficient provocation for Hack's abandoning first base—but the umps backed up Dressen.

The next year Durocher, who had been a slick-fielding shortstop for the New York Yankees team that featured the famed Murderers' Row, including Ruth and Gehrig, joined Dressen on the Reds. Between them, they had more brass than a platoon of secondhand junk dealers. Durocher got to play a good deal more shortstop for the Reds in 1931 than Dressen got to play second. But while the Reds floundered around, with or without Leo or Charlie in the lineup, a mutual admiration developed between the two men. The attraction appeared to be based on tactlessness, aggressiveness, and gall, qualities that both possessed in abundance. Durocher also demonstrated that he was a vacuum cleaner at shortstop, once going through 251 straight chances without an error. Nevertheless, Leo still could not eradicate his reputation as "The All-American Out," a nickname that Ruth, no admirer of Durocher, affixed to Leo when he'd been with the Yankees.

When Dressen left the Reds in 1932 for a brief sojourn in the minors with Nashville, Durocher remained behind. But when Leo became manager of the Dodgers in the 1940s he hired his old sidekick as a coach, figuring that Charlie's reputed ability as a sign-stealer and bench strategist would pay dividends for his club.

In 1933 Dressen escaped from the minors with a call-up to the New York Giants, to serve as a utility infielder during that team's stretch drive to the National League pennant. After the Giants also won the World Series from Washington in five games, Dressen continually claimed credit for the Giants' 2–1 victory in the fourth game, even though he didn't play a single inning.

In the last of the eleventh, with the Giants ahead, 2–1, the Senators loaded the bases with one out against Carl Hubbell, the masterful southpaw. The situation at that moment called for a Giants kaffeeklatsch at the mound, in anticipation that Washington manager Joe Cronin would send up a pinch hitter for relief pitcher Jack Russell.

In the huddle Blondy Ryan, the Giants' shortstop, convinced manager Terry that the Giants should play back for a possible game-ending double play. A left-handed batter, Cliff Bolton, with a shiny .410 mark in thirty-three games, was then announced as Cronin's pinch hitter, something of a surprise, for Cronin was going against the prevalent theory of using right-handed swingers to face lefty pitchers. In this case, Cronin gambled that Bolton could hit Hubbell's screwball better than other right-handed hitters he had on his bench.

Seeing Bolton walk to the plate, Dressen, who knew him from the Southern Association, where Bolton had played for Chattanooga, ran out to the mound, double-time.

"Is this guy fast?" asked Terry, as Charlie appeared on the scene.

"No," answered Dressen. With that curt response, he turned and walked back to the Giant dugout.

Bolton then promptly hit into a quick double play, started by Ryan on a ball hit into the hole.

All that Dressen, in his ultimate wisdom, had contributed to the crucial play was the one word "No." But for years after that Dressen managed to merchandise the notion that he had shrewdly gotten the Giants to go for the double play.

"Either he's building himself up, or he's knocking somebody down," one of Dressen's associates said. "He has a pressing need to engage in such self-promotion."

Larry MacPhail, who always liked Dressen's style, hired him to manage the Reds in 1934. Despite Dressen's compulsive attention, the Reds still remained a losing ball club. Charlie lasted in the job until 1937.

"We ain't exactly a Red menace," said Charlie. "But if these clubs up ahead of us stop too often for gas, we'll go right by 'em." They never did.

A homemade book, with a cover saying *How to Manage in the Big Leagues* by Chuck Dressen, was placed in Dressen's locker one day in Milwaukee. Inside the book there were only blank pages, with the exception of the letter "I," which appeared on every page. If Dressen got the message, he never let on that he did. But it didn't deter him, in his own way, from going about trying to outthink the opposition. He was spotted in Ebbets Field a few days later chucking dozens of baseballs against a newly installed sheltered dugout in the left-field bull pen. He was simply trying to determine which way the balls would bounce along the foul line. How could you knock the little guy for that?

Dressen was a perpetual goad to his players. "He drives, drives, and drives some more," said Pee Wee Reese. "If you make a mistake he'll criticize you in front of players, thinking that the whole team should learn a lesson."

Dressen was a percentage player, who contemplated the nine innings of each game much as he would the nine horse races at the track.

There was a warm side to Dressen, too, but it was hard to pick it up through his incessant monologues and his deprecating comments about some of his players as "goldbricks." He never failed to remind his listeners that he'd worked his way up from nothing (to extreme poverty, as Groucho Marx once added). He enjoyed the give-and-take of press conferences with the writers covering the Dodgers, and, as the Dodgers were generous with food, Charlie was generous with his time and responses. But invariably he'd end up informing his rapt audience, in a gravelly voice, that "I won exactly nine games last year on the coaching lines by stealing signs and calling pitches." Who could verify or reject this contention with any hard evidence?

When Dressen coached under Leo he often acted, ironically, as a peacemaker between Durocher and MacPhail, the team's fiery chief executive. Charlie may have been as boorish as Leo, but his more gentle disposition stood him in good stead during such altercations.

Out of the majors in 1948, Dressen managed Oakland the next two years. In 1950 he took the club to the Pacific Coast League pennant. Meanwhile, in October, Branch Rickey sold his share of the Brooklyn franchise—a club that for eight years had prospered economically, socially in the integration department, and in the won-lost column under his calculating hand—to Walter O'Malley.

It was said that O'Malley was a man who never seemed to sleep. His first wide-awake move was to wave a quick good-bye to Burt Shotton, who, like the venerable Connie Mack, always managed in his civilian clothes. Shotton had been a true-blue Rickey man all his baseball life, almost an appendage to Rickey's body. With The Mahatma gone from the premises, Shotton had to leave. O'Malley wasted no time in disposing of the body.

In November, Dressen was summoned to O'Malley's Montague Street office in Brooklyn. Within moments, he was signed to a contract as the next Brooklyn manager. Suddenly he was back in business again as a big league pilot, except this time he would directly confront his old comrade-in-arms, Durocher, who could be expected to battle him for every inch of turf whenever the clubs settled down for civil war at the Polo Grounds and Ebbets Field. Dressen's ballplayers would soon learn, too, that they'd be left to their own devices only between the hours of 1:00 A.M. and 9:00 A.M. The rest of the time belonged to Charlie Dressen.

Dressen had a tough act to follow, for the Dodgers had won the National League pennant in 1947 and again in 1949, even if they lost the World Series each time to the Yankees. In 1950, it was a bare pennant miss due to Dick Sisler's clutch shot.

O'Malley liked money—and winners—in that order. He was hiring Dressen to win.

6

The Dodgers

IN 1950 BROOKLYN was first in hitting and first in fielding in the National League. But its final record of eighty-nine wins and sixty-five losses fell short by two games of heading off the Phillies for the flag.

The new pilot, Chuck Dressen, knew he had inherited a good ball club from Burt Shotton. But the question that had to be answered was how he'd react to the team's talent and how they would react to him.

Perhaps foremost among Dressen's problems was Jackie Robinson. Playing under stringent emotional wraps in his first years in the majors, Robinson was now exposing a side of his competitive personality that offended some rivals and even a few of his own teammates.

As the first black in baseball and as Branch Rickey's hand-picked pioneer, Robinson had kept his temper under reasonable control, while all around him fell invective and abuse. A few civilized players, deeply disturbed by what Robinson was subjected to on an almost daily basis, reached out to him. Carl Erskine, Pee Wee Reese, Lee Handley of the Phillies, Gil Hodges, Hank Greenberg, and Ralph Branca showed sensitivity to Jackie's problems. But the list of active supporters was never long.

"Keep your head," Rickey had warned Robinson in laying

down the precise Marquis of Queensberry rules that he was expected to follow. Jackie obeyed, but the frustrating, repressive experience was shattering to him, almost costing him his sanity.

It has been suggested that total constraint was a primary condition when Rickey hired Jackie. Rachel Robinson, Jackie's wife, has denied this. She insists that it was up to Jackie to mediate his own behavior, according to his own judgment. The widespread story that Jackie made such a pact with Rickey was part of the mistaken mythology about her husband, said Rachel Robinson.

Approaching the 1951 season, his fifth year with the Dodgers, Robinson, for the most part, had thrown off his restrictive shackles, for he felt more secure within himself. He was now saying what was on his mind, and that was plenty! He was through acting as if he were catatonic.

With the Rickey era at an end, Robinson also had to establish a new relationship with Walter O'Malley, who lacked Rickey's crusader instinct. Jackie's dealings with O'Malley would be chilly, for he remained loyal to the man who had brought him into baseball and broken down the bars that delayed his entrance into the game. He knew he would have to deal with Dressen, too, who had been close to Durocher, whom Jackie despised.

"When I began to sound off, I was portrayed as a wise-guy, uppity nigger," said Robinson.

Baseball's self-styled Bible, *The Sporting News,* continued to lecture Robinson, a man it condescendingly looked upon as a wayward black son. In ceaseless editorials the paper scolded Jackie, suggesting that he should just play ball and stop being a missionary. But it was difficult, if not impossible, for Robinson to separate the two images.

In 1950 Jackie had played 144 games at second base, knocking in 81 runs while batting .328, with 14 home runs and 39 doubles. Yet there was never any acceptable index that could measure how much Robinson contributed to his team, no Richter scale that delivered precise numbers on the intensity of his play.

But there was a way to judge the role of Robinson's shortstop partner, Harold "Pee Wee" Reese, the former marbles champ of Louisville, whose father had been a detective with the Louisville and Nashville Railroad. By common consent, it was felt that it was Reese who kept Robinson from inwardly tying himself up in such knots that he wouldn't be able to perform at the peak of his skills.

During the years the two men played alongside each other, as the best and highest-paid shortstop–second base combination in the National League, Reese continued to be a stabilizing influence on Jackie's emotions.

If one considered Reese's background—born in Kentucky in 1918, as a war was ending, then a high school graduate who was playing minor league ball even before he could vote—it was remarkable that he would evolve into Robinson's firmest supporter, the white man from the South who dared to acknowledge that a black man deserved his chance.

In 1946 Reese was on a navy transport coming home from Guam. Anticipating his discharge, after over three years away from the Dodgers, he was also eager to regain his old shortstop position. Then he heard the strange news, coming over the shortwave: Some colored guy named Robinson had been signed by Branch Rickey.

"This watermelon eater," a navy buddy informed Reese, "is a shortstop."

The news, if true, hit Reese hard. Would this black guy take his job? Would he come home to be beaten out of his livelihood by a damn nigger?

There were some disquieting days and nights ahead for Reese, moments that were conscience-racking. Imagine, he kept thinking, if this Robinson deprived him of his shortstop post, what would his hometown pals say about that.

Slowly but surely, Pee Wee filtered out all the negatives, all those things he'd grown up with, all those prejudices and superstitions. What kind of a man could he be if he refused to compete with another man on an equal level? If the other guy turned out to be better at the job, why shouldn't he get it? Suppose Reese was the only white man competing against Robinson in a black league. How would he feel about that?

Call it Pee Wee's private code of ethics and morality— whatever it was—he came out on the right side, the side that gave Robinson his chance.

As it turned out, Reese would keep his shortstop job. He was too good not to keep it. But Jackie also reaped his own reward.

On the first road trip Robinson made with the Dodgers in his 1947 year of indoctrination, Reese made it abundantly clear where he stood on the issue of whether a man who was black could play this game without harassment. As the vitriol poured out of the stands in St. Louis, joining the mean cacophonic chorus from the Cardinals' dugout, Reese calmly walked over to Jackie near second base and put his hand on his teammate's left shoulder. There was no mistaking this as anything but a sign of support. Jackie recognized the gesture for what it was; he never forgot it.

Later, in a spring training exhibition game at Macon, Georgia, Reese again openly gave support to his teammate. Before the game Robinson had received an anonymous letter threatening that he'd be shot dead if he took the field that night. When Robinson arrived at the park his eyes searched the stands and he spied almost one cop for every paying customer. How many of those gendarmes were on his side was also questionable.

When the Dodgers warmed up, Reese noticed Jackie standing alone in the infield, his back to the stands. Pee Wee sidled over to him.

"Hey, why don't you get away from me, you human target," laughed Pee Wee. "That guy will take a shot at you and hit me!"

Robinson didn't like being a sniper's target any more than the next man. He was understandably jarred by the circumstances in which he found himself.

"But when Pee Wee kidded me about it, I loosened up. Everything was all right," said Jackie.

As different as two personalities could be, Pee Wee and Jackie represented an odd but brilliant synergistic force on the Dodgers. Pee Wee was so pale in complexion that it appeared he might have been imprisoned during the off season. His hair was flaxen, his face looked youthful and untroubled. Jackie was a dark, almost purplish black color, and his hair grew out of a tight, wiry curl. Sometimes his face in repose was brooding, though his eyes could twinkle and his smile was friendly. Reese was tiny by baseball standards, only 157 pounds, 5'10". He spoke quietly, without big words or first-person declamations. Courtesy and civility came easy to him.

Robinson was heavy-hipped, pigeon-toed, with shoulders that could have been a fullback's. Sometimes there was too much weight at the belt line and around his neck, and Jackie was sensitive about that. He liked to play at 200 pounds. His voice was pleasant, surprisingly high-pitched, and sometimes he spoke almost as rapidly as he could move on the bases.

Jackie was contentious, challenging, quick to anger. "He

would say exactly what was on his mind," recalled Carl Erskine. "There were no subtleties with him." Robinson would devour each day's newspaper with the zeal of a research analyst.

Conversely, Reese, easygoing and respectful of his fellows, was a man who never wanted to be mad at anyone. If he had a bad day at the ballpark, he chose to skip the next day's papers.

There was another major difference between these two men. Pee Wee was fond of Durocher, even if Leo was now the gauleiter in the enemy camp.

"I wouldn't be here today," he'd say, "if it wasn't for him. He helped me when I was a raw kid breaking in out of Louisville. I can't ever forget that."

When Durocher got a good look at Reese at the 1940 Clearwater, Florida, training camp he decided on the spot that Pee Wee would be the man to replace the Dodger shortstop, who happened to be Leo Durocher. Such faith on Leo's part was translated into firm loyalty on Reese's, through the dismal errors of Pee Wee's first big-league campaign, through his anemic .228 batting average in 1941, and through the years he was away in the navy.

Reese remembered that Leo was always ready to lay open his own vast store of knowledge about the game, even if he was too shy at the beginning to ask his mentor questions. One day, drawing up his courage, Pee Wee finally approached Durocher.

"I'd like your advice on something," Reese said, respectfully.

"Great, Pee Wee, what is it?" Leo asked, delighted that the young man was at last taking him up on his offer.

"Where do you get your clothes?" Pee Wee inquired.

Robinson detested Durocher, without reservations. There was an irony here, for Robinson was as grimly competitive as Durocher and should have been pleased to share that trait with him.

"If Leo lay in the street, Robinson would probably just walk around him and Durocher would respond in kind," Harold Rosenthal of the *Herald Tribune*, who covered almost every game Robinson played, once wrote.

Jackie resented Durocher's impolitic manner in the clubhouse. He knew Leo would never hesitate to bawl out players in front of an audience, whose eardrums could be shattered by his voice and the ugliness of his dialogue.

"He did it out loud, so everyone could hear," said Jackie.

When Jackie put on considerable weight one winter, after he was wined and dined regally on the banquet circuit, Durocher let him know about it in no uncertain terms. Jackie seethed with resentment. When Leo left the Dodgers to join the Giants in 1948, Jackie was the happiest fellow in the world, while the two competing boroughs bristled with hostility and disbelief.

In 1950 Reese batted .260, with eleven home runs and seventeen stolen bases, pretty much the norm for him over a full season of games. He'd even played seven games at third base, the first year he'd altered his infield geography even one whit.

With the 1951 season on the horizon, Reese was the sole Dodger player who had participated in three World Series—1941, 1947, and 1949. He was the last link to the storied Brooklyn teams of pre–World War II, with those colorful personalities who produced more anecdotes than victories. Though Pee Wee hadn't played with many of them, he was a carryover, in the eyes of the fans, to such Dodger nobility as the inimitable Babe Herman, the spirit of Brooklyn baseball from 1925 to 1931; Pete Reiser, the center fielder who defied one too many fences; spitballer Burleigh Grimes; Casey Stengel, a Dodger manager a few years before Pee Wee made his debut; the Old Dazzler, Arthur Vance, who, at the age of thirty, had yet to win a single big league game; the big smoke-balling South Carolinian Van Lingle Mungo, still throwing fastballs when Reese arrived; the mustachioed Frenchy Bordagaray; infielders Joe Stripp and Tony Cuccinello; the booze-ridden Kirby Higbe; Fat Freddie Fitzsimmons, who had pitched almost a lifetime with the Giants, then half a lifetime with the Dodgers; Ducky Medwick, who went from St. Louis's Gashouse Gang to the Dodgers. The list was endless, with its share of comics as well as journeymen. But they were all somehow connected with Reese— and you couldn't really say that about any of the other Dodger stars of the fifties.

So it was Reese, the glue of the Dodgers, the man who made the plays every day like clockwork, the social revolutionary who did it with a modest smile, and Robinson, the glowering perfectionist, who ended up fighting all the hard fights in the world. "He could have done anything he set out to do," Reese once said about Jackie. "It didn't have to be baseball. He was articulate and sharp—and when he started to speak out, easy to dislike. But he taught me a lot more than I ever taught him."

In 1951 you couldn't imagine one man without the other—or the Dodgers without either of them.

On the right side of the Dodger infield, at first base, was their 200-pound Rock of Gibraltar, Gil Hodges. A man with the durability of Lou Gehrig and the outer calm of Gandhi, he had come to the Dodgers long ago, in 1943, for a $500 bonus.

He first set foot in Brooklyn in August of that year, when he visited the Dodgers' tryout camp at Olean, New York, and played one game at third base. He had been attending St. Joseph's College in Indiana when he heard about the camp. Shortly after that, he joined the marines, spending over two hard years of combat in Okinawa and other pestholes.

When Gil returned in 1946 he played for the Dodgers' Newport News farm club as a catcher—and Rickey duly rewarded him with another $500. In 1947 he was still listed as a catcher, getting into twenty-eight games for the Dodgers.

But by 1948 there was plenty of scuttlebutt concerning another catcher, a roly-poly fellow from Philadelphia, half black, half Italian, named Roy Campanella. Campanella was catching at St. Paul, but word was that he was already better than most receivers then catching in the majors. Rickey thought so, too, and the theory was that he was on the verge of bringing up Campanella.

If Campy did come up to Brooklyn that would mean there would be three nominees for the job—Hodges, Campy, and Bruce Edwards, who had been the Dodgers' catcher in the 1947 World Series. Something had to give.

At the time Durocher had several candidates for first base— Howie Schultz, Ed Stevens, and Preston Ward. None of these gentlemen threatened to be another Dolf Camilli, or even a Del Bissonette, former Dodger heroes at the bag.

In mid-June Campy finally got the call from Rickey, and Gil was no longer a catcher. It was up to Durocher to find a new perch for him. And that's exactly what Leo did.

One day, on a sudden inspiration, Durocher walked over to Gil and popped the question: "Ever tried first base before?"

"Nope," answered Gil, who was pretty good at Gary Cooper terseness.

"Get yourself a glove and work out there," the manager directed. Somehow Durocher was convinced that Hodges could solve the intricacies of first-base play. The glove turned out to be the one Robinson had used in 1947 before he was switched to second base. Hodges used the glove for a few weeks. When he reasoned that he was set at the bag, he went and got a new one.

So started Hodges' honorable tenure at first base, although there was little certainty after his first season there, when he hit only eleven homers and batted .249, that he had won permanent possession of the post. Durocher continued to nurse a reservation about Gil's desire—he wanted the silent man to demonstrate more spirit.

"If he'd only blow up at an umpire once in a while," Durocher wailed. Hodges mulled that one over. "Would the ump change his mind?" he asked.

Rickey, at this point, also wasn't completely sold on Hodges. The next spring at Vero Beach, Florida, the Dodgers' spring training site, he made no secret of his feelings by openly searching for "pennant insurance." He even thought he'd found him in the person of apple-cheeked slugger Johnny Mize, who had just completed two back-to-back enormous home run years with the Giants. If the rumors could be believed, the thirty-five-year-old Mize was already being measured for Dodger blue. But the trade for The Big Cat was never consummated, more supportive testimony to the axiom that the best trades are always those that are never made.

By midseason of 1949 Hodges had blossomed sufficiently as a home run hitter to make the All-Star squad. His startlingly large hands were also helping to make him into a defensive first baseman with few peers. By this time he was giving the Dodgers the kind of protection at first base that Reese provided at shortstop and Robinson gave them at second.

When Reese first spotted Gil's huge paws as they rested on his knees in the dugout, in a nonlethal moment, he was astounded. "Why does the guy have to wear a glove?" he said, half seriously.

Even as Hodges became the Dodgers' most feared home run hitter—with twenty-three in 1949, then thirty-two in 1950—he continued to show vulnerability to some right-handed curveballs and outside pitches. Familiar with this batting tic, pitchers tried to exploit it. Gil often could be seen moving away—even ducking away—from such pitches, and it underlined the struggle he went through to remain fixed at the plate as pitchers worked him over.

"It's a measure of courage that Hodges fought his cringe reflex year after year," wrote Roger Kahn. "To taste fear as he did and to choke it down is a continuing act of bravery."

By 1951 Hodges had become such a permanent part of the exotic Brooklyn scene that he established a home in the Flatbush section. Shortly after that he married a dark-eyed local girl, Joan Lombardi, who had a habit of visiting Ebbets Field almost every day that the team was in town.

It may have been odd that this giant of a man, raised in the deep-vein coal-mining area of southwestern Indiana, should put down his roots among people seemingly so unlike the folks at home. As a matter of fact, almost as many people now lived in Gil's Brooklyn neighborhood as there were in Princeton, Indiana, the town of 7,000 in which he had been born. But Gil felt a strong connection with these people in Brooklyn who expressed such strong affection for him. He returned this warmth by settling down among them and hitting mammoth home runs to please them.

"You can't compare Brooklyn fans with any other," he said. "They're a separate lot. It was okay if they wanted to holler against one of their own. But they didn't want strangers to do it. They treated me so well I couldn't ever say a word against them."

As Gil gave the Dodgers another robust hitter from the right side of the plate—Robinson, Campy, Reese, and Furillo were the others—his brother Bob, at first expected to be the real baseball star of the family, had come up with a dead left arm in Class D ball. If that was a disappointment to the family, Gil tried to make up for it with his own performance.

On a muggy Thursday night, August 31, 1950, at Ebbets Field against the Boston Braves, Gil gave the whole Hodges family something to remember. Playing unkind hosts, the Dodgers had gone ahead, 10–1, in the early going, as Gil blasted two homers, one off the southpaw immortal Warren Spahn, the other off reliever Normie Roy. By the time the score catapulted to 14–1 in the sixth inning, Gil had come up with his third homer, off John Hall. By now the Hodges ménage, including brother Bob and his mother, had been alerted back home in Petersburg to the events transpiring some 1,200 miles away.

There wasn't any direct broadcast coming from Ebbets Field to Indiana, where people usually tuned in on the Cincinnati Reds.

But Hodges' folks were getting the news from a ticker in a store in town, where sucking soft drinks and making small wagers on ball games was common behavior.

Again the ticker relayed the startling message on its yellow tape. This time it told how Gil had just hit another, off Johnny Antonelli, in the eighth inning, swinging mightily from his hip pockets. This was his fourth home run of the night—and everyone in town caught on to the news almost at once. The phones were banging off the walls, and someone called Gil's father, who was supervising the night shift at the Ditney Hill Mine in Elberfeld. Nothing as big as this had ever happened before in Petersburg.

Back at Ebbets Field joy reigned. As Gil's fourth homer whizzed over the head of Sid Gordon into the left-field seats, people climbed all over each other, screaming and yelling as if nobody in Brooklyn had ever seen a home run before. When Gil crossed home plate, moving deliberately to soak up the pleasure of the moment, any Dodger who wasn't there to greet him and shake his big mitt would have been fined on the spot by manager Shotton.

The news soon spread that Hodges had joined Bobby Lowe, Ed Delahanty, and Lou Gehrig as the only big leaguers ever to hit four home runs in a regulation nine-inning game. What's more, Gil had batted in nine runs—only three fewer than Sunny Jim Bottomley's all-time high for the Cards of twelve, achieved in 1924 against the Dodgers. For the night, too, Hodges racked up a total-bases mark of seventeen, to tie the record.

Nothing like this had ever been seen before by the burghers of Brooklyn. That it was Gil Hodges who did it made it especially satisfactory.

Third baseman Billy Cox, the other regular in the infield that Dressen had inherited, could look across the diamond at Hodges and see a man who played with an intensity matching his own. But while Hodges kept his gurgling emotions well hidden under a mask of silence, Cox's reactions were on the surface for all to see. He was a taciturn and moody man, who rarely missed a ground ball. But when he did, it looked as if he needed shock treatment.

When Brooklyn had to consider parting with Dixie Walker, due to his reluctance to fully accept the presence of Robinson and other blacks in the Dodger lineup, Rickey first offered him a minor-league managerial post. Though Walker had never been indelicate in his dealings with Jackie, the situation had become inherently uncomfortable and had to be resolved.

After Walker turned Rickey down on the minor league proposal, Rickey dealt him, along with Hal Gregg and Vic Lombardi, to Pittsburgh for Cox, Gene Mauch, and Preacher Roe, a canny spitballer. When Billy the Kid or Billy the Kid Glove, as some journalists loved to call him, first came to Brooklyn in 1948, Rickey announced at once that "the boy has a good chance to become the greatest player ever to wear a Brooklyn uniform." That was certainly taking in a lot of territory and couldn't help much at contract-signing time. Prematurely comparing Cox with third-base greats like Pie Traynor, Red Rolfe, Jimmy Collins, and even Jumping Joe Dugan, as some other observers did, was also absurd. After all, Billy had played in little more than two abbreviated seasons with the Pirates and seemed to have an affinity for injuries. True, he had also hit fifteen home runs in 1947, but Rickey had gotten him primarily for defense.

Rickey also failed to reckon with Cox's fragility, as well as his hypochondriacal tendencies. Billy's psyche always had to be handled with care, for he was neither diplomatic nor particularly articulate. (It was whispered that he'd had a rough World War II. He got "shook up," as Roe once explained.) That Cox could make eye-stopping plays at third base was beyond cavil. But he was also disposed at times to become depressed or a part-time recluse. There were occasions, too, when he became critical of his teammates, which didn't sit well with them.

In time Cox won the recognition from his peers that Rickey had awarded him. But Roy Campanella once said that even though he knew how good Billy was, since he had played with him, the black leagues' star Ray Dandridge was even better. "Dandridge could outhit Billy, was as good a fielder, and could run faster," declared Campy. Dandridge was one of those black players who never got a chance to reach the majors.

When Durocher, who was still managing the Dodgers in 1948, thought he might try shifting Cox to second base, for some unfathomable reason, Billy wouldn't hear of it and sulkily disappeared for a few days while Rickey's spies were out looking for him. Rickey publicly promised Cox that if he returned to the spring training camp, there would be "no punitive measures." All is forgiven, he said. "We love the boy."

Thereupon Cox came back from his hometown in Harrisburg, Pennsylvania, or wherever his private cave was, and got his third-base job back. But injuries continued to hamper him. In 1949 he missed a month at the start of the year due to an ankle injury. After he had been in action for three months, he was sidelined again when he got hurt sliding home; it always seemed to be like that with Billy.

In 1950 he appeared in 119 games and batted .257, but injuries still afflicted him, cutting his playing time. But at the age of thirty-two, in 1951, Cox had also become a vital component of an infield—Hodges, Robinson, Reese, and himself—that for defensive brilliance could stand up against any foursome of its time.

Third base isn't known as "the hot corner" for nothing. But Cox inhaled the air down there with an insouciance that was astounding. He would stand close to the bag, a dour, long-faced man with thin strands of hair on a balding dome, wiry and unathletic-looking at less than 150 pounds. Before the ball was pitched, Cox's chain-store Davega glove hung loosely in the fingers of his throwing hand. But as the pitcher prepared to release the ball, the glove quickly shifted to the left hand and Cox snapped into a menacing crouch. The only thing menaced, of course, was the baseball. Anything hit to either side of him, no matter how fast or slow, Cox would gobble up with catlike dexterity. If the ball didn't land in the battered old glove, Cox's body would be there to knock it down, for that's what a man's bones were for. Sometimes he'd briefly hold on to the ball before letting it loose toward first, almost as if he were daring the runner to beat his sidearm throw.

Brooks Robinson came along in Baltimore a few years later to define what playing third base was all about, but Cox was still the best to many observers. "It was just that he was so underrated," said Robinson.

Peering out at Cox and the other members of the Dodger infield from his squatting position behind the plate was Roy Campanella. "You've got to have a lot of little boy in you to play this game," Campy said wisely one day—but he had a good deal more than boyishness to recommend him. Batting from a wide-open stance, Campy achieved enormous power (he delivered nine, twenty-two, and thirty-one home runs in his first three years with the Dodgers) from a burly body, with its big derriere, short, stocky legs, and powerful shoulders.

Campy was only 5′9″ tall but weighed over 190 pounds, with a belly that peeked over his beltline. "That's just my shape," he would laugh. Campy was a genial, determinedly talkative man, with smoky brown skin and a voice that could reach high tenor when he was excited. His buddies often called him "The Good Humor Man."

On the ball field he was all business, however, even if Burt Shotton often objected to one facet of his play. "They're taking advantage of you, Campy," Shotton and his teammates would scold him. "Start dishing it out." They felt he was too nice a guy to tag runners hard when they barged into him rudely at home plate.

"Aw, hell," Campy would answer. "It's their bread and butter, just like it's mine. I'm not out to hurt anybody."

Campanella was born in November 1921, in the Nicetown section of Philadelphia. Nicetown was mainly Polish—and poor—in those days, although there were some blacks there. John Campanella, Roy's father, sold fruit and vegetables to support a family of four kids, including Roy, who was the youngest.

Right from the start Campy knew the meaning of the work ethic. During the Depression he got up at two-thirty in the morning to help out his brother with a milk route. He also pitched in with his dad's delivery truck, cut lawns, shined shoes, and had a newspaper route near Shibe Park, where Connie Mack's Athletics played in those days.

Most of the kids in Nicetown didn't have enough money to buy their own baseball gloves or bats. But by the time Roy was fifteen he was invited to join the Nicetown Giants, the only black team in the Philadelphia sandlot league. When Campy played for his local American Legion team he was the only black.

Although his father was opposed to his playing baseball for a living, when Roy began bringing home sixty dollars a month, a small fortune in those grindingly difficult times, the elder Campanella recanted. In the winter of 1939 Campy went to Puerto Rico to play with the Caguas club, so his life was now a never-ending cycle of baseball—winter ball in the Caribbean, summer ball in the United States. He could scarcely hope at that time that one day he'd be asked to play ball with white men in their white man's league.

When he played exhibition games against major-league players, however, Campy's skills always elicited respectful attention. One of those impressed was Dressen, then coaching under Durocher at Brooklyn. Dressen informed Campanella that Branch Rickey wanted to speak to him. After their meeting Roy came away feeling that what Rickey had in mind was a new Negro League— and that maybe he'd get to play there. But then the news got out that Rickey had signed Robinson.

With standout performances at Class B Nashua, where he homered on opening day and got to manage one game when pilot Walter Alston was thumbed out, and in Montreal, in 1947, where he won the Most Valuable Player Award, Campy thought he might soon wind up at Ebbets Field. But instead Rickey delayed Campy's entrance into the big leagues in order to integrate the St. Paul team of the American Association.

"Mr. Rickey, I'm no pioneer, I'm just a ball player," said Campanella.

But Roy was forced to go along with Rickey's move. In thirty-five games at St. Paul, at the start of the 1948 season, Campy hit thirteen homers and batted .325. Numbers like that couldn't be hidden down on the farm.

Campy arrived in Brooklyn on July 2, 1948, just in time to take part in one of those nasty struggles with the Giants. His first time up he banged a long double. He added two more hits before the game ended. By the time the three-game series was over Campy had cracked out six more hits, including two homers. He had something to prove, after almost a decade of slogging around the Negro Leagues as a second-rate citizen, and he did it as expeditiously as possible.

Within a year Campanella had won Edwards's post. In 1950, when the National League fought through fourteen innings in the All-Star Game, Campy started the contest and remained behind the plate until the end. The durable Roy had proved he was like an old Baltimore Oriole, who could rub dirt in his wounds and remain on the field of battle.

After less than three years in the majors Campy wasn't quite Bill Dickey, Mickey Cochrane, Gabby Hartnett, or Yogi Berra. But a baseball man would have been a fool if he didn't already perceive that Campanella was one of the coming stars of the game, boasting an explosive, clutch-hitting bat, an on-a-dime throwing arm, and an incomparable esprit that many modern players lacked.

As one of the first blacks to come to the majors, Campy did carry the burden, along with the others, but he did not have the nature of a militant. In fact, in moments of pique and anger, Robinson suggested that his teammate was "an Uncle Tom." He resented what seemed to him Campy's stoic acceptance of a racist world.

But such an estimate of Campy was not quite on target. It was true that he was no agitator or radical. It wasn't his style to roil the waters—and it never would be. He simply chose to be conciliatory, for that suited his temperament.

On one occasion, recalled Dodger publicist Irving Rudd, Robinson was raising all sorts of hell about a segregated spring training hotel that blacks on the Dodgers were assigned to by management. "Campy," said Rudd, "just pointed at the hotel and said, lightly, 'Hey, we've got a better pool and restaurant here than the white folks, so why move out?' "

Campanella's personal creed was that "hate didn't get you nowhere." He was a "strong Baptist" and said prayers before each game. A confirmed Bible reader, he relied on the ultimate goodness of his fellow men.

Carl Erskine looked at Campy's noncombative demeanor this way: "Campanella was so deeply grateful at having baseball's doors finally open for him that he took his satisfaction out of that. He had never thought the day would come when he'd put on a big-league uniform; the whole thing was like a miracle to him. He thought black men like himself were getting a wonderful opportunity and he cautioned them not to 'louse it up.' Robinson, on the other hand, didn't believe in miracles. He always used to say about Campy and himself that they were totally different men and had very little in common outside of skin color."

To start against Larry Jansen, Sal Maglie, Dave Koslo, and Jim Hearn of the Giants, the Dodgers had four front-line hurlers. Erskine was one of three right-handers Dressen had on call. The others were Don Newcombe, the fastballing, prognathic twenty-three-year-old, the first black man to arrive in the majors in his productive early twenties; Ralph Branca, a Mount Vernon, New York, boy, who had been pitching for the Dodgers since 1944, when he was eighteen; and Elwin Roe, from Ash Flat, Arkansas, the senior citizen, at thirty-six, of the Dodgers' mound corps, a south-paw who could usually be relied on for a respectable performance, for it was rumored that he added a "foreign substance" to the ball when he found himself in trouble.

Weighing only 160 pounds, Erskine, who came from Anderson, Indiana, where his father was an auto parts inspector for General Motors, had a clean-cut Boy Scout aura about him. With his high forehead, brown eyes, and collar-ad looks, Erskine brought a certain class to the organization. "He was as easygoing as Arthur Godfrey's voice," Dick Young of the *Daily News* once said. And he was right, up to a point—that point was that Erskine was as keenly competitive and tough, in his own way, as any young pitcher of twenty-four could be. For one thing, he loved to pitch, even if he felt that "Ebbets Field might be the most difficult ballpark in captivity to pitch in." For another, he was willing to go out there, even if he wasn't feeling 100 percent. In his first start with the Dodgers in 1948, after being called up from Fort Worth, Erskine pitched in a drizzling rain at Ebbets Field against the Cubs. With Bill Nicholson at bat, Erskine pulled a shoulder muscle while delivering a pitch.

"In those days," recalled Erskine, "you didn't like to say much about injuries. But when it kept bothering me, I finally mentioned it to Burt Shotton. He said to me: 'You're pitchin' great. Just keep pitchin'.' "

So Erskine did, as a good trouper. But after three years of ups and downs, and a total of twenty-one games won and ten lost, he wasn't living up to his potential or the expectations of the club. But as the 1951 season approached, Erskine's curveball, an overhand pitch that appeared to swoop down at batters like a hawk searching for prey, promised to start yielding dividends. Already comparisons were being made with the curveball that Mel Harder had been tossing for almost twenty years with the Cleveland Indians.

As far as toughness was concerned, Carl didn't think he had to prove anything by throwing at batters. That wasn't in his line of work, by choice. "I didn't think it would help me to knock guys down," he said. "I guess it depends on the individual. A wild thrower, and I could think of a few, might gain by it. If such a guy threw at a hitter, then not only that batter but the next eight guys who followed him might say to themselves, 'I better not dig in against this guy, he might hit me. He's too wild.' But if I threw one close to a guy, they figure it won't happen again. So I haven't really fooled anybody, have I? The batter would just lean over more on the next pitch, figuring I'd throw it outside—and I'd have to knock him down again. So what would I gain by all this?''

From the opening moments of Erskine's arrival with the Brooklyn organization, when Rickey had to pay Carl two bonuses—the first one had been ruled illegal because Carl had entered into a contractual obligation while still in the navy—something of a love affair developed between Erskine and his new friends in Brooklyn.

"Those first days were scary," said Carl. "I was a small-town boy, not much past twenty, when I came there. My buddy, Duke Snider, felt just as scared as I did. I'd heard about the cold façade of the big city and the pressure-pot of Ebbets Field. It was like hot breath on you, all the time, people would say. But as time went by, the fans turned out to be like an extension of my own family. They were warm and loving toward Betty, myself, and my kids. There was a bond that developed between the players and the people that went beyond baseball."

After every game that Carl pitched, a local deli owner in Bay Ridge would present two bags of food to the Erskines. "Dodgers shouldn't have to pay for anything," Abe Meyerson, the proprietor, would tell the embarrassed Erskine.

The first year Carl pitched in Brooklyn he didn't know how to drive a car. Half the time going home after night games he got lost on the subway.

"After I moved near the Brooklyn Union Gas Company," he said, "I finally bought a Pontiac, my first car, and I learned how to drive on Ocean Parkway. When I really got brave, I rode on the Belt Parkway."

For Brooklyn fans, this young man must have been a strange duck, indeed. One writer called him the "conscience of the Dodgers," and Jackie Robinson said he was "one of the most fair-minded men I have ever met." He bought poetry books, played the ukulele, often meditated before games (he called this "my inside pitch"), and refused to use strong language, which was part of the arsenal of men like Dressen and Durocher. One of his first roommates, Don Zimmer, told Carl that he liked to start each day by reading the

Bible. Carl answered that was just fine, for he was a Bible student himself.

The next morning the bellhop knocked on the door at seven o'clock and handed Zimmer a copy of *The Racing Form*. "That's what I meant by the Bible, son," said Zimmer.

At 6'4" and 240 pounds, Newcombe, from Madison, New Jersey, where his father was a chauffeur to a real estate dealer, by 1951 was the best fastballer in the Dodger entourage since Dazzy Vance and Van Lingle Mungo. Maybe he was even the top right-hander in the National League, with the exception of Robin Roberts, who automatically seemed to win twenty games or more every year. In Newk's case, he'd won seventeen in 1949 and nineteen in 1950, which wasn't half bad for a twenty-five-year-old black man who had inherited a bad rap almost from the moment he first set foot in Ebbets Field.

The rap, to put it simply, said that Newk was incapable of winning the big games. He choked up, the bench jockeys had it—and they had a sweet time letting him know just how they felt.

"What's got two arms, two legs, and no guts," they taunted. Such abuse made Big Newk's disposition even more choleric than usual—and his mind became an inferno of hostile thoughts. Campanella sensed that his pitching partner needed a talking-to, so he unwound from his crouch behind home plate and went to the mound.

"Don't pay no attention to that shit, buddy, just pitch to me," Campy said, soothingly.

Pitch is what Newcombe did. He was the best hurler the Dodgers had in 1949 and again in 1950. In 1949 he had an edge over every club in the National League, except Boston, which held him to 2–2. Both *The Sporting News* and the Baseball Writers of America chose him as Rookie of the Year.

In 1950, whiplashed by Sisler's home run in the final game of the season—a game that cost the Dodgers the pennant—Newcombe was deprived of his first twenty-victory campaign. This last game was one of the pieces of "evidence" that detractors used against him as proof of his gutlessness.

The rest of the negative file on Newcombe consisted of two World Series defeats at the hands of the Yankees in his '49 freshman season. It's worth taking a look at that "evidence."

In the opener of the '49 Series Newcombe was locked in a classic 0–0 pitching duel with the Yanks' Allie Reynolds going into the last of the ninth inning at Yankee Stadium. With two balls and no strikes, Tommy Henrich, "Old Reliable" himself, connected for a homer to give the Yankees a 1–0 win. Newcombe struck out eleven and didn't walk a single Yankee in that game, while Reynolds gave up only two hits to Newk's five.

"It was a good pitch," said Newcombe disconsolately. "If I had to do it over again, I'd do it the same way."

But some amateur psychologists felt that from that point on Newcombe's memory and association were forged. They suggested that every time he had to face batters with "Yankees" written across their shirtfronts he became a snarl of emotions.

Three days later, with only two days' rest, Newk started again, gave up three runs in 3 2/3 innings, on five hits, and was yanked by Shotton. The Dodgers eventually lost that game, too.

With the exception of that second World Series start against the Yankees, Newk had pitched brilliant ball. Unfortunately, his pitching foes did slightly better.

Then why the jockeying and jibes? Is it reasonable to suggest that he was vulnerable because of his color and his size? Draw your own conclusions. Newk did, and so did many of his teammates.

In a curious way, Big Newk became a protector of both Robinson and Campanella when he arrived with the Dodgers in 1949. Rex Barney, once considered a fastballer the equal of Bob Feller and owner of a no-hitter against the Giants on a dreary night in the Polo Grounds in 1948, had been too inconsistent to be counted on. Branca was hurt. So Rickey dipped down into his farm system and brought Newk up from Montreal. That was Newk's third stop on the way to the majors—black baseball at eighteen years old, Nashua, Montreal, then the big team.

It was no secret that Robinson and Campanella had been wearing out their pants bottoms after being knocked on their butts by ill-intentioned enemy pitchers. Now, with this "big nigger," as rival benches scorched him, throwing for the Dodgers, the enemy could be expected to receive a dose—and more—of its own medicine. Thus, Newk became mound insurance, not only for Jackie and Campy but also for other Dodgers, like Snider and Furillo, who were constantly being decked.

"What are you gonna do about it?" his Dodger teammates

asked Newk. Newk didn't waste any words or pitches. "I'm gonna send every one of those sons of bitches on their backs . . . there was always that lousy talk about me choking up and never being able to win the big ones. But I never had a teammate of mine tell me that I couldn't protect him with that baseball when it was time for somebody to be sent right on his ass."

Newk was big enough when he was only thirteen years old to pitch against black men over twice his age. He had never seen a big-league game until 1946 and was a high school dropout, with little time given over to books or high-level thinking. He had literally gone from street corners and pool rooms into baseball. So if one questioned his approach to the sport, it was understandable.

When Newk got a big lead in a ball game, he was inclined to coast a bit, a situation not uncommon with many pitchers. But it was something that vexed Robinson, who believed that when you were on a ball field you never let down for an instant—you played all out every second, your intensity didn't stop, if the score was 1–0 or 20–0. If Newk looked as if his mind might be elsewhere, Robinson would walk over to him at the mound and curse him out.

"You big son of a bitch," he'd snarl, "you don't belong out here. Go home! You've got no fuckin' business in the big leagues!"

It was typical Robinson overkill. But more often than not, it worked. Newk would respond positively. "I think it made me a better pitcher," he said. "Even if it pissed me off, I got down to business."

As a right-handed pitcher for the Dodgers since 1944, when he was only eighteen, Ralph Branca had shown glittering promise by winning twenty-one games in 1947, at the age of twenty-one, the youngest Dodger hurler ever to attain that figure. It certainly looked as if he would surpass such famed Brooklyn righties as Vance and Whitlow Wyatt, both of whom were still staggering around aimlessly in the minors at that age. In the 1930s Van Lingle Mungo was hailed as Wilbert Robinson's right-handed hope for the salvation of the Bums. But he never won twenty games.

So here was Branca, a strapping 6'3", 220-pounder, who featured a screaming fastball that could go over ninety-five miles per hour, pitching every fourth day in the Brooklyn rotation and showing a willingness to start as well as relieve. In one midseason doubleheader he won the first game as a starter and took the second in relief against the Cubs. One would have bet on him for the Hall of Fame.

But Branca's winning percentages declined in the three years after 1947, and he went from fourteen to thirteen to seven victories. It was a puzzling failure, yet there was good reason to suspect that it had all started with a line drive that hit him on the leg in the waning days of 1948. An infection developed, his arm was affected, and his pitching delivery changed. As a result, what appeared to be a career with unlimited horizons became cramped and disappointing. As 1951 rolled along, Branca found himself as the team's third right-hander, behind Newk and Erskine.

But Branca contributed a good deal more to the Brooklyn cause than simple mound victories. He played a positive, supportive role in the acceptance of the beleaguered black men who had signed on with the Dodgers.

Bobby Bragan, a Dodger utility player from Birmingham, Alabama, had remarked with candor that when Robinson first joined Brooklyn he didn't care to sit down with him to eat or to play cards. Sharing a hotel room with Jackie was unthinkable. Bragan acknowledged, however, that "some of the boys, like Branca, did respond" to Jackie in a friendly way. (After exposure to Jackie and other blacks on the club, Bragan did, indeed, accept integration. "It's just a matter of getting acclimated by association," he admitted. Such forthrightness ultimately won Bragan important executive jobs in baseball. "No one questions the color of a run," he added.)

In a game in which Branca was pitching a no-hitter against the Cards in the heat of the '47 flag race, Country Slaughter hit a grounder to Eddie Stanky at second base. Eddie made a good throw to Robinson, playing first base at the time, to get Slaughter for the out. But Slaughter, with a well-deserved reputation as all-out hustler and redneck, tried to cut Jackie down with his spikes. Running at full speed, he came crashing onto Robinson's outstretched leg, just below the calf. Jackie, fortunately, was not hurt badly on the play. But Branca came over to look at the damage.

"Don't worry," he said to Jackie, "I'll get that son of a bitch for you."

Though he was seething with anger, Robinson's response was a masterpiece of restraint.

"No, Ralph," he said, huskily. "Just get those guys out."

On another occasion, when Jackie went hell-bent after a foul pop-up near the Brooklyn dugout, Branca leaped up and caught him before he could get hurt in the plunge. Branca's good instincts were applauded. It didn't hurt Robinson's morale to know that some men on his own team valued his presence.

By the time he was seventeen, in 1943, Branca, with a successful pitching record at Mount Vernon's Davis High School, had already experienced tryouts with the Giants (a team he rooted for in those days), the Yankees, who gave him a brush-off, and the Dodgers.

The Dodgers saw something there, besides Ralph's enormous feet, even if he still hadn't reached full growth. They signed him right out of Davis, and in a few days he was pitching for Rickey's Olean farm team in the Pony League.

New York University offered Ralph a basketball scholarship, unaware that he already made ninety dollars a month playing at Olean, and he accepted. He stayed at NYU for a year, playing basketball and as a pitcher starting almost every game the team played. By 1944 he was sitting on the Dodger bench, the fulfillment of any New York kid's dream.

When Ralph pitched under Durocher's aegis, he was able to handle Leo's abuse due to a wry sense of humor, and a somewhat talkative nature. He was a *parlatore*, in Italian, a chatterer. (In Yiddish a *yenta*.)

Under Shotton, in 1947, he started the first game of the World Series against the Yankees, knocking off the first twelve Yanks in a row. But in the fifth inning the Yanks battered Branca for five runs, enough to beat him, 5–3. In game six Ralph came on in relief of Vic Lombardi and got credit for the win, despite giving up six hits in less than three innings. Ralph had to be grateful to Al Gionfriddo, the little leftfielder, who robbed Joe DiMaggio of a triple, home run, or God knows what, in the sixth inning, with two men on, on a famous fly ball that nobody could have hit any harder. Rounding second base DiMag kicked the dirt in disgust, the only time anyone could ever recall him showing such emotion on a ball field.

Two years later, in the 1949 World Series, Branca worked the third game again against the Yankees. He lost it in the ninth, 4–3, after the teams were tied, 1–1, after eight innings.

From his first days as a Dodger Branca wore the number 13 emblazoned on his back. But it wasn't by choice. The clubhouse man had assigned it to Ralph because it was the only uniform his size.

"If you're superstitious, I'll be glad to change it," the clubhouse man told him.

"I took it because things like that never bothered me," said Ralph. "I even thought it might be lucky for me. I was one of thirteen kids in the family and was always the kind to defy superstition. I'd walk under a ladder or on a line on the sidewalk, which a lot of kids just wouldn't do."

Elwin Charles "Preacher" Roe was the very proper—or should it be called improper?—heir to Burleigh Grimes, the last of the legal spitballers, who pitched for the Dodgers from 1918 to 1926. (Burleigh served further penance by succeeding Casey Stengel as Dodger manager in 1937 and serving until 1938.)

Grimes didn't invent the spitter; neither did Roe. But Preacher, coming over from the Pittsburgh Pirates to the Dodgers in the December 1947 trade that relieved Dixie Walker from having to play alongside blacks, decided that since his fastball wasn't that fast anymore, he'd start throwing spitters. Only at the critical moment, of course. "I didn't throw too many of those things in one game," he explained.

With the Pirates Preacher had a hard time winning after 1945, when he led the league in strikeouts. In 1946 and 1947, when the Pirates were as solid a seventh-place club as you'd ever see, Roe won seven games and lost twenty-three. But in his first year on the Dodger mound in 1948, backed up by better sticks than he had going for him in Pittsburgh, Preacher won twelve and lost only eight. In 1949 his record went to 15–6, which gave him the league's top winning percentage. The Dodgers won the National League flag that time around, as Preacher contributed handsomely. "I wish I had four more pros like Roe," said Shotton when the '49 race came down to September.

The Dodgers were in a tight squeeze against the Cards, as they faced them in a final three-game series in St. Louis. Big Newk had lost a bitter contest in the ninth inning of a daytime game, after Robinson had been banished for making an impolite choke gesture at the volatile umpire Bill Stewart. The loss hurt the Dodgers badly. The wound could have been terminal, for the Cards were ready, before a screaming audience of hometown claquers that night in Sportsman's Park, to administer an auto-da-fé to the Brooklynites.

So who did Shotton send out to stem the Redbird tide? It was the guileful, then-thirty-four-year-old Preacher, sometime college student at Harding College in Searcy, Arkansas, a qualified high school instructor in physical education, a man who would just as soon be fishing as pitching, a fellow who looked more like a refugee from a mountaineers' convention than a pitcher about to quell a pennant threat. But quell it he did, much to the sorrow of the Cardinal fans and to the pleasure of his own folks, including his dad, Dr. Charles Edward Roe, who had once pitched doubleheaders for Pine Bluff in the Cotton States League.

With the help of a strangely robust but skinny left arm—and maybe strategic use of Beech-Nut gum (Preacher preferred that to such "foreign substances" as Vaseline, vaginal jelly, shampoo, tobacco juice, Ivory Soap, or honest sweat)—Roe drove the Cards crazy, limiting them to two harmless hits. So he rolled back the thunderheads and pulled Brooklyn right back into the pennant race.

The next night the Dodgers belted the daylights out of the Cardinals to the tune of nineteen runs. Preacher didn't bat in any of those runs himself, but maybe there was a connection between what he had done to the Cards one night and the state of discouragement that the Missourians found themselves in for the rubber game of the series.

When the Dodgers got to the World Series against the Yankees, it was Preacher again who won the only game they managed to eke out against the New Yorkers. He did a superb 1–0 job in the second game, beating Vic Raschi. Facing a Yankee lineup that had Joe DiMaggio batting cleanup, with Phil Rizzuto, Tommy Henrich, and Hank Bauer hitting up ahead of him and Johnny Lindell and Gerry Coleman behind him, Roe didn't issue a walk. The single favor that Yankee manager Casey Stengel did that day for Roe was to sit Yogi Berra down.

What made Preacher's performance even more remarkable was that in the fourth inning, Lindell, a sizable policeman in the off season, drove a rifle shot back at Roe that smashed against the fourth finger of his glove hand. Preach scrambled after the ball and threw over to first baseman Hodges for the out. When the game was over it was discovered that Lindell's rocket had broken Roe's finger in three places. For the final five innings he pitched in severe pain, while the finger bled profusely. But you never heard a peep out of the man. That's what Shotton meant by saying he'd take more men like Preacher.

How much of Roe's success was due to his "occasional" spraying around of spitballs, nobody will ever know. Fidgeting on the mound, touching his visor, scratching his ear, wiping his hand across his nose or brow, Roe was playacting the impression that a spitter was about to be born on each pitch. But that was pure hogwash—the gestures were only meant to deceive and vex, a high-class decoy. When umpires asked Preacher for a closer examination of the ball, he'd oblige, but only with a surprising loss of control. He'd throw the ball just beyond reach of the ump, where it would be picked up by Reese or Robby or Hodges, then whipped around the infield. By the time it got back to the umpire the ball was drier than the Volstead Act.

When Rickey pried Roe loose from the Pirates in 1947, there was some moaning at the bar among Dodger journalists. They insisted that Roe was too old and too frail to be of much worth to Brooklyn's mound staff. In addition, they said, Roe had fallen on the back of his head a few years before, after an altercation on a basketball court, and hadn't been the same since. Some gleefully hinted that the old master had been hornswoggled.

But Rickey had relied on the word of his loyal adjutant Shotton, who had managed Roe when the Preach was a stringbean of a kid with Columbus in the Cardinals' chain. Shotton talked about Roe's varied skills, insisting it was worth the gamble to get him. The Dodgers never regretted it.

By 1950 Rickey thought Roe pitched in a classic mold, despite his slow-motion maneuvering on the mound. "Watch this fellow when he throws his change-up," he lectured his young pitchers. "Watch him when he lets his fast one go. He always throws each pitch perfectly. He doesn't throw his curve with his fingers held one way the first time, then another way the next time. Every one is the same. He's consistent. That's why he can get the ball over—and win."

What Rickey didn't bother talking about were those spitters that splashed down and away, like drunk butterflies.

New York Giants, 1951

Back row: Sheldon Jones, George Spencer, Monte Irvin, Jack Kramer, Jim Hearn, Spider Jorgensen, Clint Hartung, Allen Gettel, Bob Thomson, Monte Kennedy, Larry Jansen, Sal Maglie, Bill Rigney, Whitey Lockman.

Center row: Wes Westrum, Roger Bowman, Artie Wilson, Dave Koslo, Leo Durocher (Manager), Rafael Noble, Henry Thompson, Don Mueller, Jack Lohrke, Fred Fitzsimmons (Coach).

Front row: Frank Shellenback (Coach), Herman Franks (Coach), William Leonard (Batboy), Jack Maguire, Sal Yvars, Alvin Dark, Eddie Stanky. (When this picture was taken Willie Mays had not yet come to the club.) (National Baseball Library, Cooperstown, N.Y.)

Brooklyn Dodgers, 1951

Back row: Billy Cox, Rube Walker, Carl Erskine, Andy Pafko, Preacher Roe, Clem Labine, Clyde King, Jackie Robinson, Dick Williams, Cal Abrams.

Center row: Harold Parrott, "Doc" Wendler, Wayne Terwilliger, Phil Hangstad, Don Newcombe, Erv Palica, Gil Hodges, Johnny Schmitz, Bud Podbielan, Don Thompson, John Griffin.

Front row: Rocky Bridges, Duke Snider, Ralph Branca, Jake Pitler, Chuck Dressen (Manager), Clyde Sukeforth, Cookie Lavagetto, PeeWee Reese, Roy Campanella, Carl Furillo. Bat Boy: Stan Strull (National Baseball Library, Cooperstown, N.Y.)

Yankee great Joe DiMaggio (left) and rookie Mickey Mantle
were teammates for the first time in 1951. (Wide World)

Willie Mays made his debut with the Giants in May 1951.
(National Baseball Library, Cooperstown, N.Y.)

In his first year as Brooklyn manager, Charlie Dressen (right)
relied on righthander Ralph Branca. (Wide World)

Around the batting cage, Brooklyn's "Boys of Summer" (left to right):
PeeWee Reese, Carl Furillo, Jackie Robinson, Carl Erskine, Gil Hodges, Don Newcombe,
Duke Snider, Roy Campanella. (*Sport* Magazine, Courtesy of George Unis)

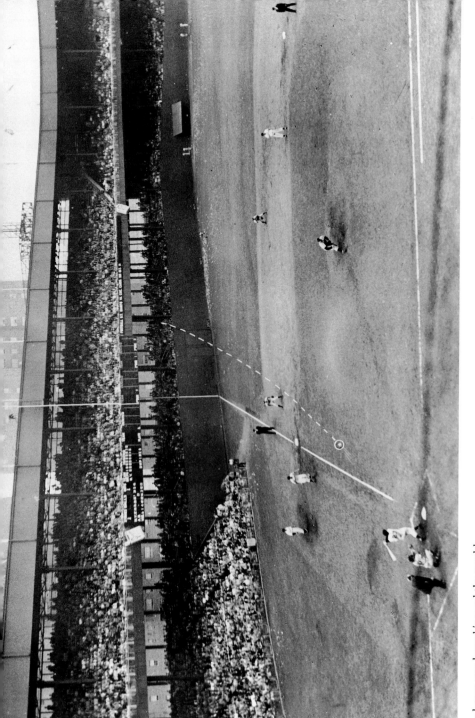

The home run heard 'round the world.

Dodger left fielder Andy Pafko watches Thomson's pennant-winning blast disappear. (Note the scoreboard that shows Brooklyn still ahead.) (UPI)

In despair, Branca walks off (right), as Jackie Robinson (42)
gloomily makes certain that Thomson touches home plate.

A mob of Giants surrounds Thomson as he carries the winning run home. (That's Mays, number 24.) (Wide World)

Celebrating the Giants' victory on the third base line: Manager Leo Durocher (left) happily wrestles with second baseman Eddie Stanky. (Wide World)

Thomson, the hero, is hugged by Giants' owner Horace Stoneham
(left) and Durocher. (Wide World)

Clubhouse celebrants: Thomson, winning pitcher Larry Jansen, and
Sal Maglie, who started the third playoff game. (Wide World)

Shrieking admirers get a wave from Thomson, on the Giants' clubhouse steps. (Wide World)

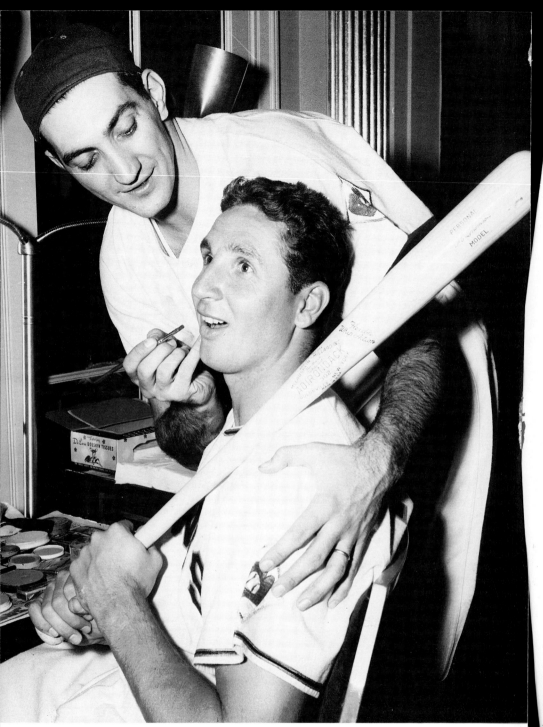

Good sport Branca applies makeup to Thomson's face before the
February 1952 New York Baseball Writers dinner. (Wide World)

Duke, Carl, and the Others

OF THE THREE center-fielding Übermenschen who gestated in
the baseball parks of New York in the 1950s, Duke Snider got there
first. He arrived at Ebbets Field in the latter part of the 1947
season. Willie Mays and Mickey Mantle, with the Giants and Yankees, respectively, appeared on the scene in the blessed (certainly
it was that for all New York fans) year of 1951.

Sun-bleached, prematurely silver-haired, prouder than a bar
mitzvah boy—and maybe as spoiled—Snider became author Philip
Roth's idea of a baseball icon: "a King of Kings, the Lord my God,
the Duke himself."

To Dodger writers, weighed down by their own self-created
Brooklyn stereotypes, Snider was always "The Dook," just as Carl
Erskine was "Oisk."

Nobody could remember when this handsome fellow, with
"steel springs" for legs (as Rickey put it), had ever been called
anything else but Duke. Supposedly, when Snider was in kinder-
garten he strutted around as if he owned the world, so his father,
Ward, referred to him as "His Majesty, the Duke." For sure, he
wasn't named after the Duke of Windsor, for in far-off California,
where Edwin Donald Snider was born in the suburb of Compton in
September 1926, they didn't pay much attention to British royalty.

In their own Duke they would have true baseball royalty—and that mattered more.

Stagestruck fathers and mothers have been known to drive their progeny onto and off the stage and screen. In Duke's case his father, a navy veteran and former semipro player in Ohio, not only inspired his son to play the game but got the normally right-handed youngster to become a lefty. "My father kept telling me," said Duke, "that since most pitchers were right-handed, a lefty would have a two-step advantage getting to first base." He also added that most parks were built to accommodate the power of southpaw hitters, with those short right-field fences.

Duke became the cleanup hitter and pitcher for Compton High School, where he also excelled in football and basketball. After he pitched a no-hitter against Beverly Hills High School, the bird dogs came sniffing around, though they were interested in Snider more as a hitter than as a twice-a-week pitcher.

So Duke and his father had to weigh the relative merits of minor-league baseball versus scholarships to West Coast colleges, such as USC or UCLA. When Dodger scout Tom Downey tapped on the Snider door in 1944, offering $750 in hard cash as a bonus, plus $275 a month if Duke would go to Brooklyn's Montreal farm club, that seemed more persuasive than spending several years staring at books, which had never been Duke's first priority.

A few days after the Duke signed with the Dodgers, a Pittsburgh scout, also having caught the Duke's act on Los Angeles ball fields, said he'd like to sign the boy for $15,000. Duke went home and told his folks he felt sick. But they reminded him that a contract was a contract. So off the Duke went to Bear Mountain, New York, not too far from West Point, where the Dodgers were conducting their frigid wartime spring training camp under the despotic eye of Durocher. Climatic conditions at Bear Mountain were unlike anything Duke had ever experienced in Compton, but he didn't have the foresight to bring along an overcoat. With teeth chattering and his mind thinking of home, where the sun always shone on him, literally and figuratively, the Duke was having hard time. The discipline demands of a by-the-numbers Rickey training operation were just too much for a seventeen-year

Wid Matthews, on hand to run the show for Rickey, was palled at what he perceived as Duke's disinterest in anything than swinging at baseballs. Thus, he informed the sulking

Moanin' low—Branca, after the loss. (Barney Stein)

man that even if it was a long ride back to California, he ought to get started. The threat worked. Abashed, cap in hand, Duke apologized, though he was not sure exactly what he had done wrong. What he didn't appreciate was that Rickey kept his own private stats on attitude and demeanor. No matter how talented a player might be, Rickey paid respectful attention to such intangible items.

The Duke spent the 1944 season with Newport News, Virginia, in the Class B Piedmont League. He batted .294 and showed off his slingshot right arm, with twenty-five assists. The next year the navy took him, supplying a bit more maturity to a growing boy. By 1946 he was ready for Fort Worth in the Double-A Texas League. Though one Brooklyn scout dubbed Snider "another Ted Williams," Duke's numbers at Fort Worth (.250 batting average, five home runs) hardly supported such a premature sentiment.

One had to be blind, however, not to see the enormous potential in Snider, with his ferocious corkscrew swing, his sprinter's speed on the base paths, and his pleasing grace in settling under fly balls. One afternoon Rickey was on hand in Fort Worth to see the boy propel a ball some 450 feet over the center-field wall.

"Judas Priest!" he exclaimed. "We've got to keep our eye on that young fellow!"

That the Dodgers did. On the night of June 4, 1947, Duke replaced Pete Reiser in center field against the Pirates, after Reiser had collided with the concrete wall and was carried off the field on a stretcher. A few days later Snider started in center field. In forty games he hit just .241, without a single home run. He was also having trouble controlling his temper, which didn't improve each time he misjudged the strike zone. Swinging mightily but at bad pitches, he demonstrated little patience with himself or with pesky left-handed hurlers.

So it was back to the minors—St. Paul—where he fared somewhat better, connecting for twelve home runs. Still, the penchant for bad-pitch hitting had to be curbed, so the ever vigilant Rickey initiated a special training course for him. At spring training in 1948 Duke was ordered to stand at the plate, bat immobile on his shoulder, and just watch the pitches roll by. His only job was to call each pitch a ball or strike, then see if his eye meshed with the umpire's judgment on the pitch. They didn't always agree, but the general idea was to get Duke to lay off those high fastballs that he loved so much. Perhaps it was a strange way to get Snider to appreciate the strike zone, but when you played for Rickey anything was possible.

Snider began the 1948 season with Montreal, under Clay Hopper. But in no time at all he got into a jam with the manager. Told to bunt one day, Duke angrily disobeyed orders—instead, he hit a home run! Such behavior didn't sit well with Hopper, even if it produced a homer. Only Snider's contrition saved the day for him. With seventeen homers and a .327 average by midseason, Duke returned to the Dodgers. Although he wasn't an instant sensation, one facet of his game had improved: he struck out only twenty-seven times in 160 at-bats, a vastly better percentage than his previous year in Brooklyn. It was a positive sign that Rickey's program was succeeding.

"The job is yours, until you prove to me you can't hold it," Shotton told Duke in 1949. So here he was, still bedeviled by his ego but full of enormous potential, on hand for a tight pennant race, in which his clutch single in the final game of the year clinched the flag for the Dodgers. He batted .292 in that first full season, hit twenty-three home runs, and covered center field as well as Reiser, once considered the most exciting star in the Dodger camp, ever had.

In his first World Series that fall, against the Yankees, Snider found that he still had plenty to learn about his profession. He was a failure. But there were reasons. The pressure in New York that year was searing. A young player like Snider could be vulnerable to the tensions that mounted almost daily, with the help of a prurient press and fans who demanded instant accomplishment.

In the first game Allie Reynolds fanned Duke three times. When the Series was over, with the Yanks winning in five games, Duke had struck out eight times, tying an unflattering record. He had only three hits in twenty-one times at bat, without knocking in a single run. During those games, wrote Tommy Holmes of the Brooklyn *Eagle*, Snider was "tighter than a bullfighter's pants."

Snider agreed. "I was as nervous as I ever was in my entire life," he said. "Ever since I'd been a kid all my dad and I ever talked about was baseball and getting into a World Series. And here I was, weak in the knees, even when I walked. I never loosened up. It all seemed so unreal. I just wasn't up to it."

If he hadn't been made of stern stuff, the experience could have been a humiliation that carried over into 1950. But Snider survived. He took heart from supportive testimonials from rivals like DiMaggio and Stengel. DiMaggio thought Duke was trying too hard to "kill the ball" but felt he'd turn into a fine center fielder. Stengel said he wouldn't mind having the guy on his team. (What would he have done with Snider when Mantle came along!)

Even when the Dodgers lost the 1950 pennant on the last day, Duke's ninth-inning single *almost* turned the tide. That it didn't was a dreadful disappointment to him and his teammates. But Snider had arrived as a full-fledged slugger, with 31 homers, 107 runs batted in, and a .321 average. The indignities of the 1949 Series were all but forgotten—and Duke looked to 1951 for further redemption.

Until he was sixteen years old Carl Anthony Furillo, who guarded right field for the Dodgers, never set foot outside of Stony Creek Mills, Pennsylvania, a hamlet near Reading. That accounted for the fact that among the Dodgers of the late 1940s and early 1950s he was probably the least worldly and sophisticated. Forced to quit school in the eighth grade, he was a hard-nosed, ruggedly handsome, black-haired man who spoke in the tough shorthand of a blue-collar ball player.

Carl was the sixth and youngest child of immigrant parents; the family was one of a handful of Italians in a village of Pennsylvania Dutch. He worked as a bobbin boy in the woolen mills and as a plumber, carpenter, and odd-jobs man. His brothers worked in the mills and as milkmen.

Ill educated as he was, Furillo had trouble responding to the simple questions mailed out by the Brooklyn front office. Arriving with the Dodgers in 1946, he was asked, as other players were, about various facets of his personal background.

The questionnaire wanted to know: *State of Health*. Furillo answered: "Pennsylvania."

Length of residence was another question, to which Carl responded: "35 to 40 feet."

Furillo was first spotted by Josh Haring, a scout for the St. Louis Cardinals, when he played for the St. Lawrence Dairy team in Reading. Haring lived in the neighborhood and was aware of how desperate the Furillos were for money, as well as the fact that Carl's mother had just died. Carl informed Haring he was making eighteen dollars a week working in a dye house of a woolen mill in town.

"I can get you eighty bucks a month with Pocomoke City in the Eastern Shore League," said Haring. Carl leapt at the chance, even when told he'd have to pay for his own meals and laundry. At first he tried pitching for Pocomoke, for Haring told him he had an arm like a cannon. But Carl had trouble getting the ball over the plate. That, plus the fact he wanted to play every day, caused him to shift to the outfield.

Before the year was out he was playing for the Reading Chicks. When Larry McPhail, president of the Dodgers, laid out $2,500 and a bus for the Chicks, Furillo went along for the ride. The bus was essential in those days, for automobiles had been earmarked for military use.

Carl was soon promoted to Montreal in the International League, where he rode a sleeper for the first time in his life. He was batting over .280 when he was drafted for the army in 1942, spending three years as a private with the 77th Infantry Division, where he saw nineteen months of action at Okinawa and Leyte, two bloody battlegrounds of World War II.

With his combat experience behind him, Carl reported to the Dodgers' Daytona Beach training camp in 1946, the same season Jackie Robinson was incubating at Montreal. Most of the Dodgers of that period—Dixie Walker, Durocher, Augie Galan, Reiser, Hugh Casey, and Kirby Higbe (who could outdrink Casey who could outdrink Hack Wilson)—were fairly quotable guys, while others like Reese knew how to get along with the press. But Furillo suffered from a chronic case of word block. This failing was mistaken for rudeness, which was a misjudgment of the man. He was simply an uncomplicated, blunt person, who tried to say what was on his mind. Asked what his aspirations in life might be, he'd mutter that it was "to play the game hard and then be left alone."

Several factors emerged to put Carl in a better light, however. His arm, recognized from the outset as one of the best in the league, kept improving in accuracy, and in every phase of the game he proved himself to be absolutely fearless. In addition, the oft-injured Reiser understandably had an uncertain future in the Dodger outfield, thus firming up Furillo's bid.

Playing under Durocher became a profitable learning experience for Furillo, even if Carl loathed Leo. Furillo acknowledged that Durocher knew a lot about the game but when the manager told Carl to "shove it" when the outfielder asked for more money in 1946, Carl never forgave that indignity. Furillo also felt that Durocher didn't know how to handle young players. "He was all out for himself," Carl said, "and not for the players."

After Durocher made his managerial switch to the Giants, Furillo was outspoken in his detestation of the man. He was also convinced that Leo had demanded that Giants' pitchers "stick it in his ear." "This guy was telling his pitchers that I was taking their bread and butter away from them," he said, "and he asked them not to let me get away with it . . . if I'm ever hit again by a Giant pitcher I'm going to let my bat go straight at that son of a bitch's head . . ."

Furillo hit .284 in 1946, on a Dodger team that battled its way into a play-off against St. Louis. He was paid $5,000 that season and believed he was worth every penny of it. The next year he hit .295, followed by a robust .353 in a six-game losing World Series against the Yankees.

At midseason of 1947, when Furillo was hitting at a .350 clip, he boasted to Robinson that he was going to beat him out in batting average. Furillo didn't particularly care for Jackie and would have liked nothing better than to edge him out at the plate. Jackie told Carl that it would be "just fine if he did, because that would give us another .300 hitter."

But the promise of midyear faded. Due perhaps to the lingering illness of his father and concerns over a newborn baby, Furillo went into a slump and never got his wish to top Robinson.

In 1949 Furillo batted .322, and in 1950 he had a final mark of .305. Curiously, in both of those years Carl demonstrated remarkable consistency, hitting 18 home runs and knocking in 106 runs each season.

In the critical final game of the 1949 season with the Phillies, Carl made a head-first slide into third base to save the game, emerging with a face full of dirt and pebbles. "It was the only way I could get around Puddin' Head Jones," he said.

Carl made a leaping grab at the right-field wall to save a no-hitter for Ed Head in 1946 and did the same thing for Rex Barney, also working on a no-hitter, in 1948.

Just as the Red Sox's Carl Yastrzemski had mastered the mysteries of Boston's Green Monster wall in left field, Furillo defiantly taught himself the pesty nuances of Ebbets Field's right-field wall. Topped by a twenty-foot screen that overlooked Bedford Avenue, the wall had as many angles as a fight promoter. Between the mesh screen that boasted of twenty or more uncertain bounce-backs and the foam-rubber pad at the wall's bottom, with its equally unpredictable caroms, Carl had his hands full. But he came to own squatter rights on the famous barrier.

One day in 1950 he nailed the Cards' Marty Marion as he tried to score from second base on a pinch hitter's drive off the right-field screen. As Furillo faded back, he looked up, pantomiming that he was about to catch the ball. Faked out of his spikes, Marion hesitated between second and third. That cost him dearly, for Carl unleashed a 320-foot throw on the fly that nailed him with plenty to spare.

"Don't run on this guy!" managers advised their players about "The Reading Rifle."

With a passion for competition, Carl had a stubborn notion about what Brooklyn fans expected of him. Asked one day by a friend why he didn't take more walks from pitchers like his teammate Gene Hermanski, Furillo glared at the questioner.

"The fans don't pay to see me walk," he said. "They pay to see me hit."

Until right fielder Dixie Walker departed from Brooklyn, Furillo and Gene Hermanski shared duties in left field. Center field was now Snider's territory, so it was just a question of who would wind up as Dixie's imitator in right and who'd go to left, on a more or less permanent basis.

As it turned out, Furillo seized right field, leaving Hermanski as the proprietor in left. In 1949 and 1950 Cal Abrams and George "Shotgun" Shuba occasionally shared time with Hermanski in left, while Marvin Rackley filled in there in 1947 and 1948. Lacking power, Rackley failed to produce a single home run in 290 times at bat. Abrams was also a disappointment, especially to the Jewish fans, for since the exit of outfielder Goody Rosen to the Giants in 1946, he'd become the sole candidate for the Jewish vote in Ebbets Field. In the long run, Dodger fans of Jewish persuasion had to settle for Jake Pitler, the white-haired first-base coach.

As the resident left fielder, the handsome Hermanski provoked the rather uninspired war cry of "There's no ski like Hermanski," hardly a threat to the rhymes of baseball-loving poet Marianne Moore. But Hermanski had a good run of it in 1948, 1949, and 1950.

Born in Pittsfield, Massachusetts, in May 1920, Hermanski moved with his family to Newark when he was five years old. He became a star in his teens at East Side High School. By the time he was twenty-one, in 1941, he had talked Branch Rickey, Jr., into a job with Olean, where he hit a hot .341 under the watchful eye of manager Pitler, who hadn't yet taken up his coaching stand in Flatbush.

The morning after Pearl Harbor Hermanski joined the Coast Guard. In the summer of 1943, after wangling a discharge from the service, he played in eighteen games for the Dodgers, on a team reduced by war to such fading veterans as Dolf Camilli, Frenchy Bordagaray, forty-year-old Paul Waner, thirty-five-year-old Billy Herman, and shortstop Arky Vaughan. Exposure to such experienced hands didn't harm Hermanski, but when Naval Aviation gobbled him up, the Dodgers had to wait for him until the war was over.

In 1946 Hermanski was back in Brooklyn, challenging for one of the outfield posts. Durocher liked Gene to the extent of declaring that he was "one of the best judges of balls and strikes I've seen in a decade." That, of course, excluded anyone he'd seen before 1936.

Dixie Walker voluntarily took Hermanski aside to teach him a thing or two about his craft. Perhaps Dixie was anticipating that he wasn't very long for Ebbets Field, in light of his racial feelings. But whatever his motivation, he was pleased to work with Gene.

"Look, kid," he said. "I know you're on your way to stealing my job. But I like you and I'm going to help you."

Thereupon, The Peepul's Cherce accompanied Hermanski to the troublesome right-field sector, pointing out what a fellow had to do to protect the wall against all assailants. As it turned out, Walker shouldn't have taken such pains, for within a year Furillo, not Hermanski, became counsel for the defense out there. Thus, Hermanski was forced to concentrate on left field.

Walker might also have instructed Hermanski on the business of hitting against left-handed pitchers, for this remained a perplexing challenge for Gene. It was not unlike the difficulties Duke Snider was having versus southpaws, aggravating him to the point where he'd sometimes beg out of the lineup on days that lefties faced the Dodgers. Hermanski, however, never resorted to such undignified tactics, thus endearing him to his bosses. But his ineptitude caused his manager to sit him down, anyway, on many afternoons that left-handers appeared on the mound.

The 1948 season, which turned out to be a good one for Hermanski, almost ended for him before it started. One day Durocher and a Brooklyn aide, Harold Parrott, who occasionally handled ghostwriting chores for Leo, invited Hermanski to join them for a ride, while the team was training in mountainous Caracas, Venezuela. The car got into a nasty collision, catapulting down a 2,000-foot incline. As a result, Gene just missed winding up in the ironic, faceless headline—DUROCHER AND TWO KILLED IN CAR CRASH—which would have accompanied such a tragedy.

By midsummer of that season the folks of Brooklyn had to be pleased Hermanski was not finished off in Caracas. On August 5, celebrating Carl Erskine's first start for the Dodgers, Hermanski pounded out three home runs in a surprising display of power. The only other Dodger ever to do this was Jack Fournier, who covered first base in the 1920s.

At the end of the season, Hermanski had amassed fifteen homers, the highest Dodger total since Camilli's twenty-six in 1942. He also got to play in 133 games, twenty-five more than Furillo. Barney Shotton might have been forgiven for imagining he had another Babe Herman aboard.

But in 1949, when Hermanski hit .299, his home run output plummeted to eight. Things got worse the next year, when he injured his ankle on a pickoff play and wound up with seven homers in ninety-four games, with only thirty-four runs batted in.

Meanwhile, his brethren in the outfield, Duke and Carl, were tearin' up the pea patch, as Red Barber kept telling his listeners. As 1951 dawned, Hermanski still had the left-field job in his grasp, but there was no certainty that he would keep it for long.

8

That Spring

EARLY IN 1951 Albert Einstein, the world-renowned scientist, had his famous head examined at Princeton, New Jersey, in order to record the patterns of the brain that had fathomed the mysteries of the atom. Around the same time many who followed the fortunes of the Giants were exclaiming that it was Leo Durocher, instead, who should have had his head examined, since he had publicly concluded that his Polo Grounds livestock were bound to win their first National League flag since 1937.

To further buttress Leo's prescience, Laraine had decided to visit a numerologist to find out what would happen to her husband's business in 1951. Many years later Nancy Reagan, the American First Lady, would schedule her husband's presidential excursions to suit her astrologist's whims. Such occult, paranormal reliances were hardly anything new for some believing people in leadership roles.

Durocher hadn't generally been a person who relied on mystical forces to win ball games. He was a resourceful man who depended more on brushback pitches, snarling competitiveness, and his own quick impulses. But he had always been as superstitious as the next man—maybe even more so. When his team was going well, Leo would eat the same breakfast every day, take the same daily constitutional, and enter the ballpark the same way. He never took kindly to black cats who invaded his space in the dugout, and although he was a fastidious man who almost went broke outfitting himself in Cincinnati in his early baseball days, he would wear the same pair of socks and underwear every day until a winning streak was broken.

If Leo was sheepish when Laraine mentioned her visits to fortune-tellers or others of that ilk, as a loyal and loving partner, he always kept his large ears attuned to what she was saying. In 1950 Laraine and Helen Fitzsimmons, the wife of Freddy, the veteran pitching coach, had consulted a soothsayer, who informed them that around the middle of that season the Giants would obtain a pitcher from St. Louis who would win eleven games for them. That was the year Jim Hearn, a lost cause with the Cardinals, came to the Giants, developed into one of the most effective pitchers in the league, and did win eleven games.

Durocher shrugged off the accuracy of that prediction, joshing that the medium had to be related to the St. Louis manager. "Eddie Dyer must have tipped her off," he said. But the coincidence stuck in his mind.

Laraine and Helen laughed about that prophecy on a number of occasions. When the Giants went to St. Petersburg in 1951, where they trained at Huggins Field (they swapped fields that year with the Yankees), the two women searched for someone who could again confide the Giants' future to them.

"Find someone who'll tell you we're gonna win," said Durocher, "because we are!"

One morning a local numerologist living close to the Hotel Soreno, where most of the Giants stayed, sat down with them and began to spell out what was going to happen on the ball field that summer.

The numerologist advised Fitzsimmons that he should wear number 6 on his uniform and always have a touch of purple about him. Freddy said he never really liked his old number, anyway, so it wouldn't hurt him to change it. As far as the color purple was concerned, he bought a purple handkerchief, then swapped uniforms with Ray Noble, the catcher up from Cuba for his first semester with the Giants. "Seis, ocho, nueve," laughed Noble, "makes no difference to me!"

In the follow-up session with the numerologist, Laraine pressed for more details. The clairvoyant daringly laid out the road map for the upcoming season: "Your husband is going to get off to the worst start of his managerial career. Then his team will start to pick up. It will gain momentum shortly after his birthday on July 27 and will be going like the wind at the end. In 1952 everything will turn out wonderful!"

Laraine couldn't wait to speak to Leo about the good tidings. When she revealed the predictions, Durocher exploded. "Next year, my neck," he said. "We're gonna make it this year. What the hell does she know!"

It remained to be seen just how accurate the mystic was or if Laraine had wasted her money.

"Blossom by blossom the spring begins," wrote poet Algernon Swinburne. In the spring of 1951 there were many blossoms—and even before the Giants and Dodgers started the season, some big winners were already dotting the horizon.

Mario Lanza, a hefty thirty-year-old former truck driver from Philadelphia, with an operatic voice and a Pickwickian syndrome at the dining table, reached his Hollywood peak in *The Great Caruso*. Method actor Marlon Brando, at twenty-seven, mumbled and glared his way to fame opposite a decaying Vivien Leigh in *A Streetcar Named Desire*. Glenn Seaborg won the Nobel Prize in Chemistry for his discovery of plutonium, and Shigeki Tanaha, a nineteen-year-old survivor of Hiroshima, won the Patriots' Day Marathon, up and down Boston's hills.

In the burgeoning TV field the wisecracking Milton Berle won a thirty-year, seven-figure contract with NBC and Senator Estes Kefauver, in pursuit of bad men like Frank Costello, won an Emmy for his Senate Crime Committee hearings. Sid Caesar took an Emmy, too, for his hilarious "Your Show of Shows."

When the Palace Theatre in New York revived two-a-day vaudeville, the irrepressible Judy Garland played over four months after being booked for only one. General Douglas MacArthur, looking like a winner over Harry Truman, was mentioned for every job in the universe, from baseball commissioner to Truman's own job of president.

A Herkimer, New York newspaperman named Lee Allen, later to become curator of baseball's Hall of Fame, discovered that a third baseman named Harry H. Raymond, a player for Louisville from 1888 to 1891, then briefly with Pittsburgh and Washington, was actually born as Harry Truman. Margaret Truman (also the name of the President's daughter), he added, had sewed the red stockings worn by the Cincinnati Reds in 1869. Such homey touches did little to enhance President Truman's standings in the popularity polls.

In Florida Durocher, pumped up by the numerologist's findings, figured to be joining other winners of 1951. Dressen, for his part, was convinced that his own manipulations in the dugout and on the coaching lines (where he often chose to appear) would go a long way to proving that he was more than just a loudmouthed puppet of Durocher.

When Durocher was asked to be specific about his high hopes for his club, he named three elements: the superb condition of his mercenaries, the invaluable experience that his front-line troops gained on the battlefields of 1950, and a fine crop of reserves, led by Artie Wilson, "the versatile Negro player," as the *New York Times* headlined it.

In the Pacific Coast League the left-handed Wilson had been almost unstoppable as an opposite-field hitter, even when manager Lefty O'Doul, who had played for both the Dodgers and Giants, came up with a "reverse shift" on him. O'Doul placed all of his infielders, except the first baseman, to the left of second base when Wilson batted, with the center fielder coming in to play short-stop. Wilson hadn't played an inning in the big leagues, yet here he was being treated as if he were Ted Williams, the "victim" of the "Williams Shift" only a few years before. In a dozen spring games Wilson batted .480, presumably making him a threat to Alvin Dark at shortstop. Few seemed to notice, however, that Wilson rarely hit more than singles.

Batting out of the cleanup position, Monte Irvin was enjoying a scorching spring training, despite the fact that newspapers still had trouble getting his name right. He was often "Irwin" in the box scores. At one point "Irwin" hit in twenty-one straight spring games, including one in which he connected for a bases-loaded home run against Cleveland's Bob Feller, in Fort Worth. He won that game with another homer in the ninth. Touring with the Giants, the Indians hit only eight homers to the Giants' eighteen in eight games.

During the course of the Giants' travels with Cleveland, overflow crowds popped up almost everywhere to greet the two teams.

There were large numbers of black fans on hand to root for Irvin, Thompson, Wilson, and Noble on the Giants and Larry Doby and Luke Easter, the first black men to be hired in the American League, on the Indians. For the first time in the history of the Nashville Park, blacks were admitted to the grandstand, and in Houston they filled almost half of it. As he had gambled when he recruited Robinson, Rickey's "noble experiment" was not only yielding social and emotional dividends for America's blacks, but it was also turning out as beneficial to the owners' pocketbooks. Who among the bigots and redneck holdouts was opposed to that?

In pregame practice and pepper workouts, Durocher often made a point to horse around, openly and convivially, with his black players. But despite such increasing acceptance in the stands and on the diamond, blacks still were segregated off the field. Few, if any, white players or executives objected to this ostracism. (Erskine, for instance, acknowledged years later that he didn't quite appreciate at the time the psychic hurt this was causing his black teammates and blacks on rival teams.)

While teams like the Dodgers, Giants, and Indians were integrated in the clubhouse, the vast majority of the other clubs weren't. Some of those segregated teams engaged in the most demeaning bench jockeying. So bad did it get at times that white players on the Giants and Dodgers, who originally had been cool to the coming of blacks into their ranks, expressed resentment at the vilification they were hearing. Desegregation was supposedly being accomplished with all deliberate speed (the new baseball commissioner, Ford C. Frick, insisted that baseball "was meeting the challenge head on, to its eternal credit"), but it just wasn't happening.

One unlooked-for problem did arise on the Dodgers, when talk surfaced about the number of blacks a team should carry on its roster. Since the Dodgers already had Robinson, Newcombe, Campanella, and pitcher Dan Bankhead, with other candidates eagerly awaiting the call from the farm system, some writers wondered whether a black "saturation point" would ever be reached on the club. For instance, would the public tolerate an infield of blacks, an entire team of blacks? Would people stay away from the ballpark? Such cynical talk about a surfeit of blacks never became a major problem. But it was often whispered about in 1951. There is little doubt it had reached the discussion level among fans.

Toward the end of spring training several route-going performances by Giant pitchers pleased Durocher. On March 31 Jansen went nine innings in a 2–1 loss, then a week later pitched another complete game against Cleveland, despite giving up nine runs in a 10–9 victory. (On the same day, Preacher Roe hurled nine innings in Atlanta, as the Dodgers won.) A few days after that Dave Koslo, scheduled to be the Giants' fourth starter, went the route for the Giants' sixth complete job. This was the sort of thing Leo relished, for he was still reluctant to depend too much on relievers George Spencer and Sheldon Jones. Even if Maglie had been scuffed around—he'd yielded sixteen runs in twenty-one innings on twenty hits—Durocher liked what he was seeing.

If extra oxygen was needed for the staff, Durocher figured that the handsome veteran Jack Kramer, who won only three games for the Giants in 1950 after several serviceable years with the Red Sox, might help. Kramer had incurred Leo's wrath by showing up late to the Giants' camp, but he started to heat up pretty rapidly, beating the Indians in Dallas on April 7, 10–3.

While these pitching developments took place with the Giants and Dodgers, as they performed their calisthenics where the sun beat down and the air crackled with the annual rebirth of the game, things were also buzzing out in the desert of Phoenix, Arizona. Casey Stengel was aiming to add a third straight American League flag to the Yankees' escutcheon and couldn't be bothered reading about Leo's brave declarations or Dressen's pop-offs emanating from the Florida coast. On the first day that the wrinkled old monologuist requested his Yankee charges to "line up alphabetically, in size place," he kept his eyes peeled on the kid with the Huckleberry Finn face. The kid's name was Mickey Mantle—imagine, having a perfect baseball name like that!—and it wasn't even made up.

"I don't think you'd get a Casey Stengel in any arena of human activity other than baseball," once wrote William Saroyan. The same thing applied to Casey's muscular disciple, Mickey Mantle.

As green as the renewal of spring, with hair yellow as the corn of his native Oklahoma, Mickey was nineteen years old when he reported to Stengel. His dad, Mutt, a zinc and lead miner and a pretty fair ball player himself in his local area, had named his son after the famous Athletics' catcher Gordon S. Cochrane, whose nickname was "Mickey."

In short order, Mickey became the hottest item on the grapefruit circuit, as his switch-hitting bat lashed the soft air of Arizona and California. Every spring writers have ceaselessly searched for the next heroes on the vine—the flowers that bloom in the spring—and then have ratified their choices with superlatives. (Witness Clint Hartung of the Giants, among others). But in Mantle they were adamant in believing they were selling the real, honest-to-goodness thing.

"The Commerce [Oklahoma] Comet," they insisted, was explosive, quicker than a frightened bunny rabbit, had legs like a prize racehorse, an arm stouter than Venus's good one, and country-boy blue eyes that could trace the wanderings of a fastball right into the catcher's mitt.

Mickey had come along just at the right moment, from Independence in 1949 and Joplin in 1950. At Joplin, he had a .383 batting average and batted in 136 runs. Even if he had accomplished that in the Western League, which was a long way off from The House That Ruth Built, those tape-measure home runs he was unloading in Arizona demonstrated convincingly that he was the real thing.

The Yankees had had the ultimate leadoff hitter, Earle Combs, roaming in center field for a decade, then DiMag had taken over, adding power, pride, and dazzling grace to Combs's consistency. Now, in this inarticulate youngster, with a face as open as the part of America that he hailed from, they began to think they had the obvious successor to DiMaggio. The irony here was that in the minor leagues Mickey had played shortstop—and not too well. Now he was in rehearsal to take over in center for DiMaggio, who, at thirty-six, was old as far as baseball was concerned and suffered from a bruised heel that was like an everyday toothache.

Stengel realized how inexperienced the boy was, yet he said he'd never seen anything like him. Few disagreed. Rickey, gone from the Brooklyn organization and now trying to solve the problems of the Pirates, stamped Mickey as "the finest prospect I've ever seen." Others said he was a combination of Cobb, Ruth, Williams, and any other superstar you could dredge up to make the point. When he hit the ball, they all agreed, it even sounded different.

Under ordinary circumstances, the Yankees would have committed Mantle to at least another year of minor-league play, not in Class C, but in Triple-A. But there was nothing ordinary about Mickey or the circumstances. Stengel already was viewing Mickey much as John McGraw relished the sight of Ott some twenty-six years earlier. McGraw at that time wouldn't think of sending the raw sixteen-year-old down to the minors. It was the same with Stengel, who nursed dreams of being Mantle's Svengali. "When you stand next to this young fella," Stengel would say, in a gobbledy-gook as hard to decipher as a doctor's prescription, "he'd look down at the ground like he was afraid his shoes were gonna walk off without him."

Casey was wise enough in the ways of baseball to know that the pressures on Mickey were mounting daily with each story filed back home by the unrelenting New York baseball journalists. Sure, the boy could benefit by unwinding from such pressures down in the minors. But how could a phenom like Mantle be buried away from the sight of Yankee fans, who already concluded that he could hit a ball farther than anyone in the world, even if he hadn't stepped into a big-league dugout?

So, based on the instant myths being created that spring training, Stengel, against the wishes of the unsentimental George Weiss, decided the boy would come east. On opening day he would be in right field at Yankee Stadium, while the glacial DiMaggio returned to center.

As the Yankees prepared for the premature coronation of a kid who was quaking in his spikes, Stan Musial, already as great as people said Mantle was destined to be, received disquieting news. The National League batting champion in 1950 with a .346 average and the only southpaw batter to lead the league four times, Musial was informed by the Wage Stabilization Board that his salary of $50,000 would not be raised. Known as a man of equable disposition, Musial didn't express envy of others or threaten mayhem. He said he would just go on about his work, which usually included tearing apart the Dodger pitching staff at Ebbets Field. Some, like DiMaggio, at $100,000, made more money than Stan the Man, while Robinson and Reese, both at $35,000, made less. Bobby Thomson would play that year for $30,000.

Other decisions were being made about the voices of summer that would fill the New York air during the 1951 season. Red Barber, with his sweet Southern phrasing, would be back to broadcast Dodger games on WOR-TV. Barber had already embellished the English language with such inventive expressions as "the catbird's seat," "the ducks are on the pond," and "the bases are FOB" (full of Brooklyn). To Barber Ebbets Field was "The Rhubarb Patch." He liked to refer to himself as "The Ol' Redhead," even if he was only forty-three that year. Mississippi-born, Barber was as unlikely a radio and TV broadcaster as one could find for the Dodgers, yet he was enormously popular throughout the borough. His heart was in Brooklyn, even if his accent wasn't.

In the Brooklyn booth Barber was flanked by the twenty-four-year-old, Fordham-educated Vin Scully and Connie Desmond, who had the reputation of imbibing too much. Scully, in his second year of Dodger broadcasting, was stylish and melodic, just as his Dodgers were brash and strident. Russ Hodges, a former hillbilly disc jockey from Tennessee, with broadcasting credits with the Cubs and White Sox, had been with the Giants and WPIX since 1948, after working with Mel Allen in the Yankees' booth. He'd also suffered through several losing Columbia seasons as a football announcer. Hodges learned soon enough that the easiest way for anyone to get a punch in the nose from Durocher was to call him "Lippy." Hodges never made that mistake on the air with the Giants—or off.

Still working for the Yankees was Mel Allen, the former law student from Alabama, whose unvarnished enthusiasm for the club on WPIX and WABD hadn't decreased an iota since 1939. Few in the New York area failed to recognize Allen's resonant pronouncements, although some did resent his open rooting for Yankee "Ballantine Blasts." Mel and Hodges were admittedly biased in favor of the home team; their voices easily revealed their prejudices. Barber and Scully, conversely, were understated and low-key, even if in their guts they yearned for Dodger triumphs.

With the season set to open, the soothsayers took a look at the National League field. For the most part, they concluded that Durocher and Dressen were chaperoning the cream of the circuit. Since Curt Simmons, the talented southpaw, was off fulfilling his commitment to the National Guard, the Whiz Kid Phillies weren't given too hot a chance. The Boston Braves had Spahn and Sain and not much more, while the Cards, under Marty Marion, once the great shortstop, didn't seem particularly potent—with Joe Garagiola batting fifth behind Musial. It was said that the Reds would hustle for Luke Sewell. They also had Ewell Blackwell, the stringbean pitcher with a disposition as wicked as his sidearm delivery. But not much was expected of them, either. The Cubs, threatening to do little, had a manager, Frankie Frisch, who could only growl about "those bases on balls" (his trademark kvetch when he broadcast Giants' games a few years before). The Pirates, eighth in 1950, appeared set again for that slot, even though they had home run king Ralph Kiner in the lineup—but, strangely, at first base.

The big news over in the American League, outside of the Bunyanesque presence of Mantle in a Yankee uniform, was that for the first time in the history of the league Connie Mack would not be managing the Philadelphia Athletics. At the age of eighty-eight, the old man with the stiff white collar and a sorry basement team in 1950 finally decided to throw in his scorecard. Jimmy Dykes, a third baseman for Mr. Mack (which is what it was obligatory to call him) from 1918 to 1932, took over the club's reins. Not only would the peppery Dykes be the new manager but the A's were scheduled to open the season at night, an all-time first for the league.

On Monday, April 16, the Giants made their preseason pilgrimage to West Point for a final exhibition. This event had become an annual ritual dating back to McGraw's time. Their hopeful spring, with all hands in shape, read nineteen wins, twelve defeats, two ties. Although not even Leo played to win in Florida, he still preferred to come out ahead. "It's a good habit to develop," he said.

The Dodgers ended their spring with fourteen victories, twelve defeats, and one tie. But baseball's loudest noise of the spring emanated from Mantle's bat. He hit over .400 and deposited nine home runs into the cloudless skies of the Southwest.

Bronzed and eager, the Dodgers and Giants returned to New York, where they confronted the words of *Times* columnist Arthur Daley, who wrote that he thought the Dodgers were by far the best team in the National League. According to form, they should win, he said.

But then he equivocated, pitifully:

"I've been listening to Durocher so long, he's so convincing a guy, that he could make a union-buster out of John L. Lewis and a red-baiter out of Joe Stalin."

Therefore, Daley prognosticated, the Giants were going to win, with the Dodgers second.

9

A Bad Start

ONLY DAYS BEFORE the Giants opened their 1951 season on April 17 at Braves Field in Boston, another more cosmic showdown took place in Washington, D.C. Harry Truman, a mere captain in World War I, summarily fired General Douglas MacArthur, feeling he could no longer stomach the general's theories about widening the Korean War. Truman named Lieutenant General Matthew Ridgway to succeed MacArthur. If Leo Durocher looked in the papers he saw in Ridgway a man who strongly resembled him. Indeed, Ridgway even had Leo's crisp voice and manner.

As might be expected, the Republicans yelled loud and long for Truman's head, some even calling for impeachment. The National League's president, Warren Giles, obviously an admirer of Mac-Arthur, said he'd like to see the seventy-one-year-old military icon named to succeed Happy Chandler as baseball commissioner. Even without Giles's recommendation there seemed only a remote chance that MacArthur would remain unemployed for very long.

Under such trying circumstances, Truman managed to retain his composure long enough to say "that it was only fitting that MacArthur should address a joint meeting of Congress, for he was one of our great military men." He said nothing about the baseball job.

Despite such low-level distractions, the Giants and Dodgers

got in their opening games in weather that made all the athletes yearn again for Florida. Someone described the Boston climate, where Larry Jansen was on the mound, as "Indian winter in mid-April." But a tough old Oregonian like Larry was used to such weather. Only 6,000 hardy souls showed up, with the wind whistling frostily from across the Charles River.

Jansen continued his spring training form with a masterful five-hit shutout, his fourteenth with the Giants, against manager Billy Southworth's team. The Braves could have been a subsidiary of the Giants, what with ex-Polo Grounders like Willard Marshall, Buddy Kerr, Sid Gordon, and Walker Cooper dotting their roster.

Leo's club that day, winning its first opener since 1946, was exactly the same one that finished the 1950 season in such a rush. It had Irvin at first, Stanky at second (all that nonsense about Artie Wilson or Davey Williams, the little Texan, taking over for The Brat was just that, nonsense), Dark at shortstop, Hank Thompson at third, Lockman in left, Bobby Thomson in center, Mueller in right, and Westrum catching. On the field for the opener the lineup worked to perfection, although Irvin, who never felt first base was his natural position, made two glaring fielding errors.

After the game Durocher, more genial and relaxed than anyone could recall, told reporters, "We probably won't lose a game all year." His mood was enhanced by the Dodgers' loss of their opener at Ebbets Field to the Phillies before some 19,000 freezing fans. Robin Roberts won it for the Phils, just as he had in the final game of the 1950 season, giving Leo a premonitory sense that history was about to repeat itself for Brooklyn.

Durocher's prediction stood up until the next afternoon, April 18, when Sam Jethroe blasted a three-run homer in the ninth for the Braves after Maglie collapsed in the sixth inning. Irvin, so hot in training, had a double and triple, causing many to wonder about all those years he had lost because of his color. What made the defeat especially bitter was that the Giants had rallied to tie the game in the ninth, only to lose.

The papers still were chock-full of news other than baseball. MacArthur had landed in San Francisco—he always seemed to be landing somewhere or other in his remarkable career—and then wended his way to Washington, where Truman, in his White House bunker, had to duck to avoid choking on the confetti pouring down on his adversary.

April 19 was Patriots' Day in Boston, a legal holiday in that city and always a doubleheader day for Boston baseball clubs. Jim Hearn picked up where he'd left off in 1950 with a 4–2 decision in the first game. But the nightcap was a harum-scarum mess that the Braves finally won, 13–12, despite another explosive hit by Irvin—a grand slam. Durocher employed six pitchers, each worse than the other, in a game started by Jack Kramer, who gave up five runs in the first inning before he could get his arm warm. Leo ended up with Koslo yielding the tying and winning runs to the Braves in the tenth inning. At the end of the torturously long day, the Giants were two-all for the year and Durocher felt like kicking himself all the way to the Polo Grounds for thinking that Kramer might turn out to be useful to him. The man didn't start another game all season.

Meanwhile, MacArthur, the artful headline-hogger, was knockin' 'em dead in the nation's capital. He told a joint session of Congress that America's Asian policy—that meant Truman's policy—was "blind to reality." He followed that with an emotional tour de force that was bound to cause the same kind of divisions between America's president and its people as had existed for so long, if you will, between the Giants and Dodgers. MacArthur had previously told San Franciscans that his "only politics was God Bless America." Now he described himself as "an old soldier just trying to do his duty, as God gave him the right to see that duty." Finishing up, he added dolefully, "Old soldiers never die; they just fade away."

Ironically, these words were borrowed from a ballad sung by Tommies during World War I. But that didn't impede MacArthur from brewing a patriotic fervor that could easily have gotten him elected to Truman's job on the spot, not to mention endless invitations to more ball games than he cared to attend.

On Friday, April 20, the Giants, who had staged their first home opening in 1876, would play host to the Dodgers for a seventieth opening in their old, rickety ballpark. Everyone in town had been waiting for this first meeting between mentor and disciple, Leo and Chuck, especially after the Giants had taken three straight from the Dodgers in Florida. The flags were whipping in the breeze, the antique green seats were shined up for the occasion, and the sun dutifully came out on a sixty-degree day, with over 30,000 on hand. But the two bitter enemies had a tough act to follow, for that morning MacArthur had received the plaudits of New York's millions in a "homecoming parade" that easily compared with the party put on by Mayor Jimmy Walker for transatlantic flyer Charles Lindbergh in 1927. Others compared the tumultuous reception for MacArthur to the welcome home for another general, Eisenhower, after World War II.

After a poor start for the morning show, due to the MacArthur greeting, Radio City Music Hall drew 6,200 capacity for its next performance, but sales in stores around the city almost ground to a halt, such was the general's mesmerizing influence. The Giants paid obeisance in their own way by pushing back the start of their game to two-thirty, one hour later than usual.

In Washington's Griffith Stadium Truman threw out the first ball in a delayed opening-game ceremony before 25,000. In the process he won a niche in the reverse record book, for not since Herbert Hoover was booed at a 1931 World Series game in Philadelphia had an American chief executive suffered such rude treatment at the hands of his countrymen. The general clearly was ahead of Truman in the public relations game at this point.

The Dodgers started big Don Newcombe on the mound in the opener, while Durocher selected Sheldon Jones, a choice that raised a few eyebrows. Possibly, the talkative Jones may have sold Leo on the assignment. "I've always had pretty good luck against the Dodgers," he said. "Some guys sort of developed sore arms before we played the Dodgers. But I like to pitch against them."

Dressen made a couple of changes in his lineup, starting Rocky Bridges at third base instead of Cox and putting lefty hitter Don Thompson in left field in place of Hermanski. The inclusion of the light-hitting Thompson put three Thompsons on the ball field that day, with Hank and Bobby (spelled Thomson) playing for the Giants. Add Fresco Thompson, an executive in the Dodger front office, and the family Thompson had to be celebrating its biggest day in baseball.

The Dodgers won, 7–3, as Irvin made another error at first base and also went hitless for the first time in twenty-eight straight games, including spring training. But the highlight of the afternoon, as far as the Dodgers were concerned, was that Dressen got a chance to unlimber his schadenfreude at the expense of Durocher. In the seventh inning Durocher sent up the much-heralded

Artie Wilson to pinch-hit for Daryl Spencer, with one out and the bases loaded. Immediately, Dressen popped out of the dugout, waving Furillo in from right field to play second base and stationing Robinson in front of the bag. The strategy called for five men in the Dodger infield, Dressen's version of the Williams Shift.

Anything Wilson hit into right field would have gone for at least a double. Since Wilson was a left-handed batter, it was considered likely he'd hit in that direction. But not in Dressen's book. Having seen Wilson play in the Pacific Coast League, Chuck was disdainful of his ability to pull the ball to right field. When Wilson hit back meekly to Newk, Dressen's plan of humiliation worked. Bill Rigney, sitting on the Giant bench, said, "Poor Artie never got over what Dressen did to him . . . it was the end of him as a player." (Indeed, Wilson was back in the minors shortly after the incident. He never played in the majors again.)

The next day, before 33,000 fans and General MacArthur in attendance, along with his thirteen-year-old son, Arthur (who threw out the first ball, which was snared by Freddy Fitzsimmons), the Giants lost again to the Dodgers, 7–3. Arthur couldn't have chosen a more typical interborough donnybrook for his first big-league game. For most of the proceedings, Durocher kept barking out orders to Jansen to brush back the Dodger hitters. The Giant pitcher was known for not having a mean bone in his body and was uncomfortable with Leo's orders. Finally, when one of Jansen's pitches, purposely or otherwise, nicked Campanella on the arm, the Dodger catcher angrily went after Westrum, the Giants' catcher.

At one stage both benches emptied, players pouring onto the field like clowns gushing out of midget autos at the Ringling Brothers Circus. When order was restored, Campy banged a double. All the fuss didn't stop Arthur MacArthur from inhaling four hot dogs, four soda pops, and two candy bars. At the end of the game he told Durocher he was sorry the Giants lost. Nevertheless, Arthur came away with a Giant baseball autographed by the whole team, a Giants cap, and a jacket with number 45 on it.

Hoping to salvage the Sunday game—it was always important to win at home on Sunday, for more fans were usually in the ballpark and thus would carry the winning message around for the rest of the week—Leo sent Maglie out to do a man's job. The Barber led, 3–1, in the eighth, then the Dodgers tied the score after another flap over one of Sal's pitches. This one scorched Robinson in the back and Jackie came out fighting, as he always did against Maglie.

In the tenth inning, Furillo pounded one into the stands, dropping the Giants to their fourth loss in a row. It was ominous for the New Yorkers that after being swept three in a row by the Dodgers *A Tree Grows in Brooklyn* opened on Broadway the same week.

Now it was up to Eddie Sawyer's Phillies, last year's National League champs, with some good ballplayers such as Granny Hamner, Richie Ashburn, Del Ennis, and Eddie Waitkus, to test the stumbling Giants. They did just that. In the first of three games, the Giants lost, 8–4, as Hartung went to right field for the day, Lucky Lohrke played third, and Irvin booted another one at first. Lohrke, so named because he had pulled out of a team bus ride with Spokane (in the Western International League) only minutes before the bus plunged down a ravine, killing eight of his buddies, remained a favorite of Leo's as a utility player.

Owner Stoneham marched on Philadelphia to see just what in hell was going on with his team, but that didn't prevent the Giants' losing skein from reaching seven in a row as the Phillies won the next two games and Durocher used up pitchers the way he spat out his mouthwash. By this time Lohrke was batting third and Hartung was still holding on in right field, which revealed more than anyone needed to know about Durocher's frustration. Things seemed to be going wrong every day, from Thomson's failure at the plate, or Irvin's obvious discomfort at first base, to Maglie's slow start, to botched plays in the field, to that other missing ingredient: no luck.

The only solace the Giants could take was that the Dodgers weren't hot yet. When Sid Gordon, their former teammate, licked the Dodgers with a late-inning homer for the Braves, they were pleased. But it was pretty hard to smile under the circumstances. Some fickle New York writers were already relegating the Giants to fourth place after less than two weeks of play.

On Thursday, April 26, the Braves visited the Polo Grounds on a superb spring afternoon and administered an eighth straight defeat to the Giants. Johnny Sain threw a shutout for his one hundredth major-league victory. Durocher had the unfortunate Wilson in at second for Stanky, and Mueller was back in right field, but nothing good was happening that day.

"This club's just going badly," said Leo, although "shitty" was what he really meant to say. "These stories about us haven't helped much, either," he added. Was he talking about stories that he himself had disseminated?

When the Giants lost their ninth straight, to Warren Spahn, only 6,500 folks showed up at the Polo Grounds. Again the Giants lineup was not recognizable: Noble was at backstop and Jackie Maguire was in right field, replacing Clint Hartung, who'd replaced Mueller. Adding insult to the general dismay were homers by Marshall and Gordon, the ex-Giants.

Writers covering the Giants started to make bets on how many games in a row the team was going to lose, although they did their joking far from Durocher's ears. Local historians emerged with the news that the Giants of 1902 had gone thirteen in a row without winning, while the wartime Hubbell-less Giants of 1944 had equaled that distressing figure. Amusingly, that fifth-place club was a success, according to Mel Ott, "because we finished ahead of Brooklyn and beat them twelve times."

The Giants were hoping that a visit to the Brooklyn bandbox over the last weekend in April might cure their ailments. But they only got more of the same. Even though Stanky produced his second home run in two games, the Giants lost their tenth in a row, 8–4. Preacher Roe wet up a few at the right time to beat Roger Bowman, a southpaw with a pretzel windup.

The highest Giant batting average at this stage of the season was Dark's .288. Robinson was hitting close to .400 for Brooklyn. Over at Yankee Stadium, DiMaggio was at .302 and not looking too worse for wear. Mantle, however, was having excruciating troubles with his fielding in right field, since he was constantly in fear of running smack into his eminence in center field while chasing fly balls. Mantle still hadn't solved the riddle of how to approach the unapproachable DiMaggio. At the plate Mickey wasn't faring too badly—but as the days passed his strikeout ratio started to increase and so did the worry lines in his face. The burning glare of publicity was scorching the devil out of him. "He was feeling the weight of the New York syndrome," wrote Donald Honig. "It wasn't enough to be a star, one had to be one with flair and style."

On Sunday, April 29, with 30,000 present on a lovely afternoon, Ebbets Field was the most idyllic place in the hemisphere for any Dodger fan. The Giants bit the dust again, 6–3, for their eleventh loss in succession, as Snider whaled a couple of homers out of sight and Hodges added another. Jansen, reputedly the solid man of the Giants' staff, failed to put an end to the Giants' miseries. The New Yorkers were now at 2–12, a gruesome start, with Boston in first place with a record of 10–5. The Dodgers were nicely positioned in second place at 8–4.

Already reduced to Singer's Midgets, the Giants had to listen to the prickly Durocher, with his total command of the language of the gutter, sound off in the clubhouse about their minimalist efforts. If some of them had grown up as choirboys, Durocher intended that they get over it.

The next night the Giants finally ended their embarrassing losing string with an 8–5 victory at Ebbets Field. Inspired by Leo's oratory, or by the birth of Whitey Lockman's first child, Linda, or by the ineptitude of a wild southpaw named Chris Van Cuyk, who threw only eleven pitches and couldn't get anyone out, the Giants came up with six runs in the first. They hung on to win for the first time since April 19, though it wasn't as easy as it looked. Feelings ran high in the packed stands; it was worse on the field.

Maglie was up to his nasty tricks again, with Robinson his principal target. The first time Jackie went to bat he had to scramble into the dirt to avoid being hit. The next time he craftily laid down a bunt along the first-base line that drew Maglie over to field it. Jackie barged into Maglie with crushing force, sending the pitcher onto his back.

Durocher lost little time creating a tempest with the umpires, always a labor of love for him, as Robinson and Maglie had to be pried apart by teammates. The two clubs were living up to their reputation for mutual dislike, and the fans ate it up.

To make matters worse, National League president Ford Frick saw fit the next day to issue a statement about the imbroglio, seeming to come down on Maglie's side. Frick warned both men to stop doing what they had been doing, referring to the incessant dusters being thrown by Maglie (and, incidentally, encouraged by Durocher) and the fierce counterreactions of Robinson. "If such things continue, there will be fines," said Frick.

Unfortunately, Frick didn't stop there. He said he was tired of Robinson "popping off" and added that if Brooklyn couldn't control Robinson, he would. Jackie had long since ceased to be a punching bag for the bigots and though Frick certainly didn't qualify for such a tag, Jackie snapped that Frick ought to try changing his color and go up to bat against Maglie.

Such intemperate exchanges altered the climate not at all, for Maglie and Robinson could be expected to carry on as they had before. But it made for interesting reading in the newspapers, perhaps preferable to hearing about the bickering going on between the Republicans and Democrats over Truman, MacArthur, Commies, and pinkos.

In the midst of such acrimony, Gil Hodges appeared as a guest one day on Laraine Day's TV program, causing a few raised eyebrows among Brooklyn's Giant and Durocher haters. Gil had consented to appear only because he was a friendly man who couldn't turn down such an invitation. How could a guy—even a Dodger— say no to such a lovely woman? There were some Dodger fans who said Hodges should have bowed out. Furillo even muttered a few curses—but the world didn't come to an end.

The Giants hadn't won a game at home as May began. Then the Cubs came to town. Poor Frankie Frisch, Chicago's pilot, could bark as loud as Durocher (who had played shortstop under Frankie with the Gashouse Gang in St. Louis), but there was scant reason for him to exercise his lungs with a team that promised to be a candidate for the cellar. Among his Cubs Frisch had Chuck Connors at first base (renowned later as "The Rifleman" on TV) and Eddie Miksis at second. Both had tried and failed with the Dodgers, although Miksis had won a moment of fame when he scored the winning run in Bill Bevens's 1947 failed World Series no-hitter.

The Cubs turned out to be good for what ailed the Giants, as they dropped two games. In one of them Al Dark hit the first bases-loaded home run of his career. To liven things up, eleven of Frisch's frustrated athletes were chucked out of the dugout for protesting an umpire's call on Cubs pitcher Paul Minner. Durocher was pleased to see somebody else get the hook for a change.

Durocher used George Spencer, the husky Ohioan, in the other game against the Cubs. The right-hander was expected to be used only in relief—in 1950 he'd started only one game. But Leo, a guy who liked to play his hunches, got a good game out of Spencer with the help of six runs in the Giant sixth inning.

The Robinson-Maglie brouhaha still refused to go away, as Dodger president Walter O'Malley took up the cudgels for his player. He said he defended Jackie's conduct on the grounds that other Giant pitchers had also used Robinson for target practice. Commending Robinson for his conduct on the field, O'Malley praised Jackie's spirit. "He gets my full support," he said. Feeling that the issue might best be put to rest, Frick didn't respond further. For the moment, all was quiet on the interborough front.

Though the Pirates didn't roll over the way the Cubs had, the Giants still managed to win two out of three from them at the Polo Grounds before sparse audiences. Pittsburgh scored four in the tenth to take one game, in which Reiser, the indomitable ex-Dodger, played left field for the visitors. Many felt that had Reiser avoided numerous confrontations with outfield walls he could have been one of the remarkable players of any era. Instead, here he was playing out the string at the early age of thirty-two. Durocher had once managed Reiser with the Dodgers, going so far as to say that Pete was "the best I ever had." He was fond of him, but still refused to give him an inch on the playing field. Protesting a called ball on Reiser, Durocher was thrown out of the game by the umpires, along with Fitzsimmons. The other event of note in the game was that Irvin made yet another error on a ground ball.

In Maglie's one-hit victory over the Pirates, his best game of the year, Pete Castiglione, leading off, tripled, scoring a moment later when Irvin bobbled again. That was all the Pirates got in the way of hits and runs the rest of the day. Monte hit a home run, proving that his loose fielding hadn't affected his confidence at the plate, as is so often the case with players having defensive trouble.

During the final weeks of 1950, Irvin had played first base moderately well, but in these first days of the 1951 season he appeared uncomfortable and out of his environment. He told Russ Hodges that he "felt like a bear trying to open a sardine can." It was only a matter of time before Leo had to come to grips with this problem.

Scoring their fifth victory in six games, the Giants licked the Pirates on Saturday on Dark's second grand slam of the year. Things were looking up a bit now, for they were 7–13 but still in last place.

In a Sunday doubleheader at the Polo Grounds, the Giants split with Cincinnati, which had the powerful Ted Kluszewski at first, a man even stronger than Gil Hodges. But they didn't have much else. The Reds literally stole the first game from under Leo's prominent nose, and the man didn't like it, for he found himself victimized by a play older than his mother: the hidden-ball trick.

Connie Ryan, the Reds' second baseman, had a reputation for being adept at this stunt. Only the Yankees' Frankie Crosetti could compare with him in its execution. The Giants should have been on their guard. In the last of the tenth in the opener Lockman was perched on second base. In that situation, with the game on the line, a base runner had to be careful. Ryan came over behind Whitey and motioned him to get off the base for a second. "I wanna straighten it out," he said.

Whitey absent-mindedly obliged Ryan, who then quickly stuck the ball in his ribs. The ump bellowed, "You're out!" It was the type of ruse that Leo would have enjoyed pulling off himself. In this instance, however, the other guy had done it to *him*—and he didn't like it. Durocher threw one of his inimitable fits and umpire Al Barlick told him to take a walk. The Giants lost, 4–3, and had to settle for a win in the second game.

In a wry postmortem, Lockman claimed that since Durocher was the third-base coach he should have shared responsibility for the disaster. "Leo would rave and rant constantly about guys watching his signals and not getting off the base," said Lockman. "But he obviously lost track of where the ball was. He had no idea it was in Ryan's hand. If he had been aware of that he would have chased me back to the bag." Lockman even hinted that Leo might have gotten himself thumbed out in order to avoid getting needled about it in the dugout. Such was life around the Giants, never a dull moment.

Meanwhile, the Dodgers, with as vaunted a group of sluggers in the lineup as any team in baseball—Robinson, Campy, Hodges, Snider, Furillo, Reese—and its first-line pitching taking shape, won enough games to stay close to first place, along with the Cards and Braves.

In one of the peak years of his baseball life, Musial checked into town with his Cardinals. Three days later he checked out, with three losses on the St. Louis ledger. The Giants got twenty-one hits, their season high, to win the second game, as Noble, their catching fill-in for Westrum, hit two home runs and Thomson tagged one. When Hank Thompson unloaded a home run the next day for a 3–2 win the club stood at 11–14. Despite their miserable start, they now found themselves only four games out of first—and also out of the cellar for the first time.

Just when things seemed to be straightening out, the Giants lost a painful contest to the Phillies, 6–5, in ten innings. In the ninth, with the score tied and none out, Thomson tripled. Manager Eddie Sawyer then ordered Jim Konstanty, the scholarly-looking right-hander, to walk the next two batters intentionally, which is the way Durocher would have played it himself. Stanky popped to shortstop for one out. Then Leo put the bunt sign on for Dark in an effort to squeeze home the winning run. But the ball plunked into first baseman Waitkus's hands instead, and Thomson, having started for home, was easily doubled up. Watching a game in civilian clothes for the first time since 1935, MacArthur hit his hand to his head in disgust, almost knocking the briar pipe out of his mouth. (At this stage, he had replaced his familiar corncob with the briar, which he had gotten accustomed to during his appearances before Senate committees.)

Whether Durocher became ill watching the ninth inning of this game, or whether he really was consumed by fever, as the press office said, the manager stayed out of action the next day. Fitzsimmons ran the club for the day and did what any self-respecting sub is supposed to do: managed a doubleheader victory over the Phillies. Jansen and Maglie pitched fine games, Noble caught both contests (Westrum had a bad finger) and batted cleanup, and Jack Maguire played right field. From his bed of fever Leo may have given orders for Noble to bat fourth. But if Fitz acted on his own, he was an undiscovered genius, because Noble got five hits during the day.

As an added curiosity, in this first month of play Maguire challenged Mueller for the right-field job. Nobody had anticipated that when the season began. Batting .400, Maguire thought he may have won himself a job, if not some respect. But the slight outfielder from St. Louis had scant power, something that Leo wanted from him and couldn't get.

One morning the Giants announced Maguire had been sold to the Pirates. "You'll like it there with Kiner," Maguire's mates said to him, as they bade farewell. Mueller suspected this move gave him squatter rights to right field.

That didn't, however, signify that the outfield situation had been resolved, since for some time Durocher had been contemplating a dramatic change. It was no secret he'd been running out of patience with Irvin at first base. Almost every day Irvin would commit another error, sometimes damaging. Finally, Monte's hitting started to sour.

In a game in St. Louis in late May, after Leo was thumbed out by umpire Lon Warneke ("the worst umpire I've ever seen," Leo always said about the ex-pitcher), the Cards rallied against the Giants. Blowing a three-run lead, the Giants lost. Listening to his team's downfall on the clubhouse radio, Leo flew into a rage. Particularly galling were two Irvin errors that helped the Cards get back into the game. To make matters worse, Monte also failed to bat home the tying run with a man on third. Instead, he hit into a double play.

The sequence of events became the catalyst for Durocher's next move. He decided to remove the bewildered and unhappy Irvin from first base and place him in the outfield, where he might regain his composure and prove his true value to the team. But who would Durocher nominate to play first base?

Going back to the early years of John McGraw, first base on the Giants had always been well tended, even if with varying degrees of efficiency. Merkle, the perennial goat, was fast-moving and more than adequate; Prince Hal Chase was a brilliant fielder, albeit sinister and unreliable; Highpockets George Kelly was always dependable; Bill Terry was magnificent, even when he wasn't hitting .401, as he did in 1930; Johnny Mize had devastating home run power, which more than compensated for his slowness.

But after Mize left to join the Yankees in 1949, the Giants experimented with a cluster of supernumeraries at first base, including Joe Lafata, Augie Galan, Sid Gordon, Nap Reyes, Tookie Gilbert (at least everybody loved his name!), and Irvin. If the Giants hoped to contend in 1951, they would have to discover somebody in their own rich tradition to play the position.

That's where Whitey Lockman came in.

In the winter of 1951, when Whitey received a first baseman's mitt from the Giants, he didn't really take it seriously. Durocher, the moving force behind the gift, had been to the movies of the 1950 World Series at Toots Shor's, the popular dining place for New York's sports celebrities. There he had exchanged shoptalk with Gil Hodges, who had himself become a pretty accomplished first baseman after Leo encouraged him to switch to the position.

"I wouldn't want to bet that Whitey couldn't do a better job than I can," said Hodges. "It's no false modesty, either—it's just that I know he has everything a first baseman needs. He's quite a ballplayer, and he'll learn fast."

"You're right," said Durocher. "He's got great hands, and he's quick and agile. He doesn't have the arm an outfielder really needs, but it's plenty good enough at first base."

Ralph Branca and Gene Hermanski, eavesdropping on the conversation, scoffed at Hodges' assessment. But Durocher listened good, as his hero, John Wayne, would say.

Lockman still refused to believe he'd be the regular first baseman, even when Durocher used him at the bag in some spring training games. It was his considered judgment that he'd be back in left field once the season got under way. He knew, too, that Horace Stoneham was opposed to the move. So when the season started Lockman was in left field and Irvin was on first base, resulting in the crisis, which now had to be confronted.

Durocher kept thinking that Whitey hadn't looked too bad in Florida at first. Yes, there were some problems Whitey had to face: when to cover the base, when to hold the runner on, when he should roam into Eddie Stanky's second-base territory, what foot, since he was right-handed, to keep on the bag in taking throws. But these things could be worked on through Whitey's good habits.

Leo still speculated briefly on giving Gilbert another shot, but he didn't think Tookie could hit worth a damn in the majors. He gave some thought to Bill Rigney, the spirited all-around man who had the heart but perhaps not the talent to play anywhere he was asked.

Wrestling with himself long enough, Durocher made his move. While hitting fungoes to the outfield one afternoon in St. Louis, Leo paused in his labors and motioned Whitey to come in to him.

"What's up, boss?" asked Lockman.

"How'd you like to play first today?" Leo said.

"In the game?" Whitey questioned.

"Yeah, in the game," Leo said.

"Well, I guess the outfield's pretty lonesome, anyway," acknowledged Whitey. "At least you're more in the ball game at first base."

That settled it. The next day Lockman went to first.

When Durocher approached Irvin, the big slugger was not sure what to expect. Things certainly hadn't been going well for him, and he wondered if he was in for another roasting from his verbal manager. Instead, Durocher simply stated, "Monte, I'd like you to play right field tomorrow."

That was the best news Monte had had since Jackie Robinson broke the color line. Oddly, Irvin didn't go to right field the next day because overnight Durocher examined the Cardinals' pitching charts and reasoned that Mueller should get another chance against the right-handers who were scheduled to start for St. Louis. So the manager penciled in Irvin for left field, with Lockman at first and Mueller in right.

The strategy didn't produce any quick miracles, although Monte's bat did come alive. He got three hits as the Giants lost to the Cards, 5–2. But in the next game Irvin's homer beat Chicago, with Maglie looking as sharp as ever.

Within a week's time "The Switch," as it came to be known on the baseball beat, looked like the luckiest move Durocher had ever contrived. To those who believed Durocher was the brainiest manager since McGraw, the move served to enhance his reputation.

For one thing, Lockman seemed to enjoy being at first base. For another, there was scant doubt how Irvin felt about being back in the outfield. To help Whitey iron out any rough spots in his defensive play, Buddy Hassett, the former fancy-fielding first baseman for the Dodgers and Yankees, was brought in to give Lockman valuable pointers. In time, Lockman fared far better at the bag than he thought he would, for he learned to relax and loosen up.

"How we got away with it, I'll never know," he said. "For a while I was afraid to come out to the ballpark because I was afraid I'd screw up the game. The Lord must have been on Leo's side—or mine!"

When it looked as if the transformation had been a success, the writers pelted Durocher with questions: "How did you know it would work out?" "How did you figure that Whitey would be a good first baseman?"

Leo's response consisted of a big grin—the man had a wonderful set of regular teeth for frontal photos—and a laugh.

"Same way I knew Hodges would be," he said.

With Irvin's bat now exploding, Durocher turned to what was happening in other outfield precincts. Mueller was still failing to hit much higher than his weight, and Thomson sometimes went for several games without nudging the ball out of the infield. Tried repeatedly in the outfield, Hartung needed a compass to direct him to ground balls. Even if he started to hit, he was a liability. Maguire had never been good enough—and he was gone. Spider Jorgensen, a refugee from the Dodgers, couldn't hit more than a single or two, and Hank Thompson appeared better off at third base, though he could play the outfield in a jam.

As far as Durocher was concerned, all of these dubious alternatives didn't amount to a damn thing. He was desperately in need of another outfielder—and all of a sudden he knew just where to find him.

10

The Coming of Willie

WITH THE GIANTS still sagging in mid-May, a young ballplayer then serving his apprenticeship in the minor leagues was summoned to the Polo Grounds. Those who had already seen Willie Mays play at such stopping-off points as Class B Trenton of the Interstate League and Triple-A Minneapolis of the American Association had passed the word along that this effervescent nineteen-year-old had the makings of a dark DiMaggio or, maybe stretching a point, a black Babe Ruth.

Was it possible that Mays, who they said could hit, hit with power, run, throw, and field—all the credentials that had been set down in Durocher's creed of ultimate professionalism—could do these things sufficiently well to provide the necessary carbonation for the Giant mix?

Always with a discerning eye for baseball talent, Durocher had gotten his only look at Willie one day early in 1951 spring training. When Minneapolis was playing an exhibition game in Sanford, Florida, Leo and Stoneham drove over from St. Petersburg to see him. Before the game Minneapolis manager Tommy Heath introduced the two men to Willie.

"I've heard a lot about you," said Leo. "Maybe I'll be seeing you around."

It was the best auto trip Durocher ever took in his life. He got to see Willie do everything the hype insisted he could do. From that moment on, he couldn't get the boy out of his mind.

Some said that Leo could sell a stethoscope to a tree doctor, if he was in the mood. Now he was in the mood to sell Stoneham on the need to promote Mays immediately to the Giants. No more waiting, do it now! Stoneham countered that Willie was too young, it was too soon, and shouldn't Leo try another outfield combination before making such a move? But Leo wouldn't hear of it. "Goddamnit," he roared. "I want this kid!"

And he got him. Stoneham gave in to Leo's urging. But before he did, an apology, almost without precedent in a sport replete with callous disregard for its clientele, was prepared for the Minneapolis fans who had been so captivated by Willie. In a quarter-page ad taken in the Minneapolis Sunday newspapers, Stoneham informed the home folks that Willie, then hitting a mere .477 in thirty-five games (and even better at home), would no longer do his zestful performing in a Minneapolis uniform.

"Merit must be recognized," the ad said. The lad "should not be deprived of his opportunity" to become a New York Giant. He hoped, said Stoneham, that the Minneapolis fans would understand. Whether or not they did, it was the last time Stoneham would ever have to pay to get the kid's name in any newspaper in America.

It would be nice to report that Willie, the latest prodigy in town (Mantle was already striving at Yankee Stadium), picked up with the Giants just where he left off with Minneapolis. He didn't. Not at first. When he arrived, as the Giants were getting ready to go to Philadelphia for a three-game series, he had something that looked like an old motoring cap on his head, a little bag in his hand with spikes and glove, and a disoriented look on his face. But he also had Durocher firmly in his corner. "He reminds me of Pete Reiser when he first came up," said Leo, as he led the cheers for his protégé.

When Willie stepped into the lineup for the first time on the night of May 25, in Philadelphia, the only Giants, outside of Leo, that he'd ever met before were Irvin and Hank Thompson. The others were all strangers. To accommodate Mays in center field, Thomson went to left and Irvin to right. Willie failed to get a hit in five trips, and on one play he ran right up Irvin's back as he went for Eddie Waitkus's liner. The ball fell for a double, but the Giants won, 8–5. After the game Leo told Irvin and Thomson that in the future they should let Mays take everything that came near him in center field. He's got the range, said Durocher, you guys just guard the lines. Hearn, the winning pitcher, said he'd never even heard of Willie before that night: "There he was, behind me in center field, making catches as if he had a kangaroo pouch at his belt line, and the first I knew anything about him was a few minutes before game time."

In the second game with the Phillies, Willie once more went hitless. But the Giants won again. The team now stood at .500, with a record of 19–19. In the third game Willie still failed to produce a hit, but the Giants won again, this time with Maglie pitching a shutout.

Back home the fans were reading all about this young man, even if they hadn't seen him in action yet. The distressed Willie agreed that after twelve hitless appearances, he hadn't produced much action for anyone to see. Maybe, he told Durocher, I can't hit up here. Just keep doing what you're doing, Leo advised.

On May 28, in his first Polo Grounds game, Willie faced a tough customer in Boston southpaw Warren Spahn. Batting third in the order, he got a nice round of applause as he came to the plate for the first time. The noise got even louder when he leaned into an inside fastball and sent it soaring over the left-field roof for his first big-league hit. (Possessor of a dry wit, Spahn explained that he had made a "perfect pitch—for the first sixty feet.") As the grinning Willie hustled around the bases as if his pants were on fire, broadcaster Hodges gave out his familiar home run call, "Bye-bye, baby!" It wouldn't be the last time he'd do it for Willie Mays.

But the home run off Spahn was all Willie could do in his first twenty-six times at bat. Since expectations for him had been so high and the pressures so intense, Willie felt, at times tearfully, that he was letting down the skipper, the club, and the fans. He pleaded with Durocher to send him back to Minneapolis, where he'd been doing so well. But that was an argument he'd never win.

"You're my center fielder," Durocher said. "I don't care what you think or what you bat. If you can bat only half as well as you did at Minneapolis, you'll be fine."

Say what you will about the many negative characteristics of the Giant manager, when it came to Willie he was a working psychologist, always reassuring, always showing affection for him.

Willie was incredulous at the support he was getting not only from Leo and his teammates but from the normally blasé New York fans. Often skeptical of the press-agented hoopla that was fed to them, the fans had fallen hook, line, and sinker for Mays. He somehow came across to them as a throwback to a more innocent time when players theoretically played for the love of it and couldn't wait to suit up for the next day's game.

Willie would run everywhere instead of walk; his cap came off in pursuit of fly balls; he could throw the ball from any part of the outfield on one bounce to the catcher, as George Spencer observed; and when he had difficulty remembering people's names, he greeted them effusively with a "Say Hey," which, in time, became his registered nickname, "The Say Hey Kid."

He played with an élan that hadn't been seen in the Polo Grounds in many a day. Even if he was immature and lacking in worldliness, coming, as he did, from Westfield, a suburb of Birmingham, Alabama, Willie couldn't be intimidated easily. When he was on a ball field, the only natural territory in his life, there was nothing he couldn't do—or think he couldn't do. When Durocher briefed him on how big-league pitchers didn't mind throwing at a man's head, Willie responded by saying he'd been thrown at in the black leagues, too. "I'm quick enough to get out of the way," he said. No problem.

As part of Durocher's cram course for Willie, Irvin, a man of enormous pride and dignity, was assigned the role of Mays's roomie—sort of a guidance counselor, adviser, and confidant. Monte didn't have too much in common with his designated buddy—outside of the color of his skin—but he took to his role of older brother with great pleasure. He was aware of Mays's potential as a ballplayer. More important, he realized how much this guileless young man might mean to the fortunes of the Giants.

"It took Willie a few weeks to feel his way around," said Monte. "It was still hard for him to appreciate he was really a big leaguer. Everything was new to him, and he was respectful and never hurt anyone's feelings. Soon Willie was doing and saying things on the bench that made everyone laugh and smile. He'd gotten his confidence and that bubbly temperament of his was charging up the whole Giant ball club. As far as Durocher was concerned, Willie simply could do no wrong on a baseball diamond. But he was great for all of us, a tonic to have around."

One day early in his 1951 season Willie actually dropped a fly ball. Monte, playing close to him, heard Willie speak harshly to his glove. "Shame on you for not catching that ball," he said, slapping the glove as if it were an unruly child. There just wasn't any limit to Willie's self-assurance on a ball field. He was simple in many ways, but when it came to baseball there wasn't anything he didn't know or his instant reflexes couldn't help him do.

There is no way of calibrating exactly how important Mays became to the Giant cause. But Bill Rigney, an insightful baseball man, believes he was indisputably the force that carried the club and made Durocher the manager he was that year.

It had long been the conventional wisdom about Durocher that he was quick to withdraw his interest from losing teams. But Rigney points out that Leo didn't lose interest in this Giant team because he felt, deep down, that it could win with Mays around.

"Even when we were in the throes of a slump that puzzled many of us, Leo was convinced that the team would get hot," recalled Rigney. "Sure, there were some pessimists who kept saying 'You guys have gotta be nuts, this team isn't going any place,' but Leo never managed any better in his life, as that team tried its damndest to get back in the race. But what really kept Leo going was Willie. He was certain, even when Willie was having a rough time at the start, that the kid would get hot and help us win. The other thing that Leo realized was that if we were way back we didn't have too many teams to climb over—we wouldn't have to crawl up a long ladder."

The Giants may have been a sullen bunch, wrote Charles Einstein, "and uncommunicative at best, but they had through some alchemy become a relaxed band of merry men."

The reason was the new man—or boy—in town.

11

The Season Rolls On

IN THE ENEMY CAMP, the Dodgers were hardly convinced of the rejuvenation of the Giants. They scoffed at the mass anemia afflicting the Giant batters—Mays down at .043, Thomson, Lockman, and Mueller flailing away in the low .200s, only Dark over .300—and conceded only that Durocher had a few pretty fair pitchers.

Several of the Dodgers had the temerity to suggest that Mays really wasn't the Second Coming. A few hinted that he wore his pants too long and looked more like a comedic Charlie Chaplin in the outfield than their own graceful Duke Snider. Much of such talk belonged in the category of normal disparagement, some of it of a psychological nature, that constantly went on between these clubs. But it may also have been a way of the Dodgers' deflecting their concerns about one obvious Dodger imperfection: the need for another good outfielder.

On June 1 the Dodgers were 4½ games ahead of the Giants, who were in fifth place. That should have been a satisfactory state of affairs to the Dodgers' front office. But there was a gnawing sense that on a team that had Reese, Robinson, and even the journeyman Cal Abrams up among the league's top hitters, there was still something lacking in the outfield—someone who might bring first-rate assistance to the Duke and Furillo. The Dodgers didn't know where such help was going to come from, for nobody was eager to provide them with pennant insurance. But that didn't mean they didn't recognize the need.

By the first of June the Giants were perched at the .500 level, with a 21–21 mark. The Dodgers were 24–15, with the six-game margin in the loss column seeming to give them plenty of breathing space. Nonetheless, when a reporter asked Pee Wee Reese one afternoon who he feared most, he named the Giants. "They're still the team to beat in this league," he said.

Durocher kept juggling his lineup. He had Willie batting third at the beginning, then dropped him to eighth. Irvin was as high as fourth and as low as seventh. Westrum, his finger repaired, batted fourth on occasion.

On June 2, way down in the lineup, Willie got his first triple, as the Giants beat the Pirates. He banged out two doubles against the Cards and scored the only run in Koslo's 1–0 shutout. It was his best day yet in a Giant uniform, the kind of performance that Durocher would come to expect from his "adopted son." Maglie, possibly the most effective pitcher in the league now, won his ninth in a row on June 5. But the next day the Giants gave the game away in the ninth inning when the Reds scored three off Monte Kennedy, a so-so southpaw who'd been with the Giants since 1946 but had never won more than twelve games. Willie hit his second home run against the Reds, a classic "Chinese" shot down the right-field line, one of the rare cheap homers that he'd earn.

With the team still bogged down at .500, Durocher, acting on one of his impulses, went to the third-base coaching line. The move had a positively electric effect—for one day. The Giants clobbered the Cubs, 10–1, with Willie's average going over .200 for the first time. But the next day the Cubs halted Maglie's streak at nine games, Leo's arm-waving and hollering failing to produce any significant hitting.

At this point in the season an exhibition game, in behalf of the National Amputation Foundation, was scheduled at the Polo Grounds. Featuring their incomparable hitter Ted Williams, the Boston Red Sox were the foes for the day. It was the first time Williams had ever played in the Polo Grounds, a park whose right-field dimensions seemed made to order for his left-handed pull hitting. Photographers dutifully rounded up Mays to pose with Williams, the crusty Hall of Famer-to-be squinting into the camera alongside the first-year man. Before a slim crowd of 5,500 people,

Willie hit a homer, while Williams had to settle for two singles. But Williams did get a chance to see Leo's choice play. Ted said he envied Willie's speed, but he thought DiMaggio looked better going after fly balls than Willie did.

Following the exhibition game, the Giants jumped all the way to second place, when Irvin hit a three-run homer in the tenth to beat the Reds, 6–3. At 28–26 the Giants were still six games behind the Dodgers, but they seemed to be showing signs of life.

The Giants won another game, with Maglie coming in in relief for the first time in 1951. Starting and relieving, The Barber could be worn out before long, for he was no fuzz-faced rookie. Was this a sign that Durocher was panicking, or did it signify that he felt his team, with a real chance to win, should battle hard for each ball game? It was not always easy to fathom all of Leo's moves, for sometimes one suspected that he manipulated things out of sheer frustration.

It now became clear that Mays was getting on track in every way. He was unleashing throws in almost every game that brought whistles of delight from viewers; he ran the bases as if he'd been born there and, just as a change of pace, made a catch one day in Pittsburgh with his bare hand. The Giants had experienced a sluggish start, but this kid with the high-pitched giggle was the wake-up call for them. By mid-June he'd even put together a modest ten-game hitting streak, which earned him a promotion to seventh place in the batting order, right ahead of the still-slumping Thomson.

On June 15, in the first closed-circuit television broadcast of a major prizefight, Joe Louis, slow and balding at thirty-seven, knocked out Lee Savold, a thirty-five-year-old ex-bartender from Britain, in the sixth round at Madison Square Garden. (The fight filled eight theaters in six cities, with the top price of $1.30 at Shea's Fulton Theatre in Pittsburgh. Other theaters charged from sixty-four to ninety-five cents for a seat.) It was another episode in Louis's attempt to win back the heavyweight title that he'd relinquished in 1949. Sadly, Louis's difficulties with the Internal Revenue Service had induced him to resume fighting at a time when he should have been reaping the benefits of a career that had made him a brave symbol to America's blacks.

But another event that day completely overshadowed, at least in the borough of Brooklyn, Louis's ill-conceived comeback. The

Dodgers finally got the one man they wanted to buttress their outfield. With the Cubs and Dodgers almost swapping rosters, an eight-man trade was completed. But the key player was thirty-year-old outfielder Andy Pafko, who had played for the Cubs since 1943. A power hitter, generally close to .300, Pafko was a fine fielder, who had played through the war years in Chicago because of high blood pressure, which gained him a military exemption. Also included in the Cubs' package were pitcher Johnny Schmitz, catcher Rube Walker, and infielder Wayne "Twig" Terwilliger. The Dodgers who were turned over to the Cubs were Gene Hermanski, Bruce Edwards, Eddie Miksis, and pitcher Joe Hatten.

There was much snickering about the trade around the National League. The consensus argued that it was a bare-faced swindle pulled off without a gun. The inclusion of Pafko in the deal, some deep thinkers said, certified a Brooklyn flag in 1951. Pafko himself, a good-spirited fellow, was crushed. He had been born in Wisconsin, but after eight years in Wrigley Field (in 1950 he hit .304, with thirty-six homers) he felt like a native Chicagoan. His wife, Ellen, came from Chicago, and if a vote had been taken among Chicago fans Andy would have wound up close to the top in popularity.

When the Dodgers were at Wrigley Field to play the Cubs a day before the trade was consummated, Pafko heard Don Newcombe yell at him from the Dodger dugout, "You're goin' to be a Dodger tomorrow, man!" But Andy brushed it off. He hadn't been told a word about such a trade. Why would Newcombe know about such a thing before he did?

Just six hours before the trading deadline Pafko was sitting down for supper at home when Wid Matthews, the Cubs' general manager, got him on the phone.

"I've got news for you," said Matthews. "We've traded you to the Dodgers."

Some ballplayers upon hearing that they've been traded to a likely pennant winner, and away from an also-ran, would have been pleased. But when Pafko got the news, he whacked the chair he was sitting on. He cried, and Ellen began to cry like a baby, too.

"It was my worst moment in baseball," said Pafko. "It almost knocked me over. Ellen and I loved Chicago and didn't want to move. All of our friends and relatives were there. I can still see the empty look on my father's face as he handed me the sports section, with the front pages full of my trade. I don't think I ever forgave the Cubs."

On the Sunday after the big trade, with the Dodgers still in Chicago, Pafko moved all of his belongings into the Dodger clubhouse.

"Suddenly," he said, "I had to change my loyalties."

That's the way baseball operated—as cold as a mortician's heart. The Dodgers were involved in a pennant race. This was no time to muse about Pafko's feelings. Certainly the Cubs didn't.

Naturally, Dodger fans were delighted. You don't deal every day for guys who can hit over thirty home runs. The Brooklyn writers, bubbling over with partisan optimism, typed that it "was time to break up the Dodgers!" What Durocher thought about the matter was unprintable. His wife, Laraine, joining in the anger felt by everybody around the Giants, went so far, even for such a genteel lady, to make some intemperate remarks about it on her TV show.

Poor Hermanski, switching dugouts, said good-bye to Dressen by assuring him that "now that I'm gone you guys are a cinch for the pennant." Even Gene figured the trade was pretty one-sided.

Edwards, second best to Campy in the Dodger catching corps, gained his revenge almost immediately. Sent up as a pinch hitter in the first game between the Cubs and Dodgers following the trade, Edwards blasted a home run to beat Erskine. Only a few hours before Erskine and Edwards had sat alongside each other on the bus going out to Wrigley Field.

"What did you throw him?" Dressen asked Erskine.

"My new slider," said Erskine.

"Well, the goddamn thing slid right into whatever that avenue is," said Dressen, reproachfully.

Despite such repercussions, the Dodgers still thought it was a splendid trade for them, and it wasn't long before Pafko became a full-fledged member of their blasting crew.

Another trade between the Cards, still considered a major contender in the National League, and the Pirates, very much a noncontender, took place at the same time as the Pafko deal. Seeking to add punch to their lineup, the Cards let their veteran southpaw Howie Pollet go to the Pirates for Wally Westlake, the outfielding roommate of Ralph Kiner, and pitcher Cliff Chambers. Westlake didn't come cheap, either, for the Cards also had to throw in pitcher

Ted Wilks, outfielder Bill Howerton, infielder Dick Cole, and Joe Garagiola, who hadn't as yet discovered he was a better talker than catcher. At the time, however, few thought the Cards had bargained themselves into the pennant with the acquisition of Westlake.

The way the season was going for the Giants, with more ups and downs than a scenic railway, the team tried to be philosophical about the addition of a player of such quality as Pafko to the Dodgers.

"We've just gotta live with it," said Leo, "even if we hate it." He was getting used to his team dying one day, then being resurrected the next. If the Giants could survive that early-season eleven-game losing binge, as they seemed to be doing, they still had a chance.

Late in June Mays' ten-game hitting streak went by the boards, Maglie became the first pitcher in the league to win ten games, and the Giants were shut out by Gerry Staley of the Cards, only the second time they'd been whitewashed since Johnny Sain inflicted such damage on them April 26.

The team's daily alignment now had Irvin in left field, Mueller in right, and Thompson at third base, replaced from time to time by Lohrke or Rigney. With such a setup, Thomson spent more time on the bench than he would have liked, but he was suffering for his soft bat. On the whole, the club was hitting much better, sparked by Mueller and Dark, both now over .300, and Irvin, who was coming up with long, game-winning hits more than ever before. Willie, of course, was Willie, putting on his show, from town to town, that broke over ballparks like a daily sunburst.

One day he hit a three-run homer in the tenth inning in Wrigley Field to beat the Cubs for the Giants' tenth straight victory in that gracious old ballpark. But he drew more appreciation in an earlier inning when, after singling, his cap dropped off as he rounded the bag wide and he stopped to pick up the headgear before hurrying to return safely to first base. Even the hostile Cub fans in Wrigley Field roared with delight at such insouciant behavior. That was just the way Willie affected people.

Such goings-on couldn't help but instill a new spirit in the Giants as they prepared to face the Dodgers again on June 26. The teams hadn't donned boxing gloves since the early moments of the season when Willie hadn't been on hand.

Naturally, Durocher trotted out his favorite Dodger-slayer, Maglie, for the first game, in front of a capacity crowd at the Polo Grounds. Before the game began the umpires gathered the combatants—Dressen and Durocher—at home plate, much as a referee would give solemn instructions to two pugilists before a fight.

"No more of those dusters," the umps warned Durocher. And Leo would look at them in all innocence. Who are you talking about? he'd say to them. Certainly not Maglie.

Pitching for the Brooks, Preacher Roe could do his share of rule flouting, too. You just had to catch him at it, but that wasn't easy. If you got hit with one of his pitches, it wouldn't hurt much, although you stood a chance of drowning. The first time Willie faced Preacher that afternoon he took a lusty swing at one of his slushy pitches and wound up with nothing but embarrassment.

"You think he's a pretty good pitcher?" asked Campanella, catching Preacher that day.

"Yeah, sort of," said Willie.

"You ain't seen nuthin' yet," Campy continued, borrowing the old Al Jolson line. "Cuz tomorrow you gotta bat against Newcombe. He just eats up young colored boys like you."

Campy always liked to talk it up behind home plate, partially to relax himself but also to distract enemy hitters. In those early days, Willie was an especially vulnerable target. The next time he came to bat against Roe Campy kept chattering away as if he were getting paid per word. That caused Willie to turn around to look at him.

"Mr. Durocher," Mays said, "just told me not to talk to you."

But all of Campy's needling couldn't put a dent in Maglie's pitching. Sal shut out the Dodgers, 4–0, moving the Giants to five behind the Dodgers. It was the first time Preacher lost all year, leaving him with a 10–1 ledger.

Although Mueller hit in his seventeenth straight game the next day, the Giants lost, thus deflating any hopes they may have had for a sweep. Mays made another one of his patented catches, this time circling, stopping, then circling again before he came to a dead stop with the baseball safely enclosed in his glove.

"What's the big idea of that dance out there?" asked Leo. "The ballet's downtown, not here."

"Skipper, I had it all the way," said Willie. "It just went further than I thought."

Irvin delivered two home runs the next day to give the Giants a 5–4 win and an edge in the three-game series. They were now at 38–31 and full of hope until they ran into a minor catastrophe the next night at Braves Field. They should have "stood in bed," instead of going out to face Boston, playing their first game at home under their new manager, Tommy Holmes, who had just taken over from Billy Southworth.

The Braves knocked out Maglie with four in the first inning, then the Giants rallied to gain a 7–4 lead, only to be blown apart by eight Braves runs in the seventh and seven more in the eighth. Where, oh where, did my pitchers go, wailed Durocher. Within hours a rash broke out on his arms. "Those nineteen Braves runs did it," he said.

Making matters worse, the Dodgers were beating up on the Phillies, 14–8, the same day. So the Giants retreated to 5½ back as July dawned.

If youth was being served in the Giant and Yankee camps, as Willie and Mickey received their initiation rites, the old soldiers still hadn't quite faded away. Nobody was asking yet where Joe DiMaggio had gone, for the great center fielder, afflicted with traumas to his body that a lesser athlete might yield to, was named for the thirteenth time to the American League All-Star team, with no protestors. Mantle still hadn't pried DiMaggio loose from his moorings. On the contrary, Mickey wasn't really even needed that first year, since the Yankees had DiMaggio, as well as Hank Bauer, Gene Woodling, Jackie Jensen, and Joe Collins in the outfield.

Still another indomitable veteran, Bob Feller, pitched a Sunday no-hitter, the third of his career, at Cleveland, though he did give up a run.

But for the Giants, on that first July day, the signal event was a three-run home run by Thomson, his tenth of the year, but his first in a month. For a long spell Durocher had chosen to play Bobby only against left-handers. Indeed, he hit his homer against the left-handed Spahn at Boston as the Giants won, 4–1. It is possible that Bobby's wallop saved his job on the Giants, for Leo was becoming more sulfurous than usual about Thomson's failings at the plate. Durocher had even gone so far as to obtain the thirty-year-old Earl Rapp, a left-handed hitting outfielder with little home run power, from Oakland. Rapp scarcely promised to solve the Giants' outfield problems—but the move reflected Leo's frustration.

When Thomson hit a two-run homer the next day to beat the Phillies, 4–3, with Hearn the winning pitcher, Durocher was so pleased with his suddenly revivified player that he hardly cared that Preacher Roe went rolling along with his eleventh victory, against Boston. To take advantage of the "new" Thomson, the Giants would need some Dodger losses.

As the Dodgers took the field on July 3, word reached them of the suicide in an Atlanta hotel room of an old Ebbets Field favorite, Hugh Casey. Said to be the last pitcher discovered by Wilbert Robinson, Casey hurled tight relief for the Dodgers from 1939 to 1948. Unfortunately, he was remembered principally for having thrown the ninth-inning third strike—rumored to be a spitter—to Tommy Henrich that got away from catcher Mickey Owen in game four of the 1941 World Series against the Yankees. With the floodgates open the Yanks went on to win, scoring four runs after two were out.

Brooklyn fans were more inclined to blame Owen for the misadventure. But the "new life" for Henrich was the ruination of a despondent Casey, who had been on his way to victory and a well-merited shower.

"When I missed the ball, I was shocked for a moment. I couldn't believe I had missed it," said Owen. "However, I always kicked myself for not calling time and stopping the game, giving Casey and me time to get over the shock and cool off the Yanks."

Casey had been a brooder and boozer, once engaging in a well-publicized boxing match with Ernest Hemingway, in 1941, when the Dodgers were training in Havana, Cuba. His sudden death, at thirty-seven, was the subject of much discussion among the Dodgers, although Casey hadn't been around to visit his old pals since he left baseball several years before.

That night the Dodgers lost to Boston, 4–3, and the Giants rallied several times to beat the Phillies, 9–8, in the thirteenth inning, for their seventh straight victory.

The final All-Star selections in the National League for the midsummer interleague game provided positive evidence why Brooklyn was expected to win. There were seven Dodgers picked— Reese, Robinson, Hodges, Snider, Campanella, Roe, and Newcombe. The Giants had to settle for Maglie, Jansen, and Dark.

With a big doubleheader (in those days scheduled twin bills could be savored for the price of a single admission) coming up against the Dodgers at Ebbets Field, the Giants, now in a resurgent mood, were prepared to cut into the 4½-game Dodger lead. Their record stood at 41–32, while the Dodgers were at 44–26. The Giants nursed visions of doing everything to the Dodgers but break down Abe Stark's pledge in right field.

The fans gathered early for that July 4 doubleheader, bringing their lunches and their lungs. Though the day was misty and not as warm as might be expected at that time of year, there were 34,000 in their seats by the time Roe threw his first pitch. Some of those present were Giant fans, venturing into hostile territory, and well advised to keep their partisan feelings under restraint.

In the opener Thomson, as he'd been doing all week long, cracked a homer to put the Giants ahead briefly. But Dressen, always "thinking of something," ordered Campy to pinch-hit a homer for pitcher Clyde King—which he did. Later Roe put down a perfect bunt to send Robinson pounding over the plate with the winning run. It ended as a 6–5 victory in a game so wildly exciting that most fans had little chance to get their pants warm.

Branca beat the Giants in the nightcap, 4–2, as Koslo gave up homers to Snider and Hodges. Again Dressen fancied himself the ultimate cerebral manager (no computers or endless stat sheets in those years) by sending up Abrams to hit for Rocky Bridges when Rocky had two strikes on him. Abrams blithely took a called third strike. So much for Chuck's strategy. Nevertheless, the Dodgers won twice.

A three-game sweep was completed the next day, as the Dodgers won behind Newcombe's blistering fastballs. The place was jammed again. Pafko hit a homer, making the trade look good, and so did Hodges, who was having a good year despite a batting average that was not as high as other years.

After the deluge, the Giants found themselves 7½ games back of the Dodgers. With the season near the halfway mark, the race had turned into a "shambles" in the eyes of John Drebinger of the *Times*. Branca openly felt that from here on Durocher "had to shoot the works with his pitchers," even if it meant using Maglie, Hearn, and Jansen in the bullpen. "He needs wins," said the Dodger pitcher.

The Dodgers' performance in padding their National League

lead over the Giants was, needless to say, enormously gratifying to Dressen. It was obvious that many others in the Brooklyn camp were joining the voluble little pilot in their smug feelings.

Dressen, however, would have benefited greatly from an epigram that philosopher George Santayana had lobbed into *Bartlett's Familiar Quotations* many years before: "Those who cannot remember the past are condemned to repeat it."

When Santayana uttered those words he had scant familiarity with pennant races. But Dressen, having been in a few himself, should have known better. At least he should have recalled how Bill Terry was hoist with his own petard in 1934 when he asked if Brooklyn was still in the league. Instead, bubbling over with success, Dressen just couldn't restrain himself at this point in the race.

"The team that beats us can win the flag," said Dressen, "but *nobody* is going to beat us. It's no longer a question of who's gonna win this race, it's now just a matter of the winning margin. We've knocked out the Giants, they won't bother us no more."

Durocher refused to buy for a second what Dressen was telling the world, even if all logic now dictated that his team was not capable of catching Brooklyn. "I don't concede the Dodgers anything," he said, "not even this much." In so saying, Leo illustrated his point by placing his right index finger a mosquito length above his thumb. "They've gotta win it on the field, not with their mouths."

The Dodgers' destruction of the Giants should have been the major news in the New York sports world. Instead, the headlines were dominated that week by the story that fourteen college basketball players from City College of New York, New York University, and Long Island University had pleaded guilty to conspiracy charges arising out of the alleged fixing of games that had taken place at Madison Square Garden in recent seasons. The metropolitan area always boasted of a rich tradition of college basketball. Its teams were among the best in the country, and urban kids from the sidewalks of New York played the game as if they invented it. The fix news was distressing, certainly the most sensational off-the-field sports scandal since Durocher had been suspended from baseball in 1947.

While others were preoccupied with this jarring insight into the "city game," the Dodgers picked up right where they'd left off against the Giants, pummeling the Phillies, 6–2. Hodges hit his twenty-eighth homer, putting him ahead of Babe Ruth's record pace of 1927, when he hit his sacrosanct sixty.

For a team that had just suffered such indignities, maybe even final rites at Ebbets Field, the Giants proved to be surprisingly resilient. At first base for the day, Irvin had four hits, and Thomson hit his fifth homer in seven games as the Giants beat the Braves, 12–10. What Durocher was most pleased about was that his team had bounced back from a five-run deficit against Spahn to get five runs in the third inning.

When Thomson hit another home run on July 7 as the Giants beat the Braves still another time, 7–6, the team showed no signs of desperation. But every time they felt they were gaining momentum, all they had to do was gaze at the scoreboard to realize they weren't moving up: the Dodgers had won again. The most remarkable thing about the latest Giant win was that Sal Yvars, the third-string catcher behind Westrum and Noble, hit his first home run in three years to keep the Giants in the game.

The twenty-seven-year-old Yvars, born on Houston Street in New York City and with the Giants since 1947, was the type of gutsy relief catcher that Durocher liked to have around. He'd been in only twenty-eight games in four years before the '51 season. The same day that he hit his home run his wife, Ann, gave birth to twin girls, Debbie and Donna, in a White Plains Hospital.

"When I was getting dressed after the game," said Yvars, "Horace Stoneham called me to come to his office. I was expecting that he'd tell me I was going to get sent down again. Instead, when I walked into his office, he smiled at me and handed me fifteen one-hundred-dollar bills. 'Here,' he said, 'don't tell anyone I'm doing this, it's not our policy. But this has been such a great day for you, it's only right to do it.' I almost fell over." At the time Sal was making $7,500 for the season.

With the All-Star Game break approaching, the Giants lost their Sunday game with Boston, 6–5, in the tenth inning. They had been winning so many of these close contests that they couldn't imagine why they lost this one—but they did, and it hurt. Brooklyn won, stretching its lead to 8½ games.

Rumors now also circulated in the New York tent that the team was on the verge of letting Eddie Stanky go to the St. Louis Browns, where the iconoclastic Bill Veeck was then ready to name him as manager of his floundering team. Stanky would replace Zach Taylor, whose pitching staff was headed up by Satchel Paige, then close to fifty years old. If Veeck wouldn't hire Stanky, there was a chance The Brat would move on to the Cardinals to take over for Marty Marion.

The stories continued to heat up, especially after the Giants brought up Davey Williams from Minneapolis, where he was supposed to be preparing to take over second base in 1952 for the Giants. Not a great hitter, Williams fielded well and looked to be a good partner for Dark around second. By coming to the Giants at this time, with a half year left, he could demonstrate whether he could earn the job the following season. But, despite all the conjecture, Stanky didn't go to the Browns or the Cards. He stayed right at the Polo Grounds.

The New York contingent in the All-Star Game at Detroit did well, as expected. Maglie turned out to be the winning National League pitcher in relief of Robin Roberts, Dark got a hit, Robinson went two for four, and Hodges, continuing his tear, hit a home run.

With the resumption of the pennant chase on July 12, the won-and-lost figures compiled by the Dodgers and Giants didn't look promising for Durocher. The Giants had forty-three victories and thirty-six losses. The Dodgers' docket was fifty and twenty-six. Subtract those devastating eleven straight defeats at the beginning of the season and the Giants would be having a splendid year. But somehow, when it was put to a referendum in Brooklyn, the burghers refused to give back those games to the Giants!

With Davey Williams at second base to start the second half, the Cards' Staley shut out the Giants for the second time. Jansen was good, but not good enough. When the Dodgers won, their margin went to 9½ games.

The next day Williams unloaded a bases-full home run, a most unlikely occurrence, and Westrum did the same thing, helping the Giants wallop the Cards. Leo asked Herman Franks to take over the bullpen coaching job as he himself returned to the third-base coaching line. Mueller, Mays, and Irvin were in the outfield, while Thomson remained on the bench. One might have faulted Leo for Thomson's removal from the lineup at a time when he was hotter than a tenement in midsummer. But he had his reasons: theoretically, Thomson couldn't hit right-handed pitching. As the Dodgers won their eighth straight, Leo still kept manipulating and maneuvering. So far, it hadn't done him any good.

Russ Hodges, the diehard in the Giants' broadcasting booth, asked the same question daily of Durocher and his players: "Does this team really still have a chance?" One of his respondents, Al Dark, replied by using a well-worn Southern colloquialism: "If everybody stays well and the creeks don't dry up, we'll be there to take it all." Dark's answer reminded some people of that amusing little play that was often put on in schools and summer camps—a play within a play—where the director keeps reassuring all hands that regardless of how bad the rehearsal looked, "It would turn out all right on the night."

Hodges could take heart from the Dodgers' loss of two games at Ebbets Field to the Cubs, of all teams. The Chicagoans were drowning in seventh place, literally going nowhere. Yet here they were suddenly rising up and bashing the Dodgers in a double-header. As if that weren't enough of a sobering lesson for Dressen, his team dropped another doubleheader the next day to the Reds. That looked like a case of raging overconfidence. When the fans started to boo the ears off the Dodgers, Dressen should have delivered one of his stirring locker-room orations. But no such philippic was ever reported in the papers.

Despite these setbacks to the Dodgers' pride, the Giants failed to take advantage of the opening. They split with the Pirates on a desperately hot summer afternoon at the Polo Grounds. The Davey Williams move hadn't done much to spark the infield, and Hank Thompson, having a struggle with his batting average (.242) and his thirst, wasn't playing up to par at third base. The Thompson problem had been worrying Durocher for a long spell. He'd have to make up his mind soon what to do there, for neither Rigney nor Lohrke could play the position regularly.

It was that time of year when those teams in contention had to make their moves, sometimes dramatic ones, to solidify their chances or to reveal that they were throwing in the towel on the season.

Over at Yankee Stadium, the Yankees, a team not known for confessions of weakness, were about to eat humble pie on Mantle. The wet-behind-the-ears Oklahoman was not living up to his adulatory press notices, the fans were getting abusive, and his confidence, always suspect, was dwindling. The pressure had been intense for Mays, too, but he was managing to live with it, and play with it, perhaps due to the unexpectedly tender ministrations of his house father, Durocher.

As wise as Stengel was reputed to be, he could be acerbic, if one could follow his syntactical tergiversations. True, he had been thoroughly sold on Mickey, but now with the boy hitting just .260, with only seven home runs, he had to publicly admit he'd been guilty of rushing Mantle too fast—maybe before he was ready.

"That young fella is great," Casey said. "But he strikes out too much. He came up here as a shortstop, but he'll be back as an outfielder. Wait and see. We'll know his name when he gets here."

That was the Stengelian way of endorsing the poor kid. Depressed and totally confused, Mickey found himself on the way back to Kansas City, where he was expected to feast on minor-league pitching and get straightened out in order to cope with Yankee pressure as well as those baying hounds of the fourth estate. Everyone in the Yankee establishment predicted he'd be back in a fortnight. But they didn't have to live under Mickey's skin.

It was now up to Durocher to confront his festering third-base problem. When July 18 arrived, he had already decided to put The Brat back on second. But what was he going to do with Hank Thompson?

Ironically, a Chicago Cubs pitcher, Frank Hiller, helped Leo make up his mind. While Jersey Joe Walcott was dispatching Ezzard Charles in Pittsburgh that night to become the oldest man, at thirty-seven, ever to win the heavyweight championship, Hiller was spiking Thompson on the foot on a close play at third base in an after-dark game. Hank had to be removed, with stitches required to close up the bad gash.

But while Hank's wound was being repaired, his ego was being carved apart by management. At the request of Durocher, Stoneham announced after the game, which the Giants lost, that Hank was being optioned to Ottawa in the International League. It turned out to be one-for-one, as the Giants called up twenty-five-year-old right-hander Al Corwin from Ottawa to give some support to the pitching squadron.

That still left the yawning gap at third base. Leo had felt that "Thompson had fucked it up so bad, that maybe nobody can ever play it." But it was now up to him to pull one out of his cap, although it is clear that when he sent the problem child, Thompson, down to Ottawa, he had already made up his mind about what he was going to do. Now he did it.

He called in Bobby Thomson, still having the most mercurial of seasons. Leo was aware that Thomson's career as a ballplayer had started at third base. That would be helpful in such a transition. But he wasn't certain if Bobby would be able to get his body in front of those scorchers down the line. On the plus side, he thought Bobby's arm would be strong and accurate enough to make the long throws across the diamond.

If he moved Bobby to third—and if the move worked out well— he would have Mueller in right and Irvin in left, around Mays, the emerging star in center field. In addition, he would keep Bobby's bat in the lineup.

"You haven't had the kind of year you should have," said Leo to Bobby.

Thanks for reminding me, Bobby thought. He wasn't the type of person who fought with other people, especially his manager. He wondered what Leo was getting at. Was he trying to tell him that he was about to be traded? That didn't make much sense, considering how hard he'd been hitting recently. In the next minute he'd learn exactly what Leo had on his mind.

"Tomorrow take infield practice at third base," said Leo, perturbed that Bobby wasn't engaging in a livelier colloquy with him. "From here on, you're my third baseman." What Durocher left unsaid was an implicit threat that if Bobby didn't make it at third base he might wind up elsewhere, certainly too far away to commute on the ferry from Staten Island.

"I've never considered myself the smartest guy in the world," Bobby said later, "but I was always adaptable. I figured I could certainly make the switch." After all, earlier in the year Bobby had made a change in his batting stance—from the classic, straight-up style favored by DiMaggio—to a shortened stride, out of a crouched, closed stance, that Durocher had suggested.

On July 20 Thomson was at third base against Cincinnati. As "The Great Experiment" began—actually it was the third of Leo's experiments that season, starting with Lockman going to first base, then Willie taking over center field—Thomson banged out three hits and Maglie gained his thirteenth victory. The same day Stoneham showed how pleased he was with Durocher's type of leadership by granting him a contract extension through the 1952 season.

The money was close to $50,000, making Leo the highest-paid member of Stoneham's enterprise.

In the first three-game series that Thomson played against the Reds, the Giants won two. Bobby collected seven hits. Though he committed several errors on ground balls and throws, that didn't change Leo's attitude a whit: Bobby was now his man at the hot corner. While the Giants were playing steady ball in the West, the Dodgers were going through one of their worst times of the season, losing nine out of twelve games. That raised Giant hopes, but the margin between the two teams still did not change dramatically.

Thomson wasn't the only Giant at this time who was banging the ball with regularity. So was Dark, so was Mays. Willie now had fifteen homers. Oddly, they were hit against fifteen different pitchers. Then one day Ken Raffensberger of the Reds put a stop to that. He gave up two homers in one game to Willie and a third later in the month. At one point, Willie had six hits in a row that were home runs—not six homers in six at-bats, but of the six hits he got all turned out to be homers.

On July 25 the Giants beat the Pirates for Durocher's one thousandth major-league victory. But the Giants lost the second game. Meanwhile, the Dodgers returned to their winning ways as Roe won his fourteenth game, against the Cubs, with Hodges hitting his thirtieth home run of the year. On track again, the Dodgers embarked on a winning streak just as the Giants started to benefit from Thomson's steady thumping and their formidable front-line pitching.

To keep their motor running, the Dodgers put in a call to St. Paul for Clement Walter Labine, a blond pitcher from Woonsocket, Rhode Island. The former paratrooper had developed a cunning sinker ball in the minors and could be used as a starter or in relief.

Bobby was up to .249 by the end of July, and though the Giants recalled Thompson from Ottawa it was clear that Hank would have to settle for part-time play in the outfield, spelling either Irvin in left or Mueller in right.

Through all these developments, including Mays's first stolen base of his career on July 29 against the Reds (after which Willie promptly got himself picked off by pitcher Willard Ramsdell), the Giants did little more than run in place. As they huffed and puffed on their successful road trip in the West, they still found themselves, each morning, behind Brooklyn by eight or nine games. It was a very frustrating state of affairs.

At times, because of their inability to cut the Dodgers' margin, the Giants began to look indifferent. That's what being nine games back can do to a team's morale. The Giants' sometime performance fit right in with Ty Cobb's deprecating comments about modern-day players, made that week before a congressional investigating committee in Washington. The legislators had invited the old churl to come in and talk to them about baseball's reserve clause, which he defended angrily on the grounds that it was necessary for the life of the game.

"Baseball," he said, "has made it possible for hundreds of young men to improve their lot in life." In no way, Cobb insisted, could players be considered "peons." It was another opportunity for him to evaluate negatively the modern players as opposed to players of his era. "These present-day guys seem to be a particularly fragile lot to me," Cobb growled.

Well, maybe the Giants *were* feeling fragile these days, even if they weren't peons. They kept working their butts off and nothing much happened vis-à-vis the Dodgers.

To underline this depressing situation, on the last day of July Thomson hit two gigantic homers to beat the Cubs, 4–3. But the same afternoon Newcombe defeated Pittsburgh for his fifteenth victory and the Dodgers' tenth in a row.

As August began, the Giants split a doubleheader with Chicago and the Dodgers lost one, with General MacArthur, looking imperious even in his civvies, in attendance. This meant that the Giants were still twelve down in the loss column, the only statistic, according to baseball's Euclids, that was worth looking at during a pennant race. Thus, with fifty games to go, or less than a third of a season, the Dodgers had what appeared to be an insurmountable lead.

"We were so far back of those guys, it wasn't even funny," said Willie.

But if Willie had bothered counting how many games the Dodgers lost when MacArthur was in the Brooklyn ballpark, he would have pressed Irving Rudd, the lively little director of Dodger flummery, to keep inviting the general back every day. Maybe even provide him with carfare.

According to figures released by Rudd himself, the Dodgers

never won when MacArthur was in an Ebbets Field box. Rudd said he was there thirteen times, enough to lose any National League race, even the current one.

Despite this shameful record, Rudd persistently kept calling MacArthur's Waldorf-Astoria suite to entice him out to the ballpark—and the general never turned him down. "You haven't lived 'til you've visited Ebbets Field," Rudd told MacArthur. So the general was now living. It's possible, too, that his frequent appearances in Ebbets Field kept MacArthur highly visible for the open baseball commissioner job.

But from the look of things, MacArthur should have returned to West Point, where he had served as the celebrated superintendent following World War I. On August 2, ninety cadets, many of them stars on Colonel Earl Blaik's football team (including his own son), were evicted from the corps for cheating in the classroom. It was said that even with the purge of these men— "scapegoats," said Colonel Blaik—the cheating was more extensive than reported.

All in all, with the recent basketball skulduggery and now the West Point mess, it had turned into a shockingly bad summer for sports scandal.

12

The Winning Streak

IN HIS FIRST seventeen games at third base Thomson had turned into Durocher's most successful guinea pig. He hit .345 over that span, with five home runs and eighteen runs batted in. But on August 5 the Dodgers took both ends of a doubleheader from Cincinnati, keeping them 9½ games in front. It didn't matter that Corwin, developing into the Giants' secret weapon, beat the Cardinals, with Maglie in relief.

A three-game series with the Dodgers now was on the Giants' agenda. New York fans were envisioning a sweep at Ebbets Field that could catapult their team back into the race. Two out of three would do little good. What was needed were three wins to prevent a pennant runaway, said the writers covering the two clubs. Few could disagree with such an assessment.

When the first game on August 7 was canceled because of rain, that presumably set up a doubleheader for the next day. But Walter O'Malley, that exemplar of the free enterprise system, preferred to feed ball games to his baseball-hungry patrons one at a time— for separate admission fees. There would be a game in the afternoon, after which the park would be emptied out. To get into game two that night fans would have to pay again. O'Malley may not have been enamored of his predecessor, Branch Rickey, but he didn't hesitate to follow closely in the image of the shrewd old horse trader, now in his first year in the Pittsburgh front office. Rickey would have loved him for charging twice for the two games.

Even if the Dodgers were many lengths ahead of the Giants, that did not diminish the heat of the battle when these teams clashed. The steam that poured out of Maglie's nostrils when he scowled darkly at Robinson from the mound was no less than it had been two or three months earlier. The flow of scatological lava from Leo's mouth did not cease because the Giants were so miserably far in the rear. Stanky's passion to win had not abated, nor did his distracting tactics come to a halt; Dark's competitive juices had not stopped gurgling, and Furillo hated Durocher as fiercely as he ever had. Nor did Robinson believe that the millennium had been reached in interracial relationships or that he should at last still his tongue in deference to a concordat with Rickey that, in fact, never really existed. The two stars, Maglie and Robinson, would continue to "spar on the edge of homicide," as Thomas Kiernan once wrote, and the fans would be there to eat it up.

The presence of such partisan crowds in Ebbets Field precluded any lessening of jockeying, brushbacks, and beanballs, all of which had come to be the spice of this rivalry between the two New York teams. Leo and Chuck, both leadership goads in their dugouts, loved the smell of baseball combat. It was a certainty that their zest for playing and winning hadn't been reduced an iota by the nature of the one-sided race.

Despite the perfect setting for mutual mayhem, the first game went quietly enough. Unloading three home runs by Snider, Hodges, and Furillo, before a packed house, the Dodgers won, 7–2. Giant fans, if there were many in that claustrophobic, loyalist madhouse, had little to cheer about, as their favorites were bombed into submission.

But the second game was certainly more in keeping with the scenario projected for these confrontations.

Maglie, ever the provocateur, worked on Jackie, as he always had, pitching him dangerously close, gesticulating, snarling, baiting. Robinson, his bat held proudly high, swung at each pitch as if he were trying to decapitate his tormentor. In the past the Giant pitcher had used his low-and-away curves and his tight pitches to thwart Jackie more often than not. But on this evening Robinson's bat was hotter than his temper. On the bases he was more than that: he stole second, he stole third. Threatening to steal home, he took daring leads off third base, mocking Maglie all the while. He bunted adroitly down the first-base line, trying, with bad intentions, to lure Maglie into close quarters if the pitcher tried to field the ball. But Maglie was having none of it. He let the hesitant Lockman try to make the play, while Robinson joyously ran past the first baseman to reach base safely.

By the time the game was 6–3, in the Dodgers' favor, with Jackie knocking in runs and scoring them, the crowd was wild in appreciation of the spectacle. When Durocher finally removed Maglie the pitcher could have opened up a grocery store by collecting all the garbage that came raining down on his head as he belligerently stalked off the premises.

(Maglie came to work almost every day with an aching shoulder. Before he pitched, The Barber had to be worked over by the trainer for at least twenty minutes. But that never inhibited his competitive instinct. Sal Yvars told of a typical Robinson-Maglie set-to, when Maglie kept shaking off Yvars's call for a curveball on a two-two count. Maglie wanted to throw Robinson his fastball, but Yvars was so annoyed that he unwound from his crouch position to go out and argue with his pitcher. "Whatsa matter with you," said Yvars, "throw your goddamn curve!" Maglie glared back at him. "Forget it," he said. "I feel like knocking him on his ass." That was Maglie.)

The byplay on August 7 wasn't limited to the exchanges between Robinson and Maglie. Giants pitcher Sheldon Jones sent Reese scrambling into the dirt with his "purpose pitch," then repeated his intimidating tactics with Campy, who, unlike Robinson, invariably arose with a sweet smile on his face. When umpire Jocko Conlan started for the mound to deliver a warning to Jones, Durocher bolted out of the dugout as if he'd been shot from a cannon. No sir, Durocher wasn't going to miss all this fun! Minutes later, Durocher and Westrum charged that Dodgers pitcher Clyde King was quick pitching. This time umpire Bill Stewart, tossing Leo out of the game, waved his arm majestically at the Giants' manager, whose every appearance roused the collective growls of the crowd. In short, it turned out to be everything a Dodger-Giant game was cracked up to be.

Refusing to quit, the Giants tied the game with three runs in the ninth inning with the help of a two-run single by Irvin. That set the stage for an ending that hurt the Giants to the depth of their bones. In the bottom of the tenth inning, with two out, the Dodgers filled the bases on singles, none of them particularly hard hit. Then Billy Cox hit one past the straining glove of Thomson at third for the winning run.

Both games had gone to the Dodgers, Robinson had never been more brilliant or contentious, Maglie had never been more surly, and all of Durocher's operatic sorties onto the field hadn't amounted to a bag of peanuts.

There had been many euphoric days for Jackie since he had faced down the abuse from rednecks like Phillies manager Ben Chapman, Country Slaughter, and others in the early years. But this day was the best of all. When he returned to the Dodgers' clubhouse after the game, he was gleeful. "Hey, we showed those sons of bitches, didn't we," he shouted in his high-pitched voice. "We did it to them!" He added insult to injury by pounding his bat on the Giants' clubhouse door, now closed to the world. Other Dodgers could also be heard, loudly proclaiming that the Giants had had it.

These inflammatory words could be picked up easily in the Giants' quarters, situated, in a masterpiece of dreadful social planning, alongside the Dodger clubhouse.

"Listen to that black bastard," snapped Eddie Stanky to Al Dark and Bill Rigney, both close by. "We'll stick that bat up his ass!" Realizing almost at once that Irvin was within earshot, Stanky turned to look at his black teammate. Stanky's private brand of logic, baseball-style, was that such nasty epithets were permissible. He had always believed in using rough, tough language as he launched into his bench jockeying. Jackie played the game the same way, figured Stanky. He always argued that Robinson himself was a master of the coarse insult. Robinson had been beating up verbally on Durocher all year, hadn't he? asked Stanky.

Whatever Stanky's rationale was, Irvin must have agreed because he looked over at Stanky and said, softly: "That's okay with me, Eddie."

In commenting later, Monte said that "somehow this incident struck a chord with the whole team . . . I can't explain exactly what it was, maybe pride. It was like right then and there every man made some private decision that we were going to take it to them, that we were going to make a run of it, no matter how hopeless it looked. From then on, we really started to play some ball."

Irvin's memory played tricks on him. The Giants still didn't really start to "play some ball," for the next day Brooklyn mopped up the three-game series with a 6–5 victory, propelled mainly by Campy's two home runs. Rudd's theory was knocked into a cocked hat that afternoon, as General MacArthur was in attendance—and the Dodgers had won. Branca hadn't lost a game to the Giants at Ebbets Field since August 1945. His record remained intact with this win.

Following the twin loss to the Dodgers the day before, Roscoe McGowen of the *Times* had openly despaired for the Giants. "Maybe the Dodgers wrapped up the pennant last night in a wild game at Ebbets Field," he wrote. With the Giants being drubbed once again by Brooklyn, McGowen's words took on special meaning.

It looked even worse on August 11, when the Phillies' Robin Roberts, always a haunting presence against the Giants, shut them out, 4–0, putting the Giants fifteen down in the loss column, and thirteen games behind the leaders. Though it was a Saturday game at the Polo Grounds, only a meager audience of 8,000 looked on. The fans appeared to share McGowen's write-off of the Giants.

Durocher himself at this point, according to some of his players, including Dark and Rigney, was giving signs of total retreat. He'd been saying since late May that Mays was going to be the alarm clock, and his moves with Thomson at third base and Lockman at first had worked out satisfactorily. Yet the Giants kept falling further behind.

"I'm not sure if Leo cared anymore," said Rigney, "and the team played against the Phillies like a bunch of robots." Durocher, often the master psychologist, didn't seem able to stem the rising tide of defeatism.

"I wouldn't say that Leo was suicidal," said Laraine Day at one point, "but I give myself credit for saying nothing that would put the idea in his head."

The next day the Giants were to play a Sunday doubleheader with the Phillies. It threatened to be not only a long, dreary afternoon but an unpropitious time to have a special day for Westrum, as good a team player as anyone on Durocher's roster. But the good people of Poughkeepsie, New York, Wes's residence, had decided long ago to honor their friend on August 12. They would bring down gifts and all sorts of bibelots to present to the catcher, but Wes was afraid the Giants would play like a bunch of whipped dogs. "If they did," said Westrum, "I'd feel just like a horse's ass."

But thanks to some first-rate pitching by Maglie and Corwin and clutch hitting by Irvin and Thomson, Wes didn't have to feel guilty about the long trip made by his Poughkeepsie pals. The Giants won both games, 3–2 and 2–1. They were tough games, too, the kind that a team has to play hard to win. Only 17,000 showed up, although nobody did a nose count on just how many were from Poughkeepsie. Irvin's three-run home run won the first game, then he raced all the way around from first base on Thomson's double to win the second game. The rains came down hard during the second game and the Dodgers also won that day, behind Newcombe, but the Giant clubhouse was a happy place for the first time in a month.

In the Monday game against the Phillies the Giants won again, to make it three out of four in the series. Pitching in a groove, Jansen was the winner. He was helped along to his fifteenth victory by Lockman's three-run homer and another spectacular grab by Mays, a diving, shoestring catch of Willie Jones's sinking liner, accompanied, naturally, by Willie losing his cap. (This cap-flying-off ritual had now become so popular among the fans that one suspected that Willie had manipulated it down to an art.)

In all the fuss about Mays and the heralded transfer of Thomson to third base, Lockman had been virtually ignored. Hitters like Whitey, proficient at hit-and-run, going for the holes, hitting them where they ain't, don't generally win headlines. That continued to be the case with the North Carolinian. But he was having a productive year, and Leo knew it.

The Dodgers kept pace with the Giants, beating the Braves on Hodges' thirty-third home run.

Coming up, the Giants had three games with the Dodgers at the Polo Grounds. Normally, in a close pennant race, this series would have been characterized as "crooshal" by the "ink-stained wretches" in the press box, as Red Smith was fond of calling them. Now the series looked to be little more than one team marching irresistibly to the flag, with the other looking on passively. Under such conditions, how could anyone regard these games as "crooshal"?

At 12½ games back and with their luck at a low ebb against the Dodgers (the Giants had been whomped six in a row by the

Brooks), the New Yorkers might still have nominated Maglie and Jansen to work the games. But both men had pitched recently and Leo was forced to reach out to his auxiliaries, in this case George Spencer, a workhorse in relief but only an infrequent starter. By pitching in the first game with the Dodgers, Spencer was starting for only the third time all year.

"Sure, I was surprised Leo picked me," said Spencer, "but he always liked to play hunches and I guess that's what I was—a hunch. Leo also had a memory like an elephant, and he knew I usually did pretty well against Brooklyn."

The recent surge of the Giants plus the fact that the Dodgers were in town brought out a surprisingly large crowd of over 42,000. There had been a feeling that the fans had thrown in the towel on their team, but this night they came back, in a sense, testing the credibility of their favorites.

The Dodgers, packed with right-handed power, lined up this way: Furillo, Cox, Snider, Robinson, Campanella, Pafko, Hodges, and Bridges (in for Reese, who was ailing). Only Snider batted from the left side. The Giants, with a settled lineup at last, fielded Stanky, Dark, Mueller, Irvin, Lockman, Mays, Thomson, and Westrum.

That night, as Spencer's fastball and sinker worked as never before, the Giants won, 4–2. Durocher was all smiles. Where have you been all my life? he was asking about Spencer. Later, the pitcher readily acknowledged this as "probably the best game I ever pitched."

Also helpful to Spencer's cause was the failure of the Dodgers' Erv Palica. The twenty-three-year-old right-hander had won thirteen and lost eight in 1950, with two shutouts. But his work in 1951 had been mediocre. For a month prior to this game he had complained of a sore shoulder. Nevertheless, Dressen was uncompromising in his feelings that there was nothing wrong with Palica. He constantly chastised him for "not wanting to pitch," insisting it was all in Palica's head.

But in three innings that night, Palica unfortunately proved his point. He gave up home runs to Mueller and Lockman and had next to nothing on his pitches. So Leo won his gamble on Spencer, and Dressen lost his on Palica.

"Sometimes if you did lousy," said Spencer, "Leo wouldn't talk to you for weeks. Other times, he wouldn't talk to you for weeks, even if you were going good. He was a tough guy to figure out."

If the Giants needed additional momentum, they got it in the next game from Mays. Hearn and Branca were in a tense mound duel, 1–1, in the top of the eighth inning. With one out, the Dodgers advanced Cox to third base and had Branca on first. Furillo then hit a drive to right-center, fairly deep and catchable, but certainly, under "normal" circumstances, designed to score Cox from third. But Willie was already in the process of rewriting the baseball dictionary: normal to him didn't mean a thing.

He came over fast from left-center, where he had been playing for the right-handed Furillo, and made a good glove-handed catch. Cox, meanwhile, had tagged up at third and headed home. He was a slight man and as fast as most other Dodgers, with the exception of Robinson, Reese, and Snider. But he never made it. And the 21,000 Giant fans who saw him fail, and Mays succeed, probably still can't believe it. As Willie grabbed the ball, running full speed, he stopped dead, planted his left foot, and pivoted to his left. For an instant, his back was to center field. Then he was full around and unleashing the ball. It zoomed toward Lockman, the cutoff man at first base, who wisely let it go through. When Cox arrived at home plate, the ball, which Westrum caught on the fly, was waiting. Not only had the throw—later called "The Throw," for the sake of formalizing the growing Mays legend—nailed Cox dead to rights, but it wasn't even close. Cox was out by almost three feet. As Cox kept staring at the plate, the crowd roared with delight.

Westrum hadn't even bothered to remove his mask. Later he said the ball, thrown some 325 feet, was "a strike, right over the heart of the plate." Eddie Brannick, with the Giants for a half century, in every role from office boy to traveling secretary, said he'd never seen a "greater play made by any other outfielder." Even if you confined that statement to Giant outfielders, that was covering a lot of territory, including Stengel, Irish Meusel, Ross Youngs, Freddy Lindstrom, Ott, and Jo-Jo Moore. Furillo, with an arm he had reason to be proud of, mumbled "impossible" at what he had just seen.

Perhaps the most flabbergasted party in the Polo Grounds was Dressen. In a moment that should have rendered him catatonic, he still found words, revealing more about himself than the play he had just been privileged to see.

"I'd like to see the guy do it again, then I'll believe it," he said. Mays, in the years to come, would not only oblige Dressen but many others.

Almost as if it were prearranged, Mays batted first for the Giants in their half of the eighth. Again the crowd applauded mightily. Willie did what he was supposed to do; he singled. Westrum then hit a two-run homer. When the Dodgers were retired peacefully in the ninth, the fans went home happy.

In the clubhouse after the game, Lockman decided he'd have some fun with his manager.

"What would you have done if I'da cut that throw off?" he asked. Durocher blinked at him. "You'd still be running," Leo said.

It was only the fifth win for the Giants in seventeen games with the Dodgers and they were still down thirteen in the loss column, but they had something to talk about.

On August 16, in the final game of the three-game set, the Giants won again, 2–1. Maglie was as sharp as he'd ever been, containing Robinson in the process. Birdie Tebbetts, the catcher and later manager of the Cincinnati Reds, believed that "in one spot, in one ball game, I'd rather have Robinson up there than any other man." But in this game Jackie didn't have a chance. When Thomson scored on a wild pitch by Newcombe in the seventh inning, the Giants had their sixth win in a row. The Giants' batting averages, even for their third-string catcher, Yvars, were more robust than they had been all year. Yvars, in only a few games, was hitting .382. Dark was at .316, Irvin at .304, Mays at .284, and Mueller at .283. Thomson had come all the way up to .252 and was hitting like gangbusters.

Durocher was still upset, however, by the number of errors his team made. Thomson had hardly become a Pie Traynor at third base, Dark and Stanky made too many miscues to be rated the best double-play combination in the league, and Mueller had a weak arm. But how much of a right or left fielder did you need with Willie roaming far and wide in center?

Leaving home to go to Philly, the Giants felt good about themselves, though nobody was daring enough to talk pennant or comeback. They were too far behind for such nonsense. In third place, seventeen games back of the Dodgers, the Phillies were about as realistic a threat as the Giants. The Phillies of Richie Ashburn, having a splendid year as one of the league's top leadoff men and center fielders, Dick Sisler, and Granny Hamner were playing well but not well enough.

The Giants beat the Phils in the first game, with Spencer getting credit in relief. The big pitcher suddenly loomed important in the Giant scheme. Meanwhile, the Dodgers split two with the Braves, winning, then losing.

The next day Jansen pitched a four-hit shutout, licking Roberts, a good sign for any team, for, although Robin tossed up an inordinate number of home run pitches, he was one of the great right-handers in baseball and always difficult to beat.

But Roe won his sixteenth game, despite a sore arm, and the Dodgers stayed serenely in front of the Giants by nine games. In the loss column they had the Giants by eleven.

On Sunday the Giants beat the Phils for the third straight time, Corwin picking up the win. The whole pitching staff now was contributing. In Durocher's lineup, Willie was still batting in the sixth slot, with Thomson behind him. It was Bobby's twenty-third homer that helped the Giants to their latest victory.

When the players crowded into the clubhouse after the game— their ninth win in a row—a couple of them inquired what the Dodgers were doing against the Braves. It had been a long time since anyone had given much thought to each day's Brooklyn score. Scoreboard-watching was the name of the pastime, but it was not a game to play when your team appeared to be irrevocably out of the race.

Someone informed Al Dark that the Dodgers had just lost to the Braves by the lopsided score of 13–4. "That means we're eight games behind them now," said Dark, who failed to add that that was the closest the Giants had been to the Dodgers in a long time.

A few others commented that for the league leaders to be drubbed by Boston in such a way wasn't exactly fitting. But sometimes, as all these players knew, it's better to lose a laugher by 15–0 than to get beaten, 2–1, in the ninth inning. It doesn't hurt your nervous system as much. Strange ideas were now percolating in Giants headquarters, once as lugubrious as a bear's cave. What was going on here, anyway?

Something was going on in St. Louis, too. But that was in the other league. That same Sunday afternoon, to help celebrate the fiftieth anniversary of the American League, the Browns, owned by baseball's premier maverick, Bill Veeck, played a doubleheader with Detroit. Thirty-seven games back of first place, the Browns were a feeble imitation of a ball club, and Veeck would have been the first to acknowledge that. For one fleeting moment that day he thought he'd bring some joy into the despairing lives of the 18,369 (the largest Sportsman's Park crowd to gather since 1947) who had come to sun themselves.

As the Browns batted in the bottom of the first inning of the second game, a tiny man emerged from the St. Louis dugout, waving three bats.

"Number one-eighth, Eddie Gaedel, batting for Saucier" was the message from the loudspeaker.

All eyes in the ballpark focused on the gnomelike figure strutting to home plate. That included the eyes of Bob Cain, the Tiger pitcher. What they were looking at was a 3'7" midget, twenty-six years of age, weighing about as much as your pet bulldog.

Crouching at home plate, as he faced Cain, Eddie had a strike zone that was nearly invisible. Certainly it wasn't visible to Cain, who walked the imposter on four straight pitches that were intended for a six-foot batsman.

After the deed was done, it was said Veeck had been inspired by James Thurber's short story "You Could Look It Up." But Veeck supplied the real answer: John McGraw had once told his father that he often yearned to send up to bat a little hunchback who was kept around the clubhouse for good luck.

To get Gaedel into the game Veeck paid him $100 for the day's work, actors' scale for a midget act. He also had to sign Gaedel to a standard player's contract. Many charged at the time that Veeck had made a mockery of the sacrosanct national pastime. At the least, some spoilsports said, he "was exploiting a freak of biology."

But for Veeck, and most people, it was a moment of unalloyed sunniness. Gaedel would be remembered forever, even in the record books, for his single at-bat—a walk (better than most of the Brownies could do). And Veeck, the consummate showman, could settle, whether he liked it or not, for being "the guy who sent the midget up to bat."

The rest of the summer in baseball, especially as far as the Giants and Dodgers were concerned, would be grimly serious business. But as Veeck saw it—and rightly so—the world could always use an occasional light touch, a little fun, where nobody, including the Tigers, would get hurt. Hell, the Tigers didn't even let Gaedel come around to score!

The day after Gaedel played his first, and last, game, Mickey Mantle again became the big news in New York, rather than the Giants and Dodgers, who had one of those rare open dates on the schedule.

Mickey had been recalled from his Elba, in Kansas City, where he had suffered a disastrous start, going 0 for 22. After that, the chronology of events in his life played like an overwrought dime novel.

In despair one morning Mickey called his father, Mutt, back in Commerce.

"I don't think I can play baseball anymore," Mickey said.

"I'm coming to see you," answered Mutt.

The next day Mutt Mantle showed up in Mickey's hotel room. Within minutes Mickey's belongings had been chucked into a suitcase.

"What are you doin', Dad?" the bewildered Mickey asked.

"I'm packing your stuff, son. You're going back home, where you can come work in the mines with me," said Mutt.

If there was anything more frightening to Mickey than the prospect of again facing that double-talking Stengel, it was those godawful mines, where the sun never shone and you never saw a single blade of green grass.

Mutt Mantle made his point: the boy had better start concentrating on baseball. The suitcase was unpacked, and Mickey, who had regarded the demotion to Kansas City as punitive rather than instructive, began to play the brand of ball that Mutt Mantle knew he was capable of. In the next forty games at Kansas City Mickey hit eleven home runs and amassed a .361 average.

In later years, in thinking about the episode, Mickey admitted, "It was the turning point of my life."

By recalling Mantle now it was as if the Yankees were telling the Giants and the Dodgers that Mays and Snider weren't about to monopolize all of New York's future headlines. With DiMaggio's center-field dynasty drawing to a close, the Yankees were putting their money on this new youngster, just as the Giants had put theirs on a black kid from Westfield, Alabama.

On August 21 the Giants beat the Reds at the Polo Grounds, 7–4, for their tenth in a row. At one time the Reds led by 4–1. But in the eighth inning, the Giants banged three home runs, one by Westrum with one on and singletons by Stanky and Lockman.

It was a remarkable game in one sense because the Reds were deprived of another run in the seventh, when Hank Edwards was thrown out at home on a desperate try for an inside-the-park home run. On the play almost everybody in the ballpark, except the hot-dog vendors, handled the ball. Edwards hit a long one to the right-center corner of the field, where Mueller scooped it up and tossed it, laterallike, to Willie, who came running over. Willie then relayed to Lockman, who threw to Westrum, who put the ball on Edwards as he came sliding in.

Almost every time that Spencer pitched on these August days Westrum would come to his rescue with game-tying or game-winning homers.

"Next year when you sit down to talk salary," Westrum told Spencer, "tell them to put aside half of your dough for me."

"Try and get it!" laughed Spencer.

Since Brooklyn didn't play that day, the Giants found themselves 7½ games out.

Facing Ewell Blackwell, the fierce sidearming pitcher, on August 22, the Giants won another squeaker, 4–3. They fell behind 3–1 in the seventh, then things began to happen. In nine previous pinch-hit appearances Earl Rapp had failed to hit the ball out of the infield. Nevertheless, Leo sent him up to bat in the seventh and Rapp hit a 430-foot fly to bring in the man at third and tie the score. Jones came on in relief of Jansen and Koslo to get credit for the victory—but not before Durocher almost got nervous exhaustion in the ninth. After Jones retired two, the Reds reached him for two singles. When Sheldon went to a 3–0 count on Connie Ryan, Leo had had enough and sent for Corwin, who finally got Ryan to ground to Dark for the last out.

While such nerve-racking events were transpiring at the Polo Grounds, the Dodgers were trimming the Cardinals twice, 4–3 and 8–7, both games lasting ten innings.

With eleven victories in a row, the suddenly renascent Giants may not yet have projected themselves into the National League race but they had started to compel the attention of their fans. They were a hot team, suddenly confident, coming from behind in the late innings, each day growing new heroes. In offices, stores, and homes around the city, portable radios crackled with late news and play-by-play of Giant games. Only a few weeks before people had stopped listening.

The Giants didn't play on August 23. When the Dodgers lost to the Cardinals, the Giants moved to 7½ games behind the leaders.

With Mantle back in the Yankee lineup in right field, where he could look over his right shoulder and glimpse the gloomy icon DiMaggio in center field, the Yankees were again inexorably marching to the American League pennant. But on this day they received news about their budding star that left them with mixed feelings. Mickey had been pronounced 4-F by army doctors due to bone disease in his left leg, presumably the result of a high school football injury.

This was the second time Mickey had been turned down by his Oklahoma Selective Service Board in less than two years, at a time when the Korean War was still killing and maiming young American soldiers. The decision to reject such a radiant-looking specimen (wouldn't any teenager in the country have been willing to swap his own body and muscles for Mantle's?) caused the usual eruptions from many of those whose own sons had been snapped up by the military draft and from others who might have designated themselves as superpatriots.

As apolitical as most baseball players, Mickey had suffered denunciation from the letter writers. They accused him of being a shirker, a draft dodger, a "Commie," and a coward, while all along he innocently suggested that he was prepared to serve if his country chose to take him. The abuse only added to the burden that he was already carrying as an outfielder manqué.

The Yankee establishment was pleased to learn that Mantle's career would not be halted, even temporarily, by military service. Yet they were saddened to know of the seriousness of the physical impairment, which might affect his performance in the future. They knew, too, that the abuse of his character would persist, for these were times that brought the reptiles out of the woodwork.

On August 24 the Cards visited the Polo Grounds and nursed a 5–4 lead going into the last of the ninth. But the resilient New Yorkers rebounded again to win, 6–5. It was the fourth game in a row that the Giants had won with a late-inning rally. Yet the crowds were not breaking down the turnstiles to get into the Polo Grounds. Only 14,000 attended, including 4,000 Ladies' Day invitees. The radios might still be carrying the inspiring message of Giant resurgence, but the fans were not coming.

Strangely, all three of the local teams appeared to be running hard to equal their attendance figures of 1950, when the Yankees dipped to 2,081,000 from their 1949 2,283,000 figure; the Dodgers went from 1,633,000 to 1,185,000, and the Giants barely made it to 1,000,000, some 200,000 less than their 1949 attendance. The enormous turnstile counts following World War II were dwindling, certainly for the Giants and Dodgers, and only a fiercely fought final month could restore their health at the gate.

Branca's 1–0 shutout over the Cubs kept the Dodgers from losing any ground, even after the Giants won their twelfth in a row.

The next day the Giants fell behind the Cards, 3–1, in the third inning. The way they had been playing it was natural to expect that they'd come back to win. The rains came first, however, and the game was called. Thomson lost a homer as a result. But the Dodgers dropped one to the Cubs, 5–1, narrowing the loss column by another game.

Chicago now journeyed to the Polo Grounds, where a scheduling quirk, brought on by postponed games that had to be made up, had them playing a Sunday as well as a Monday doubleheader. At the same time, the Dodgers would play hosts to the Pirates in two twin bills. The race had begun to resemble trial by torture.

With 30,000 people (still much less than capacity) urging them on in the Sunday bargain bill, the Giants won both times, 5–4 and 5–1. That man Spencer again gained the first victory in relief, and Hearn pitched elegantly in the second. Hearn's nerves, questioned from time to time by others on his own team, were holding up admirably. In the first game Maglie went all the way until he unceremoniously blew a three-run lead. With the score knotted in the last half of the inning, Westrum unloaded one into the left-field seats. With Spencer pitching, Wes had become a rival to Babe Ruth! (In addition, Westrum caught all four games in the two days, a tribute not only to his spirit but to his body.) In the nightcap, Willie tried out his legs, stealing home for the first time in his life, against pitcher Walt Dubiel. This was the type of thing expected only of Jackie Robinson—now Mays was doing it.

Throughout the long afternoon, thousands of fans kept apprised of the goings-on at Ebbets Field, with radios stuck in their ears. What they heard was only half-satisfactory. The Dodgers pulled out a wild one, at 12–11, then lost the second, 4–3. After the day's action, the Giants were six games behind, seven in the loss column.

The Monday doubleheader attracted 16,000 fans to the Polo Grounds as the team looked for its fifteenth and sixteenth victories in a row. Would the New Yorkers be able to challenge the great winning skein of twenty-one, mounted by the Cubs in 1935 to cop the National League pennant?

For a few devastating moments in the twelfth inning it looked like the streak had sprung a leak, as the Cubs scored a run to go ahead. But in the bottom of the inning, Bill Rigney came off the bench to pinch-hit a long fly to win the game, as a runner scored from third. Squirming in and out of trouble, Jansen, the quiet man from Oregon, went the distance. After the game, the Giants' doctor, Anthony Palermo, claimed that his medical head-quarters had been besieged with requests for aspirins from the fans, a certain sign that Leo's players were holding up better than many of their supporters.

In the second game things went rather easy, as Corwin subdued the Cubs, 6–3. When the news came in that the Dodgers had split again with Pittsburgh, losing the second game, the Giants were five games behind. The Dodgers now led with a mark of 79–45, trailed by the Giants at 75–51. In the course of the sixteen-game winning streak the Giants had sawed off eight games from the Brooklyn lead, which had once seemed air tight. And it wasn't even September, the traditional stretch drive month in baseball, when pressures multiplied and pitching staffs often melted.

With twenty-six games left for the Giants and twenty-eight for the Dodgers (only four games remaining between the two rivals), the Giants still felt they had more than a slight chance. Now the Dodgers knew they had a battle on their hands, whether they would openly admit it or not. Could the Giants keep winning? Was that too much to ask of a team that had already strung together a heart-stopping string of victories?

The answer came the next day. One of the most execrable clubs in baseball, Pittsburgh, came into the Polo Grounds. They were twenty-seven games out of first place, with a team that was hardly breathing. Manager Bill Meyer had Ralph Kiner, infielder Danny Murtaugh, and a few qualified major-league pitchers, led by

Howie Pollet, Murry Dickson, Bob Friend, and Vernon Law. Other than that, they were a team just finishing the schedule.

So what happened? Pollet pitched a 2–0 shutout, ending the sixteen-game streak and proving, if anyone needed such proof, that on any given day any one team in baseball can beat any other team.

Thomson tried hard that afternoon to prolong the streak before only 8,800 fans. He stroked three hits, including two doubles, as many hits as the Pirates got during the entire game. But the wildness of Jones, plus key errors by Stanky and Mueller, plastered the first defeat on the Giants since August 11.

It had been two weeks of nirvana for the Giants, from August 12 through August 27, raising the hopes of the players and bringing fans to their radios, if not to the ballpark. Now it was history.

During the streak the pitching staff, headed by Spencer's four victories, had done remarkably well, with the help of late-inning clutch hitting. Corwin had three wins, Jansen had three, Maglie won twice, Hearn took two games, and so did Jones.

The day the streak came to an abrupt end, the Dodgers won, 3–1, over the Reds. Brooklyn now had a five-game lead.

In an anticlimactic note, the Giants announced they were bringing Hank Thompson back from Minneapolis, where he'd been hitting .340.

13

September

MAYBE MOST OF THE GIANTS didn't believe that black cats were demonic—and maybe most of them placed little credence in the efficacy of hexes, broken mirrors, four-leaf clovers, or rabbits' feet. Or maybe they didn't concern themselves about walking under ladders. But during their long streak many of them did pay obeisance to their own varied superstitions.

One of the Giants wore the same pair of socks each day of the streak, and when the hapless Pirates put an end to it he finally removed them from his wardrobe.

"You don't have to send them to the laundry," yelled Stanky, "just point 'em in the right direction and let 'em walk!"

Each day of the winning spell Durocher never failed, if the games were played at the Polo Grounds, to come to the ballpark the same way. When he got there he refused to use the steps in center field. Instead, he insisted on walking underneath the stadium.

Durocher's spooky behavior was a throwback to the days of McGraw, when The Little Napoleon was convinced it would bring his team good luck if his players spotted any beer barrels before a game. (Needless to say, he went out and enlisted platoons of beer trucks to rattle down the avenue.)

McGraw also hired an eccentric fellow named Charles Victor

Faust, from Marion, Kansas, to pitch for the Giants in 1911 because he felt Faust was a good-luck charm. One day before the season began Faust approached McGraw and informed him that a fortune-teller had predicted that if he pitched for the Giants they'd win the pennant. McGraw signed Faust to a contract and he pitched batting practice every day. On the last day of the season Faust pitched one inning against the Dodgers and gave up one hit. The Giants did win the pennant that year. Three years later Faust was committed to a mental institution. One wonders whether it shouldn't have been McGraw.

Bobby Thomson was never particularly superstitious. Yet when the streak started he was wearing a pair of shorts that had ants imprinted on them.

"The guys started to comment on it, so I continued to wear them every day," said Thomson. "All through the sixteen games, they hung there next to my locker before each game, so the guys could see that I was going to wear them."

The shorts "helped" Bobby get three hits on August 28 against the Pirates. But the Giants still lost—and the streak went down the drain.

Durocher's role in the streak—aside from his daily ritual—was fascinating, although managers can't pitch for pitchers or hit for hitters.

He had started the season noticeably more restrained than usual. He seemed more reasonable and likable than before—and that was saying a good deal, for Leo was never an easy man to like. He appeared less inclined to lash out at his men or even the enemy.

Some attributed this change in style to the fact that his team was staggering. Thus, he had turned into a soft-hearted bench philosopher. Writers with the club had long taken note of the fact that when Durocher's teams were losing he became more affable and easygoing.

In the first part of the '51 season, Durocher revealed a sensitive side of his personality that shocked his detractors right out of their negative opinions. One day when George Spencer got into a two-out, bases-loaded, ninth-inning jam against Chicago, he botched a surprise bunt by the Cubs' Eddie Miksis. Had Spencer thrown home quickly and accurately he would have gotten a sure force-out. Even a quick throw to first base would have nailed the third out.

Instead, George hesitated, then made a dreadful throw home to Westrum. The ball eluded the catcher, two runs scored, and the Giants lost another game. Instead of sharing the fury of any self-righteous Giant fan after the game, Durocher refused to knock Spencer for his poor execution. But he did have some unkind words for the clubhouse man!

"Why didn't the son of a bitch tell me what happened to George's baby?" said Durocher.

Apparently, right before the game got under way, the news that Spencer's wife had lost her child in birth reached the clubhouse. Feeling that the news might upset the manager, the clubhouse man never told him.

"If I'd have known about it," said Leo, "I never would have brought him in to pitch. It's a wonder he didn't throw the damn ball over the grandstand."

What Durocher kept saying as his team kept losing was that they would come back, that they were good enough to win, that they would be there at the end, and so on. It all sounded so predictable, an outpouring of managerial clichés that few felt Durocher really believed. Leo, possibly as complicated a character as ever set foot in a baseball dugout, had chosen not to rave and rant.

When Willie Mays joined the team in late May, Durocher evolved into a loving, adoptive father. He coddled, patted his back, reassured and laughed with—and not at—the young man. To Leo, his protégé was a combination of Sammy Davis, Jr., Jascha Heifetz, and Joe Louis, and he was determined to treat him with exquisite delicateness. Willie appeared to flourish under such benign handling.

There is no telling what might have happened to Willie under another mentor at that stage of his development. While Mantle had not exactly thrived at Yankee Stadium in 1951 under the sometimes incomprehensible tutelage of Stengel, Willie had fared considerably better under the sponsorship of his own soft-soaping Svengali.

All through this early period of "the new Durocher," some Giant players continued to fear Leo's scorching language—"verbal punctuations," Charlie Einstein had dubbed it—but for many he remained something of an odd genius. They felt he knew more about the strategies and intricacies of the game than any other manager and respected him for it. They admired his guts, brains, and vitality, even if they could have done without his playacting and posturing.

As the streak moved along in late August, however, Durocher reverted to the man that baseball folk knew only too well—and that many hated. Once again, he was a driven, raging, embattled figure. The veins stood out on his neck as he argued with umpires, harangued his foes, and deprecated his own players. His vocabulary was rancid, his manner angry, as he stalked back and forth in the dugout or on the coaching lines, where he could be closer to the action. He was a man obsessed with the need to win—and to continue to win. Players now reacted like well-trained marionettes, and pinchhitters magically responded to his call. As people always said, it was the way Durocher acted when he had a team with a shot at victory.

"With a chance to win," said Russ Hodges, "Durocher was hardly fit to live with. He could see only one thing—the pennant. He wouldn't settle for anything less, wasn't interested in anything less, and wouldn't talk about anything less. The closer he got to the Dodgers, the tougher Leo got."

There were two games left with Pittsburgh before September came. In the first, on August 29, Hearn pitched after only two days' rest, at his own request, showing the kind of selfless, newly acquired spirit that made Leo love him. Jim won, 3–1, on a three-hitter. The Dodgers won, too, 13–1, over the Reds, so the teams kept pace with each other.

The Giants played errorless ball for Hearn, something they hadn't been able to do for several weeks. If their hitting and pitching had taken on new life during their sweet-sixteen streak, they still did not qualify as a team of golden glovers. Aside from the heroic defense supplied by Willie and the steady catching of Westrum, even with a damaged finger, the Giants were leaky and suspect in the field. They hardly stacked up with the Dodgers in stopping the ball, making the accurate throws, and turning double plays.

Perhaps most important in the 3–1 win over the Pirates was another switch that Durocher engineered in his lineup. For almost a month Willie had been batting in the sixth slot, ahead of Thomson. But since August 4 Willie, although hitting as high as .295 on occasion, had not connected for a home run. Leo now dropped Willie behind Bobby in the pecking order. For the most part, that's the way the lineup would go to the umpires for the rest of the season.

In the second game against the Pirates the Giants suffered what may have been their most upsetting loss since the dreary days of April. With the Giants ahead, 8–1, in the top of the sixth, the Pirates scored six times. In the eighth they added two more. In the ninth Kiner belted his thirty-seventh homer of the year to give Pittsburgh the victory, 10–9. The 8,000 fans on hand couldn't have been blamed if they believed this was the Giants' valedictory for the year.

What made it even more painful was that Mays hit two home runs, breaking his long drought. Spencer, so solid during the streak, blew sky-high in the ninety-degree afternoon heat, in his fiftieth—and least effective—appearance of the year.

Such a defeat might have totally deflated a lesser team, or a lesser manager. Just when the Giants seemed to be making a serious bid to catch the Dodgers, they'd thrown away what seemed a sure victory against a team that had no right to beat them in such a manner. Twice in three days the Pirates had upset them.

"We still didn't let it get us," Dark said. "Although I guess it should have gotten us down."

Thomson said that "maybe it wasn't meant for us to win, after all . . . but we figured there was still a month to go . . ."

It is no exaggeration to suggest that pennant pressure can be as numbing and overpowering as one of Bob Feller's blazing fastballs right in the face. Even the strongest of men can leak oil in that month. Some may manage to control their tensions and anxieties better than others. Some may learn to live with it and thrive on it, while others succumb to it. But as the "stretch drive" commences, pennant pressure rolls in as inexorably as the San Francisco fog.

"September can be the roughest few weeks in a ballplayer's life," said Vin Scully, Red Barber's young partner in the Dodgers' booth. "It's the month of sweating palms, pounding hearts, and acid stomachs. I've seen players sit in the dugout, their heads in their hands, for many minutes, crushed in spirit, after making a bad play or a crucial out in a critical game. During the regular season that's a sight you'll rarely see. There's a lot written in the faces of the players, some with a harried look, others with dark circles under their eyes. All of them have an enormous desire to win—that produces a tension that can eat you alive!"

Testimony from hundreds of baseball men who have been through it is the best corroboration that pennant pressure is no hype or false slogan. When men go to bat with "olives" in their throats, you know pennant pressure is as omnipresent as the crisp fall air.

The onset of September in 1951 saw the Giants seven games behind Brooklyn and eight down in the loss ledger. The standings stood Brooklyn, 82–45; New York, 76–53. The schedule makers also had the foresight to begin the month with a two-day series between the two contending teams.

Though he was riding high, Dressen didn't show up for the September 1 game. He had the flu. Under the circumstances, it might have been psychosomatic—maybe Charlie knew something that others didn't. The Dodger hero of the 1947 World Series, Cookie Lavagetto, handled the club for the day and probably wished he had stayed home too.

While a screaming, beseeching crowd of 41,000 looked on at Saturday's game at the Polo Grounds, the Giants, not the Dodgers, played as if they were the league leaders. The winds were chilly and surly, but the mood on the field was hot, as it always was for Giant-Dodger tussles.

With Maglie on the mound, gunning for his eighteenth victory, inevitably tempers flared. True to reputation, Sal let one loose at Robinson that seemed to glance off Jackie's bat. But Jackie stormed at the ump, claiming he'd been hit in the wrist. Without any medical exam to substantiate Jackie's charge, the ump waved him to first base, forcing in a run. This propelled Maglie to join Durocher and Westrum at home plate in a shouting match, causing the fans to set up a partisan din that shook the flaky green paint off the seats in the ancient ballpark. But the misadventure didn't thwart Maglie or his teammate, Don Mueller.

An expert at hitting the ball "where they ain't," Mueller probably could hit bad pitches better than any player in his league. Choking up on his thirty-two-ounce bat about two inches, he rarely moved his feet in the batter's box and always had an idea where he was going to hit the ball; more often than not, he swung at the first pitch that came along, using his flexible shoulder movement. But on this fall day Mueller suddenly became a power hitter, defying a stereotype that had pursued him in his years with the Giants. Three home runs came flying off his bat, astounding the crowd and, no doubt, all hands on the Giant bench.

To add to the Giant picnic, Thomson banged the Giants' fourth homer off Branca, putting the game beyond the Dodgers' reach at 8–1. When Dark and Stanky collaborated on the season's first triple play in the National League, an atmosphere of euphoria was rampant in the stands. What more could any Giant fan ask for?

On Sunday, September 2, on Larry Jansen Day, the place was almost packed again. Once more the Giants, who had had little experience on the positive side of "laughers" during the season, came away with an easy 11–2 decision, behind Hearn. At one point Dressen, back on the bench after his transient bout with the flu, became so inflamed about what he was seeing, and how the umpires were ruling, that he led all his players not in the game on a march to the clubhouse. The demonstration accomplished nothing, although it brought yowls of derision from the crowd.

With beanballs flying, umpire Al Barlick threw out Dick Williams and Branca, then thumbed out Newcombe, Labine, and Robinson. For a sick man, Dressen looked pretty lively when he wailed about a strike call on Pee Wee Reese. In the seventh inning, by which time the Dodgers were well thrashed, Phil Haugstad, a skinny right-hander with a single victory to his credit in three years of pitching for Brooklyn, plunked both Mays and Thomson with errant pitches. Why Barlick permitted Haugstad to remain on the premises is a mystery, considering his previous exertions in throwing other Dodgers out of the game. But it made no difference in the outcome.

Overlooked in the ambiance of acrimony were two more home runs off Mueller's bat, giving him five for the two games. This was a lovely piece of long-distance hitting that only Ty Cobb, Ralph Kiner, Cap Anson, and Tony Lazzeri had accomplished before that day. Mueller was as mystified as the next man in his effort to account for his transformation on that September weekend.

"I guess it was something working internally," he said. "The whole thing was a traumatic experience for me. On Saturday when I hit the three homers I was thinking of my wife and our overdue baby back in St. Louis. It sounds funny, but maybe those home runs were 'premonitions.' "

When Don connected for his fifth home run, in the eighth inning, he had gone to bat knowing that his six-pound baby had finally been born. Waiting in the on-deck circle, Irvin had walked over and whispered the happy news to Don, a piece of information he'd picked up in the dugout only seconds before. Bang!—came the fifth homer in two games.

As he rounded the bases, Mueller grinned crazily at each Dodger defender, none of whom were privy to his secret. Passing Leo in the third-base coaching box, Mueller yelled, "It's a boy, it's a boy!" (Though he met the ball well for the rest of the month, Don hit only one more homer.)

Leaving the Polo Grounds after the victory, Durocher said to Laraine: "I guess that one of these days they'll be running box scores on confinements and maybe even pools on whether it'll be a boy or a girl!" That night Leo could abandon his practice of watching professional wrestling on television, a habit he'd gotten into during the year whenever his team bungled a game.

After the smoke cleared from the disastrous weekend for the Dodgers, a British journalist, George Whiting, observed that these "Dodger-Giant games were three hours of hilarious insult and near murder . . . a British Cup final would be tea at the vicarage compared with this annual American mayhem. These games certainly are not glorified rounders." Nobody ever said they were.

With his club moving to within five games of the Dodgers, Durocher sniffed victory more than ever, and acted accordingly. He had stopped addressing the writers traveling with the team, was snapping at almost everybody, and disputing every decision on the diamond that went against his team. As the club moved on to Philadelphia for a Labor Day doubleheader with the Phillies, the feelings of the players were almost as giddy, a sure sign, perhaps, that Leo's best-laid plans would go astray. That's exactly what happened.

Despite the momentum the team had after the two lopsided wins over the Dodgers, the Giants fell to the Phillies in the first game. Many New York fans took the train down to Philadelphia, accounting for part of the crowd of 32,000. But they were disappointed when Al Corwin lost for the first time, 6–3, in a game in which the Giants had Robin Roberts on the ropes on more than a few occasions. Contributing to the defeat was Mays, of all people. Willie generally could do no wrong in Leo's eyes. But on that Labor Day he made the horrendous mistake of forgetting to touch third base as he tried for an inside-the-park home run.

"I sorta glided over the base, never touching it," acknowledged poor Willie.

When the Giants registered only a minor exception to the ruling, it was clear Leo's heart wasn't in it. Obviously, he'd seen what
the umpires had seen.

After the loss Durocher ate out Willie, one of the few times
during the season he chose to do that. What Leo emphasized to
Willie was that the single run may not have made much difference
but that a home run might have persuaded manager Eddie Sawyer
of the Phillies to yank Roberts. Thus, the Giants may have gotten
a shot at a new pitcher. The tongue-lashing by Leo may have chas-
tened his young outfielder. Nobody could recall Willie failing to
touch a base in any other game he played that year.

It was a hard defeat for the Giants to take, but they came back
to win the second game, 3–1, with Koslo on the mound. By winning both ends of a doubleheader with the Braves at Ebbets Field,
the Dodgers were able to increase their lead to six games.

With an off day on Tuesday, the newspapers trotted out their
usual thumb-sucking articles about the Giants' chances, providing
a bit of historical analogy, none of which was particularly relevant
to the case at hand.

The essayists pointed out that in 1914 George Tweedy Stall-
ings, a Virginia Military Institute graduate, had led his Miracle
Braves all the way from last place on July 19 to win the National
League flag. They failed to note that on that July day the Braves
were only eleven games behind the league-leading Giants, after
losing eighteen of their first twenty-two. By mid-August the Braves
had moved to within 6½ games of the Giants due to a fine pitching
staff of George Tyler, Dick Rudolph, and Bill James, not to mention
the spitfire second baseman Johnny Evers and the lighthearted
Rabbit Maranville at shortstop.

Such comparisons with the current hazardous position of the
Giants just didn't hold much water, although it did make good
"rainy day" reading.

Perhaps a more striking parallel to the Giants' situation was
the Phillies-Dodgers 1950 race, of more recent memory. The Phillies were ahead by seven on Labor Day, only to squeak through on
the final day of the year, thanks to Sisler's home run. But what had
placed the Phils in jeopardy was their own poor play at the end of
the year, plus injuries to key pitchers and left-hander Curt Simmons's departure to military service.

More comparable than either the Miracle Braves or the fading

Phillies to the Giants' late-season heroics in 1951 was the plight of the Cardinals in 1930. Manager Gabby Street always believed he had the best team in the National League, with such sluggers as the bespectacled Chick Hafey, first baseman Sunny Jim Bottomley, and the Fordham Flash, Frankie Frisch, at second base. But on August 9 the Cards found themselves twelve games behind Brooklyn. By September the Cards had advanced to 4½ games behind the Cubs, who were then in first place. The Robins (which is what they were then called, instead of the Dodgers) had fallen to third place. Ultimately, the Cards swept a Labor Day doubleheader from the Reds. They then took on the Robins in late September, moving into first place, despite the purported kidnapping of their ace right-hander, Flint Rhem. More likely, Rhem was a victim, not of underworld intrigue, as the fantasists of the press suggested, but of bathtub gin.

None of these scenarios were quite comparable to the Giants' present plight. Yet when such precedents were recycled, it gave new hope to Giant aficionados.

When play was resumed on September 5, the Giants won a doubleheader from the Braves in Boston, 3–2 and 9–1. In one of those games Sheldon Jones, an in-and-outer all season, went the route for the first time. Maglie won the other, for his nineteenth victory. The Dodgers beat the Phillies, 5–2, so the margin was 5½ games.

It rained on September 6, neither club playing. A day without combat in September would seem to be a good time for a few moments of relaxation. But if Durocher's men had their choice, they would have played. Sitting around hotel rooms, the sudden Cinderellas of the baseball world did not have a second of peace. Writers wanted to talk to them and friends besieged them with demands for tickets for remaining games at the Polo Grounds. They also anticipated the final two meetings of the year with Brooklyn on September 8 and 9, at Ebbets Field, contests that might, they thought, go a long way toward deciding the outcome of the pennant race.

But before the Dodgers and Giants would meet, the Giants finished their series in Boston with a 7–3 victory. Thomson put together his best day ever in a Giants' uniform, with a five-for-five performance, as Jansen captured his eighteenth game to stay close behind his sidekick, Maglie. Irvin hit a 500-foot home run to become the first player in either league to knock in 100 runs. The Giants were rolling again—but the Dodgers also won, over the Phillies, 11–6.

As the two-game series with the Giants began, the Dodgers still couldn't quite believe their bid was for real. Rocky Bridges echoed what most of his fellow Dodgers thought. "It still didn't enter our minds at that time," he said, "that those guys *really* had a chance to win."

Dressen chose to start Newcombe in the first game on Saturday, September 8, against the Giants. Heading for his first twenty-victory season, Newcombe could quickly disillusion the toughest of foes with his frightening fastball. Aware as anyone that Newk had constantly been disparaged for his presumed failure to win clutch games, Dressen didn't believe such nonsense for a minute. Neither did the Dodgers. Newk had always shown himself to be a willing worker, who could pitch on three days' rest but didn't mind going on two days, either, if Dressen called on him.

On this occasion, Newk came up with one of his better performances. He was helped along when the roof fell in on the Giants' starting pitcher, Hearn, in the fourth inning. The Brooks won, 9–0, but there was no element of forfeit about this game as far as the Dodgers were concerned. They walloped the Giants for the seventh straight time at Ebbets Field and the ninth time in ten appearances there. Though the Giants had bounced back to win five straight against the Dodgers before this game, they failed again to overcome the terrors of Ebbets Field.

Oddly, the crowd was relatively small—some 23,171 showed up. Was it possible that the normally pessimistic Dodger partisans had become arrogant in their belief that their team couldn't lose?

Thomson continued to pound the ball, singling in the second inning for his eighth straight hit. Newk, however, finally put an end to that with a strikeout. But the dynamic role Robinson played—three hits, three runs, and an artful squeeze bunt, with the Dodgers already comfortably ahead, 8–0—may have planted the seeds of revenge for the Giants and disaster for the Dodgers.

Why a team wasn't expected to steal bases when it was ahead by many runs or add to its score when it had a considerable lead has long been one of the game's mysteries. Thus, in keeping with this cock-eyed tradition, when Jackie bunted to bring home an additional run late in the game, the Giants became openly furious.

They regarded the skillful move as unseemly, "bush," just plain "chicken shit." They felt that Jackie was trying to show them up—of course, he was—before his screaming supporters, sticking salt into their open wounds. They despised him for it.

In the clubhouse the Giants fumed and cursed at their tormentors, principally Jackie, and vowed to get even. If ever a team had been psyched up by a loss—a rough loss, at that, that sent them 6½ games back—this was such an instance.

To further exacerbate matters, when Bill Rigney pinch-hit for the Giants when the game was beyond recall, Newcombe greeted him by throwing a pitch precariously close to his head.

"My glasses went flying, as I hit the dirt," said Rigney, "and I busted a lens, but all the Dodgers stood out there laughing at me. When I got back to the clubhouse, I kept yelling to the guys, 'We've gotta rip 'em tomorrow'—something I picked up from Stanky during the streak. Damn, if it didn't catch on, like a slogan!"

During the torturous month of September baseball can evolve into a game of contesting wills and resolve. There is no simple way to calibrate the effect of Robinson's perfectly legitimate actions on the belief of the Giants and their manipulative manager that Dressen's Dodgers were out to grind their faces in the dust.

The next day the Giants retaliated—this time Ebbets Field was packed—with a tough 2–1 decision, as Maglie took his twentieth of the year. If the Giants ever had to win a game this was it—a jackpot contest. "Everybody except the Giants players had quit on us after Newcombe's victory the day before," said Mays. "If we'd have lost this one, the players might have thought that way, too."

But Maglie was always at his best when the chips were down and everybody's stomach was gurgling. He protected a two-run lead provided for him by Irvin's two-run home run off Branca in the fourth inning, wriggling out of trouble time after time.

Suddenly, in the eighth inning, Snider doubled with one out and Robinson tripled, narrowing the score to 2–1. Now the natives were howling. They could smell impending defeat for the Giants and a win that would give their favorites a 7½-game lead.

As Robinson taunted Maglie at third base, only ninety feet away from a tie, Durocher dared to walk to the mound to hold a kaffeeklatsch with his pitcher. Leo knew he could start a small riot in Brooklyn just by sticking his bald head out of the dugout. Now he was right there in the epicenter of the diamond, the focus of all hateful attention, a role he admittedly relished.

But there was always a reason for Leo's moves. This time he sought to slow down Brooklyn's momentum, always precious at such a time. Thousands of waving handkerchiefs greeted the Giants' manager, although one might have wondered why they continued to wave them in the face of their own Andy Pafko, the next batter.

The public address announcer, Tex Rickard, as familiar a voice in Ebbets Field as Red Barber, pleaded with the customers to stop. But trying for such a cease-and-desist order, Rickard was as likely to get results as a Mafia don requesting less bloodshed against sworn enemies.

When the game resumed Pafko sent a hard one-hopper in the direction of Thomson at third base. Bobby made a good snag of the ball and in the same motion swipe-tagged Robinson, who had been dancing several feet off third. Then Bobby whipped the ball to first base to get Pafko for the third out in what might have been the most important double play of the year for the Giants.

With sixteen games left to play the Giants were 5½ games back of the Dodgers, who had nineteen to go. Even if the Giants could keep winning at their same remarkable pace, the three extra games that Brooklyn had to play could be to its advantage, for in a crunch these were games it could win. Furthermore, the Giants already had seven more defeats than the Dodgers, games that were irredeemably stuck in the loss column. "No way you can ever make up games on the loss ledger" is a hoary cliché in the baseball world. It happens to be true.

Though Durocher never was much at formal clubhouse meetings or inspirational pep talks and wouldn't think of calling on past Gipps and ghosts or invoking the memory of sainted Giant figures, his enthusiasm on a daily level in 1951 was truly contagious to his troops. Some Giants may have cringed at his language ("Let's get those cocksuckers," one of his more colorful exhortations, was, of course, never reported in the daily press), but most of the players admired his hunch-playing and aggressiveness.

"He was a great cheerleader," said Sal Yvars, "even if he used so much perfume that the whole clubhouse stunk from the guy. But in those last days of 1951 he would use everything to win. He got his scouting reports from Tom Sheehan, who was out on the road for us, picking up little things about players on the teams we were about to play. This guy can't steal, Sheehan would say, this guy's hurting, this guy's arm is lousy, this guy can't hit an inside pitch, this guy's ass is dragging, all that sort of stuff. Today they've got it down to a fine art, I guess, but in those days it wasn't as common.

"To keep Willie happy and take the pressure off him, Leo played around with him before almost every game, whether it was pepper or throwing with him or just kidding around with him. I don't think any of the other guys resented this favored treatment because they sensed what Willie meant to us. Yeah, Leo believed in us. 'We're gonna win this thing, we're gonna win,' he'd keep saying. And you had to believe the guy."

Bill Rigney agreed that Durocher's attention to detail and his total involvement rubbed off on his players. "We learned how much we loved the game," Rigney said.

In those last weeks of the season Rigney said that because there was no food served in the clubhouse the players had to adjourn to somebody's hotel room. "On the road each night after every game, a bunch of us—Stanky, Dark, Lockman, Irvin, Jansen, Thomson, Westrum, myself—would go up to a room and sit around and talk about the next day's game. I kept my own little book on the pitchers we were scheduled to face and we'd go over that stuff. We'd also talk about the other team's hitters and where to play them. It was sort of like an exchange of information among the guys. But we did it because we were all believers and kept thinking we could still win. We felt it in our bones. A couple of my fly balls won games during our streak. You remember such things, and want to keep on contributing."

Another crucial element in those fading days of the race, according to Rigney, was that the Giants knew they had only one team to hurdle in order to win. That was the Dodgers. "Maybe it never would have worked out, if there were other clubs to pass in addition to the Dodgers," said Rigney.

By this time Durocher was having some trouble with his stomach. Just keeping food down was difficult. But he probably wasn't the only man in the Giant clubhouse whose stomach was in a daily rebellion caused by the mounting pressure.

When the Giants had a Monday off, on September 10, Durocher told the writers that from now on his three top pitchers— Maglie, Jansen, and Hearn—would work in rotation. Presumably that would give each man about five starts and would leave Jones, Corwin, and Koslo available in case someone's arm wore out or exhaustion took over. Spencer, still indefatigable, was ready to go in relief.

Returning to action on September 11, the Giants split a twin bill with the Cardinals in St. Louis. They lost the nightcap, 4–3, after Westrum had hit his third grand slam of the year in the first game and Irvin had stolen home for the fifth time. For a large man, who weighed over 200 pounds, Monte was amazingly quick, a reminder that one didn't have to be small and wiry to steal home. (Built like a dray horse, Lou Gehrig accumulated fifteen steals of home during his Yankee career; even Babe Ruth, mirabile dictu, had ten.)

In the second game the Giants staged a three-run rally in the ninth that fell short. As a result, Brooklyn increased its lead to 6 games after a 7–0 victory over the Reds on the same day. With fourteen to play, the Giants were down eight in the loss column, enough to discourage anyone in a Giant uniform and certainly anyone who carried the team around in his heart. When such statistics showed up every day in the sports pages, in big, black type, it served as a constant reminder that things still were pretty bleak for the New Yorkers.

"Sure, it was a frustrating time for everybody," said Dark. "After all that we had done. And now it seemed to be adding up to nothing. But there wasn't a single guy in that clubhouse giving up. Every day that we came to work, Stanky or someone else would yell, 'Let 'er rip!'—and the guys responded to it. We didn't keep winning games by accident. Maybe it was predestined."

Dark also underlined the Durocher factor: "I think he kept us alive. He knew which guys that he could get on and those that he had to lay off. He knew his pitchers, starters, and bull pen better than they knew themselves. Fitzsimmons, his pitching coach, was also a big help, handling young guys like Corwin. There wasn't a thing Leo didn't know about the guys in the other uniforms—but he also knew his own lineup like the back of his hand."

When the Giants were still out west on Wednesday, September 12, their ballpark was taken over for a widely heralded fight between Sugar Ray Robinson and the European and British empire champ, Randy Turpin. In his early thirties, Sugar Ray was still an extraordinary hitter and stylist, possibly the best anyone has ever seen in his weight class. In the tenth round that night he knocked out Turpin to regain his middleweight title.

There were over 61,000 in the Polo Grounds to witness the battle (more than the Giants had ever drawn to the ballpark, but you couldn't compare the figures, for on fight night seats occupied both infield and outfield space where ballplayers roamed). The Turpin-Robinson bout was also seen in movie theaters, with seats priced at $2.60 against a normal movie price, at the time, of 99 cents.

While Sugar Ray was pummeling Turpin, the Giants were rained out in St. Louis. But the Dodgers, also out west, in Cincinnati, lost to the Reds, 6–3, and the Giants gained some ground. It was back to 5½ games for them in what seemed like a teasing treadmill.

When the weather cleared the next day in St. Louis, Maglie was set to add another win to his mounting record. But the Cards blasted him for six runs in the second inning and held on to win, 6–4. Again the Giants tried desperately to scramble back into the game, adding two in the sixth and two more in the eighth—but to no avail.

There was a peculiar footnote to this day for the Cards. After facing the Giants in the afternoon game, they played the Braves that night and lost to Warren Spahn. One club playing two different rivals on the same day hadn't happened in baseball since 1883. As far as the Giants were concerned, they only wished that the Cardinals hadn't showed up for the matinee.

Continuing their long western swing, away from the daily pressures aroused by the New York press and the fans, the Giants moved on to Chicago, a team that had been either seventh or eighth since 1948 and wasn't about to do any better this year. With the wind blowing out in Wrigley Field, Chicago can be a nightmare even for the best pitchers. On Friday, September 14, the capricious wind was no factor, although the Cub fielders made five errors anyway. The shoddy defensive work led to a 7–2 Giant victory.

In this game Mays snapped out of a slump, with two hits, and Thomson's average rose to .277, fifty more points than it had been when Durocher had decided to sculpt him as a third baseman. More significant than the victory, however, was the explosion of the usually serene Westrum. Like every athlete on the Giants, Wes was experiencing the emotional wear and tear of the daily pennant drama. So perhaps it shouldn't have shocked anyone when the catcher lost control of himself following a play at home plate that Wes later insisted was "the worst call ever made against me."

With Frankie Baumholtz on third base and one out, Hank Sauer banged one into left field. It looked long enough to enable Baumholtz to score easily after Irvin's catch. But Monte unleashed a dart to Westrum that had the runner dead to rights.

"I had the plate blocked off and Baumholtz hadn't touched it yet," said Westrum. "I didn't have to move two inches to take the throw."

But when Westrum turned around to get Al Barlick's affirmation of the out, he learned that the umpire had pronounced the runner safe. Westrum blew his top. Before Durocher could race to his rescue, Wes had given Barlick a rude push, baseball's ultimate act of lèse majesté. As a result, he was fined fifty dollars and suspended for three days. At this time the Giants could ill afford such absenteeism. It meant also that Noble and Yvars would have to handle the catching chores in Chicago.

Meanwhile, with the sore-armed Roe still working his magic for his twentieth win, the Dodgers defeated the Pirates, 3–1.

On September 15, with Noble behind the plate, the Giants beat the Cubs, 5–2. Thomson, Mays, and Mueller all connected for home runs. It was Mueller's first circuit shot since his five-home-run barrage against Brooklyn. Jones was the winning pitcher, breaking up Leo's three-man rotation. There was nothing written in blood, as Durocher continued to play his hunches, winning some, losing some.

Since Pittsburgh drubbed the Dodgers, 11–4, the Giants again found themselves five games back, precisely where they had been when their sixteen-game streak was terminated.

14

Two Weeks to Go

THE HISTORY OF THE 1951 Giants to this point had been one of stumbling ineptitude, followed by a smashing revival, followed by frustration. The Dodgers' story, conversely, had been one of season-long command and a haughty disbelief that anybody, including the Giants, could truly challenge their hegemony.

But all through the long, hot summer the voice of Leo was heard throughout the land. Now it kept saying: "Don't you worry, we'll get 'em before it's through. We're gonna take it all." Durocher would then emphasize how things like this had happened before. For example, he'd been a victim himself back in 1942, when his Brooklyn team led the Cardinals by 7½ games with five weeks to go.

"Those damn Cards won forty-three out of their last fifty-one," recalled Durocher about Billy Southworth's team. "Everyone thought we couldn't be headed off. They said it was impossible. It wasn't; we got licked."

Durocher had made his point, in case the pessimists didn't get it.

Back on August 28 it was the veteran lefty Howie Pollet who had stymied the Giants as they tried for their seventeenth straight victory. Now, on Sunday, September 16, with just two weeks left in the campaign, Pollet got still another chance to dampen the Giants' hopes, pitching the first game of a doubleheader in Pittsburgh.

This time, however, Pollet, twice a twenty-game winner with the Cardinals, wasn't up to it. In the seventh inning, when the game was still close, the Giants shelled him for four runs, helping Jansen to a 7–1 triumph.

Did Jansen himself think the Giants were going to win? "I thought it wasn't very likely," he said. "But our team's mood continued to stay loose. In baseball, you've got to take it day by day, the bad with the good. You keep on hoping that you're gonna catch them."

In the second game of the doubleheader, Maglie, working on only two days' rest, held on for a 6–4 win, for his twenty-first victory. As tired as Sal was, he agreed to take a shot at it after Leo prevailed on him to "get out there and see what you can do." Durocher originally had intended to start Jones. But with a chance, at long last, to cut the Dodgers' margin to below five games, Leo was inclined to gamble with a bone-weary Maglie over an unpredictable Jones.

In the two games the Giants exploded for twenty-nine hits, their season high. Thomson hit a homer in each game, further proof of his rebirth. But in the second game, after uncharacteristically protesting a called third strike, Bobby was ushered off the premises by the umps, soon to be joined by Leo and coach Herman Franks. In such days of tumult and drama Durocher never missed an opportunity to back up his players or to test his hectoring on the umpires.

Even without Leo on the scene, the Giants scored two in the ninth to win the second game. With Westrum still muttering to himself over his brief suspension, Noble rose to the occasion by singling in Lockman, with the sixth run after Hank Thompson had hit a fly to score Irvin from third with the go-ahead run. Since neither Noble nor Thompson had contributed much for some weeks, their sudden production underlined how the team, as a whole, was now coming through.

Though the Dodgers also won at Chicago, 6–1, behind Clem Labine, their margin sunk to 4½ games. Of French-Canadian extraction, Labine was from Rhode Island. As soon as he joined the club in mid-July from St. Paul, his name had become the subject of speculation among his fellow players, the fans, and the writers. Just how did you pronounce it, anyway? Was it Labyne or Laybin or Labean? Should it go trippingly off the tongue, rhyming, say, with Jean Valjean?

Originally signed by Branch Rickey to a Newport News contract in 1944 for a $500 bonus, Labine had served in the paratroops for over two years during World War II. Garbed in sports jackets, with his blond hair in a crew cut, Labine was verbal, bright, and insightful, even at the age of twenty-five. When he was called up by Dressen, Clem hadn't expected to be injected into the starting-pitcher alignment—but here he was on the front line against the Cubs, using a sinker ball that would turn out to be increasingly effective.

Though the Dodgers' pitching staff had had its occasional woes during the year, with Roe and Erskine suffering constant miseries, their sluggers hadn't been as vulnerable to the usual injuries that mount up during the course of a 154-game season. But on Blue Monday (for the Dodgers), September 17, Campanella, always a wonderful rotund target for the headhunters, was beaned by Cubs right-hander Turk Lown. The Dodgers lost, 5–3, to Chicago, amid the usual suggestions that once again a black man had gone down in malice.

It wasn't clear how long Campy would be out, and the Dodgers assigned Rube Walker to fill in for him. Walker was one of the players who came over to the Dodgers from the Cubs in the deal for Pafko that was supposed to wrap up the National League flag for Brooklyn. Although he had never come close to hitting .300 in the majors, Rube was an able, though slow-footed, defensive catcher. He was certainly no Campanella.

With the loss, the Dodgers were now four games ahead of the Giants, who had no game scheduled that day. The next day, in Cincinnati, the Giants pulled out a one-run victory over the Reds, as Koslo got the victory, aided by Spencer in relief. This fifth straight win for the Giants, their tenth straight in Cincinnati, brought them closer to the Dodgers. With Campanella still out, the Dodgers lost to the Cards, 7–1, and began to show the signs of a club in imminent peril.

But Roe did his bit on September 19, with a shutout over the Cards, putting to rest for the moment the burgeoning mood of panic back in Flatbush. Since the Giants didn't play that afternoon, the Brooklyn margin went back to 3½ games, with five in the loss column.

On September 20 the Giants dropped a dismal 3–1 game to the Reds, sending their latest streak into the ashcan. Compounding their heartburn was left-handed junk man Ken Raffensberger, who threw pitches that made overeager batters look like suckers. The Giants had taken it on the chin at a most inappropriate time, for the Dodgers beat the Cards, even with Campy still on the sidelines.

The distance between the two clubs went back to 4½ games, and the newspaper necrologists again looked for a burial place for the Giants. The *Times* ran the gloomy pronouncement that "the Giants' pennant hopes were sunk," also reporting that Ford C. Frick, the National League president and one-time ghostwriter for Babe Ruth, had been elected baseball commissioner for seven years. In part, the Dodgers owed their current eminence in the standings to Frick, for, in his finest hour, several years back, he had sternly warned a group of wildcatting bigots on the Cardinals that they would wind up back on the farm or pumping gas if they struck over the appearance of Robinson in a Brooklyn uniform.

With both teams due to return to familiar territory, at Ebbets Field and the Polo Grounds, the odds still sharply favored Brooklyn. Though their last western trip of the season had seen the Dodgers lose more ground (they lost four out of nine, while the Giants lost three out of nine), their supporters still had reason to remain optimistic. The facts spoke for themselves. With a week and a half to go, the Dodgers had a 92–52 record and ten games to play. The Giants had seven to play and a 89–58 mark.

In the worst-case scenario for the Dodgers, if the Giants marched off with all seven of their games, the Dodgers would still only have to win half of theirs to win the "gonfalon," as Red Smith was disposed to call it.

By any calculations, the Giants' chances looked gloomy, yet they had one spiritual element going for them in addition to their own desire. That part of the civilized world that really cared about such matters as baseball pennant races was almost wholly in their corner. People prefer underdogs, especially the genre that repeatedly comes off the floor, as the Giants had done all year. Outside the borough of Brooklyn, it seemed as if everyone was pulling for the Giants and each morning's radio report of the latest ball scores became a daily adventure of high anticipation.

With the arrival of their heroes back home on September 21, the Flatbush faithful began lining up in the predawn hours for

World Series tickets. By 8 A.M. 1,400 people had queued up outside the Montague Street office of the Dodgers. By nine-fifteen more than 5,000 applications for tickets had been distributed. There may have been some moments of doubt when the Dodgers had been struggling through the west against "The Creeping Terror" (as sports columnist Bill Corum described it), but with the boys safely back in Ebbets Field everything pointed to another pennant winner in Brooklyn.

That day the Dodgers started Labine again. Clem had chalked up four straight complete-game wins, amassing twenty-two strikeouts, as he came to the aid of a weakening pitching corps. Now he was confident he could beat the Phillies. In the first inning, however, the Phils loaded the bases, bringing up Puddin' Head Jones, one of the team's Whiz Kids. Puddin' Head took a good look at Clem's sinker ball and sent it out of the lot for a four-run homer. It was a devastating blow for the Dodgers. They never recovered, losing a carelessly played game, 9–6. After the contest, Dressen, always quick to place blame or exonerate himself from it, insisted that he'd been "trying to attract the attention of my catcher [Walker], so he wouldn't call for that pitch . . . but the guy never looked toward me on the bench." Labine, who felt as rotten as Dressen did, knew he was about to be flung into Dressen's doghouse, for that's the way his manager operated.

"Dressen always wanted me to take a full windup," said Clem, "but I told him I wouldn't take a full windup. I guess that should have taught me to keep my mouth shut."

The gloom thickened around Brooklyn headquarters the next day, after the Dodgers lost again to the Phillies, 7–3. After almost a week's absence, Campy returned to the Dodger lineup—Lown's dart in the ear couldn't keep him away any longer, for Campy was a "gamer"—but he couldn't turn things around.

With three runs in the eighth, on an Irvin triple and a Mays single, the Giants won at the Polo Grounds, 4–1, before a few more than 11,000 in the stands. The folks may have been tuning in their radios for their daily suspense, but an aura of disbelief still prevailed at the box office. With this win the Giants inched to within three games of the Dodgers, as Jansen took his twenty-first victory, giving the Giants twenty-nine wins in thirty-five games.

On September 23 Maglie won his twenty-second, again by a 4–1 score. This time 18,000 showed up, leaving two thirds of the seats empty on a Sunday afternoon glowing with sunshine and promise. Roe kept pace with The Barber, winning his twenty-second of the year against the Phils. With 20,000 present at Ebbets Field, one had to wonder where all those diehard Dodger fans were hanging out. The Giants were still three games behind, after traveling at a pace for well over a month of five wins for every loss.

Monday, September 24, was the last home game of the year for the Giants. Despite the admirable effort the team had made to get back into the race, the crowds still were not coming to cheer the team on. To add to the riddle, the Giants had been playing well in their home roost all year, winning every series with the other seven teams in the league.

When the Giants came into the sixth inning with a three-run deficit to the Braves, the doomsayers were waiting in the wings. But one more time the Giants rallied. With their usual resourcefulness, they scored two in the seventh and another in the eighth to tie the game. In the ninth Mueller singled and went to second on a bunt by Rigney. With two out, it was Stanky's turn to bat. The feisty little infielder was having one hell of a time getting base hits. Unlike some others in the cast, his average had been slipping away. But that didn't mean he didn't want to be the man at the plate in this situation. Durocher pretended to scan the faces on the bench for a pinch hitter, an act so demeaning to Stanky that if looks killed Leo would have been a corpse. Finally, Durocher nodded to Stanky. "Get up there and get a goddamn hit," he snarled.

Eddie obeyed orders. He slammed one past third base, where Sibby Sisti, sent in for Bob Elliott by manager Tommy Holmes, couldn't come up with the grounder. Running for Mueller, Davey Williams came scooting across home plate with what proved to be the winning run. In this instance, the fact that Elliott had come up lame in the eighth inning trying to run out an infield tap probably donated the game to the Giants, for he was a better third baseman than Sisti, who normally played second.

As Durocher sweated out the last of the ninth, he watched Koslo, in relief, get two Braves to pop up with men on second and third and only one out. After such a tight squeeze, he couldn't restrain himself for the millionth time from paying tribute to his men. With his team now only 2½ games behind Brooklyn, he was more convinced than ever that his Giants were going to win. And it didn't make any difference if they did so through sheer fight and skill, or the "predestination" that Al Dark mysteriously talked about.

"These guys are playing for all they're worth," Durocher said. "Anybody who thinks this race is over is crazy. The worst we'll get is a tie. You heard it here. We'll win all four of our last games. They've got to lose some of those seven games they have to play. All the pressure is on them now. We have no worries or pressure. We'll make the pressure as tight as we can for them. You can bet on that!"

The man wasn't talking in a haze of fantasy, either, for the Dodgers were now behaving like a team in a straitjacket. They were straining desperately to keep what they had long thought had been firmly in their grasp: the National League pennant. Once they had taken it for granted that they had it all wrapped up in fancy paper. Now they were tight, nervous, and disorganized. All of Dressen's entreaties and spur-of-the moment strategies weren't able to stem the tide.

"We didn't really panic," said Clem Labine. "But it had to be discouraging for us to see that every day the noose got tighter. Now we knew that the Giants were for real. No, we weren't playing that badly. It's just that they were playing too well."

Campanella's perspective was slightly at odds with Labine's. He said that only a month before the Dodgers had been loose and cocky but now they were constantly looking over their shoulders or staring each day at that brooding scoreboard, which invariably relayed a message of despair.

Once scrappy and unconcerned, Dressen now conceded he was in a battle. "It'll be all right, it'll be all right," he assured one and all. But it was getting harder for people to believe him—or to believe that he believed it himself.

There are many turning points in a race as hard and unending as the 1951 season of 154 games. There are bad bounces and good bounces, good hunches and bad hunches, slumps and streaks, good luck and bad luck. The weather plays a role. So do bones that don't break and pitches that do. Baseball's wise men insist that all these factors balance out in the end and that over the long haul the best team will win. Talent will triumph, they say, after all is said and done.

But if there was a single day that may have turned the tide against the Dodgers in 1951 it was Tuesday—yes, Black Tuesday—September 25.

The Dodgers had returned to Boston's Braves Field for a doubleheader. The end of summer in New England can often be glorious, but there is always a dazzling uncertainty about it. When the Dodgers arrived in Boston it was chilly and damp, perhaps an accurate reflection of the team's mood.

A frostbitten crowd of 5,500 was on hand for what turned out to be the last rites for the Dodgers. The Braves had played .500 ball for most of that year. With a Warren Spahn or a Johnny Sain on the mound they could be tough on anyone, despite their record. But when Brooklyn came to town Sain was no longer there, for the Yankees had grabbed him for their own pennant insurance. That left it up to the great Spahn and a former American League right-hander, Jim Wilson (with a mediocre record of 6–8, from 1945 through 1949), to pitch the two games.

Branca lost the opener, 6–3, to Spahn, for his fourth consecutive defeat and his tenth overall. Clyde King, coming in to relieve him, didn't help very much. But facing the nondescript Wilson in the second game, the Dodgers conceivably should have fared better. They didn't. Erskine was massaged early and often and the Dodgers lost miserably, 14–2.

You could hear the jangle of nerves in the Dodgers' clubhouse after the double defeat, though it was unlikely you'd hear anything else. It was a team in agony, now almost deathly afraid of itself, muted by distress. There was no more high-pitched note of optimism from Robinson or the egotistical braying of Dressen.

"A dropped book on the floor or somethin' else would send a guy right through the ceiling," said Rube Walker. That's the kind of last week it had turned out to be for a once proud Dodgers team.

While Spahn was beating them in the first game, the Dodgers got the news soon enough in their clubhouse that the Giants were winning, 5–1, in Philadelphia. That meant the Giants were only three down in the loss column—and it could be two by nightfall.

How the Giants won was revealing, too. Again it was Maglie, this time in late relief of Hearn, cranking it up once more, after Jim faltered after seven splendid innings.

"This team had guys helping each other all year," said Rigney. "We didn't play errorless ball at the end when we were winning, and there is no way we could have been considered a good defensive team. But nobody got on anyone for mistakes. It was one guy helping another guy—like Maglie going in there to help out Hearn."

Hearn had thought he could make it through the last two innings. When he realized he couldn't, he could only smile ruefully when Sal raced—or was it trudged—to his rescue. "Hell, I realized his arm was as dead as mine," said Hearn.

When the Black Tuesday of Dodger sandlot baseball came to an end, the Giants and Dodgers both had won ninety-three games. But with fifty-six losses, the Dodgers had two fewer than the Giants, with fifty-eight.

Now one game separated the rivals, with only a handful of days left in the season. No longer could the Dodgers win one, lose one, as they had been doing for too long.

On Wednesday, September 26, the Giants, sniffing blood, smothered the Phillies, 10–1, in Philadelphia. Jansen, with an easy game for a change, won his twenty-first, as Irvin blasted a homer, triple, and double.

It was still dreary in Boston. But for a few moments the Dodgers revived. Newcombe took his nineteenth win and Campanella had three hits to lead Brooklyn to a 15–5 victory. Even though both teams won that day, it was a plus for the Dodgers, for still another day in the race was past without their lead diminishing any further.

Adding to the psychological pressure on the Dodgers, the Giants announced that they would start accepting requests for World Series tickets. It would be an all-New York World Series, the first since 1937 (when Lou Gehrig and Carl Hubbell were the stars), the Giants' front office merrily predicted. The Yankees, of course, would be the opposition, though they hadn't quite clinched the American League pennant (they did that the next day), but they could sit back and enjoy the fraternal strife that was occupying the other league.

The next two days, September 27 and 28, were off days for the Giants, a piece of scheduling that might ordinarily have benefited them, for theoretically they could relax and watch the Dodgers squirm. But momentum, which the Giants had at this time, could be sidetracked through inactivity. The Dodgers had to finish with the Braves in Boston—or were the Braves finishing them?—and then move on to Philadelphia, where they would play out their final three games. The Giants had only to play two weekend games with the Braves, hoping they wouldn't experience the same treatment that had befallen the Dodgers.

Down the stretch Preacher Roe, with his multiassortment of pitches, slushy or otherwise, had been brilliant. He'd won ten games in a row and was probably as responsible as any other Dodger for keeping the club in front. He didn't relish pitching in Boston's tundralike weather, but there he was, on September 27, trying to prolong his own streak (he'd lost only two games to this point), while preventing further disaster for his teammates.

Going into the last half of the eighth inning the game was tied at 3–3. The pesky Braves then got two men on base, causing the Brooklyn bullpen to start heating up in a hurry. Sam Jethroe was on first and Bob Addis, an outfielder with only fair speed, was on third. Dressen's prescription was for his infield to play in in order to cut off the run. The left-handed-hitting Earl Torgeson then cooperated nicely by hitting a hopper right at Robinson at second base, which is just what Jackie was hoping would happen.

Robinson made a clean play on the ball and with the same motion threw hard to Campanella, waiting at home to block the plate from the on-charging Addis. When the smoke cleared, with Campy bowled over from the collision but still holding on to the ball, umpire Frank Dascoli flashed the sign that Addis had beaten Robinson's throw. Simultaneously, the chilled 2,086 Boston fans let out a roar that could only further inflame the Dodgers.

Campanella howled out his disbelief to the skies. "He's out, he's out!" he wailed, jumping up and down at home plate. "Man, I had him!" Within seconds, Campy was joined by his irate teammates, who were shouting and screaming in support of their catcher.

"He was safe," Dascoli adamantly proclaimed. Turning his back on his detractors, he pretended to concentrate on wiping off home plate with his whisk broom. By this time Campy's mask was in the air and his mitt was on the ground. When Coach Lavagetto joined Campy's protest, Dascoli evicted both of them.

For all of his howling, Dressen remained on the bench, although almost everyone else was cleared out by Dascoli, leaving only a skeletal ball club to finish the game.

And it was finished, too—finished for the Dodgers. They got Reese on second, with a double in the ninth with one out. Since Rube Walker had replaced Campanella, it was his turn to bat. But

Dressen sent up Wayne Terwilliger, a right-handed batter, to hit for Walker against Chet Nichols, the Boston southpaw. "The Twig" grounded out, and Pafko fanned to end the game.

The Dodgers' growling didn't cease with the conclusion of their grim 4–3 loss, which left them just a half game ahead of the Giants, with only one less defeat. After the game "somebody" on the Dodgers, perhaps Robinson, in his typical pigeon-toed style, kicked in the panel of the door to the umpires' dressing room, located right next to the visitors' clubhouse. The door was left a splintered mass and though suspicion centered on Robinson and Roe as the malefactors, Robinson always denied doing it. "I know who did it, but I won't tell," he said.

Whether they were actually guilty or not, Robinson and Roe were fined $100 and $50, respectively, while Campanella was hit for $100. Campy was insistent in declaring that "I never called Dascoli nuthin'."

In the aftermath of the episode, the Dodgers not only angrily questioned Dascoli's judgment on the safe call but also for tossing their catcher out of a ball game that meant so much in a close pennant race. Dressen moaned that Dascoli was an "incompetent umpire who had had five run-ins" with his club during the season. Jackie observed that "you expect tempers to be frayed at such a time . . . he had no right to throw Campy out."

As for Dascoli's call, pictures that were shot of the disputed play failed to provide substantial support for the Dodgers' grievance. Close examination of the photo sequence showed Addis's left foot hooked across the plate, while Campy desperately tried to make the tag. Campy's body had flipped over the runner, seemingly after Addis's toe had touched the plate.

The controversy revealed less about the eyesight of Dascoli than about the collective state of mind of the Dodgers. "I watched my heroes with a shaken faith," said Frank Graham, Jr., then working in the Dodgers' public relations office. Dressen's club, to put it mildly, was in panic. Things gradually had gone from bad to worse. When a composed athlete like Campanella could blow up, it had to be symptomatic of a team that had lost control of itself.

A group of Giant loyalists, including Stoneham, Durocher, and Hubbell, the director of the team's farm system, followed by radio the turbulent proceedings from Boston in the Giants' 42nd Street offices. As they listened to the play-by-play, with the crazy denouement in the eighth inning, their cheers literally rattled the windows. Even the sangfroid screwballer, Hubbell, couldn't resist a laugh and a smile.

"I think we've got 'em now," shouted Leo.

The curious aspect of the Dodgers' tantrum was that pressure also fell on the Giants. Now that they were *this* close, their own nerves began to jangle. When they heard what had happened to the Dodgers in Boston, they instantly realized that there was increased pressure on them, too. For so long they had been loose and without anxiety, because few really anticipated that the race would come down to a nose-to-nose finish. Their own success had caught up with them. Having nearly a whole country pulling for them was an awful load to carry. "Our stomachs were starting to get to us," said Hearn. "Sleeping didn't come easy those last nights," said Bobby Thomson.

Idle for the second straight day on Friday, September 28, the Giants were barracked in Boston's Kenmore Hotel, where they spent their time listening to radio reports of the game in Philadelphia between the Dodgers and the Phillies. If the Dodgers lost, the Giants would be in a flat-footed tie for first place.

With Erskine working on the mound and gunning for his seventeenth victory, the Dodgers got off to an early three-run lead. But the Phils chopped away for one run in the sixth, narrowing the margin to 3–1. In the eighth inning catcher Andy Seminick belted a two-run homer over Shibe Park's left-field wall, tying the game at 3–3. In the last of the ninth, while the Giants held their breaths around their radios, Puddin' Head Jones, already ensconced in Brooklyn's Hall of Infamy thanks to his bases-loaded homer earlier in the month against Labine, singled Richie Ashburn home with the winning run. Most of the 18,000 in the ballpark enjoyed the demise of the Brooklyn team, hooting at the Dodgers through most of the game. When Ashburn came racing home they stood and applauded, as if the Phils themselves had been rocketed back into the pennant race.

With only two victories in their last eight games, the Dodgers had let the race get away from them. On the same day that Brooklyn's loss threw the National League race into the last weekend, the Yankees clinched the American League flag, as Allie Reynolds tossed his second no-hitter of the year.

Now a whole borough shared the suffering of its baseball team.

Nobody described the frustration and disappointment better than baseball writer Howard Sigmand. "They closed the Brooklyn Bridge today at both ends," he wrote.

Never missing a chance to grind his foes even further down than they were, Durocher said there was no reason Robinson shouldn't have been suspended, over the door-bashing, just as Wes Westrum had been a few weeks before. It really wasn't an issue anymore—but Leo always knew how to hurt a guy, didn't he?

15

The Final Weekend

IT WAS HARD to believe. The Giants and the Dodgers, after the sweating, mauling, and nerve-twitching, had come down to the final weekend with exactly the same account sheets. Each had won ninety-four games, each had lost fifty-eight.

The final games on Saturday and Sunday, September 29 and 30, would tell the story. The Giants had two games to go with the Braves in Boston. The Dodgers would play two with the Phillies in Philadelphia.

At this stage, the almost identical records of the Braves and Phillies mattered little, for often such also-ran teams would rise up and smite down the mighty. In such a hotly contested race, anything could happen. The Braves, having already humiliated the Dodgers, could do the same thing to the Giants. The Phillies could hope to do no worse against the Dodgers, after they had already inflicted a tormenting defeat on the Brooklyns the day before.

The intensity of feelings in Brooklyn about the pennant race had reached a new high—or a new low, depending on how one looked at it. Braves manager Tommy Holmes revealed a batch of telegrams that he'd received from angry Dodger fans, in which they bitterly protested "the Braves' treatment" of the Dodgers in the closing days of the race. These telegram senders asked how Holmes, a native of Brooklyn and one of their own neighbors, could countenance such behavior on the part of his team toward the Dodgers!

What did these people want, asked Holmes. Did they expect him to direct his men to take it easy on the Dodgers—or, even more unthinkable, lay down for Brooklyn? Holmes had to remind them that this was not the way the great American national pastime was played. The incendiary matter served to underline just how high emotions ran in 1951, especially for Dodger fans.

Even though he was known as a considerate man, Holmes could not be expected to consider the many past miseries of Dodger fans—Sisler's pennant killer of a home run in 1950, Owen's missed third strike on Casey's pitch in 1941, an unassisted triple play against them in the 1920 World Series, the constant forgetfulness of Wilbert Robinson and the frequent peccadilloes of Babe Herman. Did these many Brooklyn hurts excuse what some Brooklyn fans were now shouting at Tommy Holmes? Of course not.

One didn't have to be a budding mathematician to comprehend the forty-eight hour scenario now facing the Dodgers and Giants. The newspapers were mired down in the various possibilities, even when statistics weren't as rampant in the sports pages as they have since become.

It boiled down to this formula:

If the Dodgers and Giants each won two games, they'd end up tied. If they each lost two games, they'd also be tied.

If the Giants won only one of two and the Dodgers won two, the Dodgers would have the pennant. If the Dodgers won only one of two and the Giants won two, the Giants would win the pennant.

If the Dodgers split their two games and the Giants also split theirs, that would mean a tie.

For that Last Hurrah weekend the Giants and Dodgers settled on the lineups that had gotten them there.

For Durocher, it was Stanky, Dark, Thomson, Irvin, Lockman, Mays, Mueller, Westrum, and the pitcher. (Mueller was penciled down for sixth in the order because Durocher expected to face Spahn, the left-hander, in the Saturday game.)

For Dressen, it was Furillo, Reese, Snider, Robinson, Campanella, Pafko, Hodges, Cox, and the pitcher.

With Spahn nominated to start for Boston on Saturday, Leo picked Maglie to oppose him. The old hunch-player wasn't playing any hunches here. He was riding with his best against the Braves' best. Maglie proved he was up to the task, limiting the Braves to five hits in a 3–0 shutout, for his twenty-third victory.

"No doubt about it. It was the most important game I ever pitched," said Maglie. "I'm the happiest guy in the world." Sometimes it was hard to tell how happy Maglie was, for he didn't smile much. But he had a lot of company in the Giant clubhouse.

All the necessary momentum that the Giants needed in this game came from Mays. In the second inning, after Willie walked, he came off first base as if he were totally oblivious of Spahn's well-earned reputation as the pitcher with the trickiest move to first. Spahn was capable of picking runners off if they so much as leaned an inch or two the wrong way. But Willie refused to buy the legend. After Durocher gave him the palm of his hand— the go-ahead sign—Willie set sail for second base and made it easily.

As Spahn cuddled the ball on the mound, Willie then lit out for third, making it with feet to spare against the pitcher's late throw. He came home on a groundout for the first run, which proved to be all that Maglie needed that day.

"Willie took the pressure right off the whole club," said Durocher. "He won the game for us right there." (Considering that Mays stole just seven bases in that freshman year, he had certainly chosen the right moment to get his legs moving.)

There were only 8,000 fans in the Boston park. But judging from their squeals for Willie's steals, and for two subsequent runs that the Giants scored, most of them had come to root the Giants home.

In Philadelphia that night, the Dodgers were already aware that the Giants had won. How unkind could things get for them?— the Giants playing in the afternoon, while they had to wait for the evening. Nothing had been lost yet, but the tension in the Dodgers' clubhouse was like an unseen presence.

Besmirched so often and unthinkingly for his supposed "big-game" failures, Newcombe was Dressen's choice to start against the Phillies. Lose this one, the Dodgers knew, and the whole world would be convinced that they had taken the apple, that they had crumbled in the clutch.

Newcombe did what he had to do that night, shutting out the Phils, just as Maglie had done against the Braves. He scattered seven hits. Each inning he got to look bigger and bigger on the mound, an intimidating figure, as he won his twentieth game of the year.

For the 28,000 in Shibe Park it was, oddly, a welcome win, for any upstanding baseball fan had to be pulling for that quintessential finish: two teams tied on the final day.

So it would all come down to Sunday, September 30. The day started out as if it were going to be New England's best—crisp and clear. But by noon the ominous clouds moved across the skies of Boston. The umpires said that if the teams hoped to get the game in, it would be best to push up the starting time by a half hour. So it was done.

With twenty-one victories already in his pocket, Jansen was Durocher's selection for a game that had to be won. It was a fulfillment of Leo's superstitious nature that Jansen would try to end the season as he had begun it last April 17, at Boston, when he had shut out the Braves in the opener. With the gods on his side, and a few base hits, Jansen might repeat that performance.

The Braves scored once in their first at-bat, arousing a quick sense of despair in the Giant fans among the 13,209 at the ballpark as well as those thousands of partisans listening in at home or in their cars. But when Bobby Thomson shot his thirtieth homer over the wall to tie it in the second inning, Giant fans regained their composure.

The Giants added runs in the third and fifth innings, the last on a slashing single by Irvin. That gave Jansen two runs to work with. In such a tense environment, Jansen remained cool. At one stretch he retired twenty-two Braves in a row, as he outpitched Jim Wilson, Max Surkont, and Vern Bickford.

Then, with two out in the last of the ninth, with everyone in the Giants' camp aware that the Dodgers were trailing Philadelphia midway through their game, Jansen suddenly weakened. Bob Addis, whose toe had beaten Campanella at home plate just days before, now became a thorn in the Giants' side by hitting a long double. Sam Jethroe followed with a dying-quail single, Addis stopping at third base. No sense getting thrown out at home when the Braves needed two runs to tie.

Next up was catcher Walker Cooper, still burned off at Durocher for chasing him out of the Polo Grounds as soon as he took over the Giants' helm. Wherever announcer Russ Hodges' fateful message of this game was being carried, hope mixed with anxiety among his listeners. Was it possible that the heavy-hitting, ex-Giant Cooper would write a cruel finish to the season-long pursuit by the New Yorkers?

When Cooper's tantalizing high hopper to Stanky at second handcuffed the Giants' infielder, Addis scored. One of the league's slowest runners, Cooper managed to beat Stanky's throw to first. Now it was Jethroe, a speedster, at second base with the potential tying run, and Cooper, the winning run (to break Giants' fans hearts), at first.

That left it up to Willard Marshall, once a good home run hitter for the Giants, to make the third and last out of the game—or end the Giants' dream.

Three pitchers grazed in the Giants' bull pen. Spencer was right-handed and overworked. Koslo was left-handed and probably the best bet to thwart the lefty-hitting Marshall. Corwin was right-handed and perhaps too inexperienced to be inserted into such a numbing situation.

All eyes now were on Durocher as he hopped across the third-base line (touching the lines was verboten for him) to visit with the exhausted Jansen. Would he decide to yank his pitcher and bring in Koslo? Would he gamble with Spencer one more time?

"How do you feel?" asked Leo. Did it really make any difference, at this stage, what Jansen had to tell him?

"I've got enough left," said Jansen, huskily. "Let me finish it. I'll get him." Just one more out, thought the pitcher, that's all I need. That would give him his seventh victory over the Braves for the year. But he wasn't counting such things right now.

If a manager peers into his pitcher's eyes, can he tell what he's thinking or feeling? Is there any way to measure what the pitcher has left, outside of heart? Probably not—but Leo stared into the tired lines of Jansen's face, anyway. He may have seen fatigue and determination there. He also saw the best man he had at that moment. He knew Jansen wanted to stay in. Durocher would play his last hunch of the season and let him pitch to Marshall, now standing at the plate bemused by the huddle of Giant strategists.

Finally walking away from Jansen, Durocher shot back over his shoulder, "Get him out!" Durocher, the born gambler, was now gambling that the weary Jansen could deliver one more out for the Giants.

Alone now on the mound, Jansen stared past the muscular

Marshall at the big catcher's mitt of Westrum. He got his sign as Marshall wiggled his bat once or twice mockingly in the pitcher's face. Jansen threw. The pitch came in low, a slider that slid too far. It was a ball.

The rhythmic clapping of the fans was not a precise barometer of their feelings. Were they rooting for Marshall to fail or for Jansen to succeed? It was hard to tell.

Marshall connected with Jansen's next delivery and sent a scorching foul into the right-field corner. On the next pitch, Jansen gained his pitcher's advantage—it was a good strike, on the outside corner of the plate. He was ahead in the count, one-and-two.

Jansen looked down at Westrum. Marshall stepped out of the batter's box for a moment, then edged back in. His bat curled in a semiarc, then was quiet. The umpire leaned forward, behind Westrum, part of the tableau, prepared to make his judgment. Jansen wound up and threw, a fast pitch, away. Marshall caught the ball at the end of his bat, sending a lazy fly into left field, where Irvin waited.

"I went racing over from center as fast as my legs could carry me," said Mays later. "I still didn't know what I was going to do about anything. Monte was there, waiting. I shouted over at him. He patted his glove a couple of times. I shouted some more. Then Monte made the catch and I jumped all over him, just out of plain joy."

The game was over. Jansen had done his job. In fact, he'd done it so well that the game had lasted only one minute past two hours, one of the fastest contests of the year.

The players scrambled off the field and rushed to the clubhouse. But not to celebrate. Yes, there was satisfaction in what they had accomplished. But it wasn't time yet for champagne popping or the postmorten interviews of triumph, for the other part of the story hadn't run its course. All of the returns from the outlying district of Philadelphia hadn't come in yet. That struggle was still going on, even as the Giants showered, dressed, and prepared to take the five o'clock train back to New York. In the background, Red Barber's play-by-play from Philadelphia could be heard, first reassuring for them, as the Dodgers trailed, 6–1, in the third, then growing unsettling, as the Dodgers battled back.

By the eighth inning Rube Walker's two-run pinch-hit double had tied the game at 8–8. Barber's account, once elegiac, underlay the fact that these Brooklyn players were not quitting, especially in the face of the Giants' victory in Boston.

Dressen was shuffling pitchers in like infantry replacements. The lame-armed Roe had started, lasting only two innings. Then came Branca, then Labine, then Erskine. When the Giants arrived at the railroad station to get on the train, Newcombe was pitching. Hadn't the big guy gone nine shutout innings only hours before? He had. But now he was the fifth Dodger pitcher of the afternoon.

"There's no tomorrow," said Dressen by way of explanation for Newk's appearance, uttering the well-worn cliché of all managers at such a last-ditch moment.

There was a telephone on the Giants' train, something of an innovation. Hodges, the Tennessean broadcaster who was as fervently loyal to the Giants as owner Stoneham, immediately surrounded it and got in touch with radio station WMCA in New York. WMCA was receiving the game from Philly, but the Giants weren't getting it on the train.

With the Giants' entourage huddled around the broadcaster, Hodges took the play-by-play on the phone, then relayed his brief summaries to the anxious crowd. Sometimes the connection was poor and Hodges had difficulty hearing it. The persistent clack-clacking of the train's wheels didn't help matters, either.

"Everybody quiet," yelled Durocher.

As the game went into extra innings, cheers greeted each report of Philly base hits. Groans and oaths sputtered after every mention from Russ Hodges that a Dodger had reached base.

In the twelfth inning, with one out, the Phillies got men on first and second. Then Jones walked, loading the bases. With slugger Del Ennis due to hit, it appeared as if Dressen might take Newcombe out.

"Hell, no, he won't," said Durocher. "Ennis is a right-handed batter."

Durocher was right. Newcombe stayed in to face Ennis and got him on strikes. With two out, that left it up to Eddie Waitkus, the first baseman. Two summers before Waitkus had been the unwitting gunshot victim of a crazed nineteen-year-old girl in a Chicago hotel room. After miraculously surviving, Waitkus became something of an exotic baseball legend as well as an important member of Philadelphia's Whiz Kids.

Dressen still elected to stick with Newcombe, even though

Waitkus was a lefty batter. Hodges strained to hear what was happening, his ear glued to the telephone. The Giants didn't utter a sound. Durocher was white-faced, his jaw set grimly at attention. For the first time in months, even Willie was quiet. Then Hodges started to speak:

"Waitkus belts a low line drive to the right of second base . . . Robinson caught it . . . the Phillies are arguing that Robinson trapped it . . . Warneke says no, he got it . . . the Phillies are out . . . the Dodgers are out of the inning."

Red Smith recorded it this way: "Robinson flings himself headlong at right angles to the flight of the ball, for an instant his body is suspended in midair, then somehow the outstretched glove intercepts the ball inches off the ground. He falls heavily, the crash drives an elbow into his side, he collapses . . . stretched at full length in the insubstantial twilight, the unconquerable doing the impossible."

Not a soul on that Giant train bound for New York had ever wished Jackie Robinson well. He had been their implacable enemy. But what they had just heard, accompanied by their own head shaking and muttering, convinced them, if they hadn't been convinced before, that they were up against a man who never quit.

For several minutes Robinson lay still, while his teammates gathered around him. When he finally arose groggily, he walked slowly and uncertainly toward the Dodger dugout. Still buzzing over his catch, the crowd roared in appreciation of what they had just seen.

The decision in Philadelphia was still on hold.

In the thirteenth inning Newcombe retired the first two Phillies batters, then suddenly weakened and walked the next two. Dressen made a path to the mound again, taking the ball from his right-hander, who had pitched 5⅔ innings of heroic relief after shutting out the Phils the day before. In came Clarence "Bud" Podbielan, a twenty-seven-year-old right-hander from the state of Washington. Dressen was asking him to get the third out. He did.

"How long can this goddamn thing go on?" asked the frustrated Durocher. Nobody answered him.

In the fourteenth inning, Roberts, in his sixth inning of relief, retired Reese and Snider on pop-ups, so it looked like he had gotten through another round of Dodger batters. But he failed to reckon with the astonishing recuperative powers of Robinson. With a one-

and-one count, Robinson turned savagely on one of Robin's fast-balls and sent it soaring into the left-field stands for a home run. The Dodgers were now ahead, 9–8, in this marathon. In the gathering gloom of Shibe Park, Dodgers' president O'Malley and his general manager, Buzzy Bavasi, rose from their seats, wild with joy and relief. Jackie had rescued them again.

Now it remained for Podbielan to get three more Philly outs. When Ashburn opened the last of the fourteenth with a single, one of his four hits during the torturous afternoon, Russ Hodges dutifully passed the word along. "Maybe it's not over yet," said Dark, hopefully. Fingers were crossed all down the line on that Giants' train.

Puddin' Head Jones sacrificed Ashburn down to second base, with the tying run. One out, a man on second. Going to a full count on Del Ennis, Podbielan got the slugger to pop to Gil Hodges at first base. Two out. Waitkus, moments before robbed by Robinson, then lifted a game-ending fly to Pafko in left, causing the entire population of Brooklyn to exhale.

"Dodgers win, 9–8," said Russ Hodges, hoarsely.

The regular season was over. The Dodgers, once regal and prideful, had clawed back, in their own way, to survive. But the Giants shared the National League lead with them. Both teams had records of 96–58.

The Giants had won thirty-seven of their last forty-four games, twelve of their final thirteen, and their last seven in a row. From August 12 on the Dodgers had won twenty-six out of forty-eight games. But they had dropped six of their last ten. Had the Dodgers folded up or had the Giants simply played too well to be denied?

However one assessed what had happened in this most unpredictable of seasons, the Giant players on that train had the look of pallbearers. They had had it in their grasp, then it had slipped out. Robinson, that damn Robinson!

There were mumbled suggestions among them that they'd "get 'em tomorrow," but the lengthy bloodletting between the two clubs had taken its toll. At that moment the collective morale among the Giants was lower than a dachshund's belly.

When the Merchants Limited pulled into Grand Central Terminal at a little after nine o'clock, 5,000 fans were on hand to greet their adored Giants, all of them proud of the fight their team had waged. In their own happiness they didn't appreciate the disappointment that had clouded that trip home from Boston.

Over at Penn Station, a grateful crowd of Brooklyn supporters welcomed their battered warriors, now forced to face the Giants in a best-of-three play-off to start the next day.

That Sunday in New York anyone not familiar with the harrowing details of the Dodgers' come-from-behind triumph in Philadelphia or Jansen's workmanlike job against the Braves wasn't living on this planet. The word was out, on street corners, restaurants, in shops, theaters, in parks, hospitals, in homes in Harlem, Park Avenue, Brownsville, Flatbush, and in the Bronx, where the Yankees reigned, that the Giants and Dodgers had fought to a tie.

Even the *New York Times*, often reluctant to showcase sports events on its front page, ran a headline that clarioned the deeds of September 30: BROOKS' VICTORY IN 14TH LEAVES FANS LIMP.

16

The Play-offs

WHATEVER IMPELLED Chuck Dressen to elect to play the first play-off game at Ebbets Field on October 1, will forever remain a mystery. Having won the coin toss, Chuck chose home territory for the game, which meant the two teams would migrate back to the Polo Grounds for the second and third games, if a third became necessary.

Dressen had little precedent to go by. In the only other National League play-off in history, in 1946, after the Cardinals and Dodgers posted 96–58 records, Durocher, then managing the Dodgers, won the coin toss. He chose to open at Sportsman's Park in St. Louis, presumably giving the Dodgers the home-field advantage in the next two games. But there was no such advantage, for the Cards won two straight, one at home, one away. Had Dressen set out to do just the opposite of what Durocher had done in 1946?

In 1948, in an American League one-game play-off, the Cleveland Indians beat the Boston Red Sox. The site of that game was also decided by coin toss. The game venue went to Boston. Where was the home-team advantage?

No doubt Dressen figured to win that first game in Ebbets Field, giving him the momentum. He would entrust that game to Branca, who, coincidentally, had been the starting pitcher in the first game of the 1946 play-off. On that occasion the twenty-year-old Branca, bothered by a sore arm much of the year, was so disconcerted before the contest that he left his glove at home and his wallet, containing $200, under a pillow in his hotel room. He also left much of his high, hard one, as the Cardinals routed him within three innings.

Now, five years after that negative play-off experience, Branca was his manager's choice again. Dressen had few options. He certainly couldn't nominate Newcombe, for that willing man had already spent the weekend in strenuous labor, and Roe and Erskine, the other big winners for Brooklyn, were nursing questionable arms.

Durocher had no such dilemma. Maglie had pitched Saturday, Jansen had worked Sunday. It was now up to Hearn, with his 16–9 record and two wins in five decisions against the Dodgers. (Branca had beaten the Giants only twice in six games.)

On the last day of the season, Hearn had warmed up alongside Jansen. Since Larry's arm felt tight there was a chance that Durocher would call on Hearn to pitch against the Braves. But when he decided on Jansen, Hearn sat down.

"I never liked to warm up the day before I'd start a game," said Hearn. "But I didn't have any idea at that time that we'd end up in a tie and that the next day I'd get the call as the starting pitcher."

On an Indian summer afternoon, with the temperature reaching a high of seventy-four, Hearn worked as quickly and efficiently as Jansen had the day before.

Pafko roused Brooklyn's hopes with a second-inning home run, but the Dodgers could do little against Hearn after that blow. Those right-handed sluggers spread throughout the Brooklyn lineup couldn't match the right-handers in the Giants' lineup.

In the fourth inning Thomson hit a two-run homer off Branca to put the Giants ahead, 2–1. It was his second home run of the year off the Dodger pitcher. Then Irvin hit a bases-empty homer in the eighth, increasing the Giants' margin to 3–1, which is the way the game ended.

Monte had found Branca a favorite target all year—this was his fifth homer off him during the season. In all, the Giants had connected for ten homers off Branca to this point.

Over the second half of the '51 season Thomson had, more or less, set the compass for his homer off Branca. From April to July

13 he hit National League pitching for a disappointing .231 average. It looked like a repetition of his efforts during the 1948 and 1950 seasons, when he had finished with marks of .248 and .252.

Then, as if a genie were guiding his every move on the playing field, Thomson found himself and his potential in late July. That was when Durocher made his move, putting him at third base. As time went on, Durocher was hailed as a genius. More likely, it was just one of the things that sometimes happen in baseball.

With the change in environment, a shortened stance, plus the addition of a slight crouch, Thomson's batting eye cleared away the mist. His average zoomed, and so did the Giants. From July 14 to September 15, Thomson batted at a .385 pace. When the going was the most critical, from September 15 to the end of the regular season, Bobby was a menace at the plate, batting .449. Aside from Irvin, whose clutch hitting was remarkable, Bobby had become the single most important cog in Durocher's machine.

Following the opening-game victory, the Giants' chances to win went sky-high. They were now going back to the Polo Grounds for two games and hoped one would be enough. Down the stretch Maglie had pitched with two days' rest, and some suspected that Durocher might bring back the bearded Brooklyn-basher, even after such short vacation time.

Hearn, however, felt so good after his Monday victory that he told Durocher he'd love to pitch again on Tuesday. "I think I can pitch tomorrow, if you want me," Hearn said to Leo. "I don't feel tired at all."

Ordinarily, the manager would have brushed off such euphoria, but he was acting like a very supportive fellow these days. "Ya know, I just might use you, Jim," he said. Was the manager being facetious? Not even Hearn knew. But Jim was sincere when he made the offer.

As things turned out, Durocher didn't use Maglie or Hearn. He didn't even have Hearn in the bull pen on October 2. Instead, he played another one of his hunches. The hunch, in this case, was "Available" Jones, the twenty-nine-year-old right-hander from Tecumseh, Nebraska, who had won thirty-one games and lost twenty over the 1948 and 1949 seasons. In 1950 he slumped to 13–16, when it seemed that he walked as many batters as he struck out, not a productive ratio. Certainly, this should have given any manager pause, especially in such a crucial game.

A talkative, pleasant man, Jones hadn't done too much winning in 1951—six games, to be exact. But he did manage to win another nickname during the year. Many of his buddies, inspired by Al Capp's "L'il Abner" comic strip, took to calling him "Seldom," a conversion of his first name of Sheldon but also a wry commentary on his inability to win.

Nevertheless, though he hadn't pitched since September 24, Jones was on the mound for the Giants in the second play-off game. "The guy was well rested," said Durocher. "Maglie was tired as hell."

I remember that Jones game only too well, for I was at the Polo Grounds that bright, sunny day, along with 38,000 other people. Mrs. John McGraw was there, with her left arm in a cast, and Bill Terry, McGraw's successor, was there too. Sitting behind first base, with my wife, Phyllis, who was pregnant at the time, and Fred, my father-in-law, a lifelong Giants' fan, I recall how testy Fred became as soon as he was aware of Jones's selection. Fred had been watching, under his generous but quizzical white eyebrows, as Jones took his warm-up tosses. He was convinced that Sheldon would be useless that day—and hardly "Available."

"Durocher can't be serious about starting him," Fred growled out loud, the first of many negative assessments he registered that afternoon about the state of the Giants. Fred was entirely right, of course.

The Giants had come into this game on a roll. Having taken seven straight games to close out the season, they had added an eighth with Hearn's play-off win. But within minutes of the start of this game, Robinson had stepped up and banged a two-run, first-inning homer. Jones was like "a man walking a tightrope across Niagara Falls from the start of the game," wrote Arthur Daley of the *Times*.

After 2⅓ innings, in which he gave up two runs on four hits, Durocher pulled Jones out of the fray. Spencer didn't do any better, giving up four runs in 3⅔ innings. Corwin ended the agony for Giants fans by yielding another four runs. The final score was 10–0.

Hodges, Pafko, and Rube Walker added the other Dodger homers, while the Giants' defense had its worst day in months. Thomson, Mays, Jones, and Spencer—Spencer with two miscues—contributed a total of five errors.

Perhaps the oddest aspect of the Dodger win was the pitching performance of Clem Labine. A resident of Dressen's doghouse ever since the September day when he'd given up the grand slam to Puddin' Head Jones, Labine redeemed himself with a six-hit shutout.

Dressen would have preferred starting Roe. But the veteran pitcher told him, "I can hit harder right now than I can throw." So Dressen reached out for Labine. Despite the knowledge that he was going to start on October 2, Labine, always a cool customer, had no trouble at all sleeping the night before the most important game of his life. When he arrived at the park looking particularly well rested, Labine informed Doc Wendler, the Brooklyn trainer, "This is the day I find out whether I'm a man or a boy."

So much for Dressen's unerring instinct about pitchers. Where had Clem been those last two weeks of the season?

At the start of the game Dressen had complained about Jones's "spitballs" to umpire Larry Goetz. But after Robinson hit one of those "spitters" out of the park, Dressen cut out his whining.

In the third inning, when the Giants were still in the ball game, Thomson, their hottest hitter, struck out with the bases loaded, on a three-and-two pitch.

"It would probably have been a ball if he hadn't swung," said Labine. But Dressen suggested that that's exactly the way he'd planned it.

"Ya think I'm gonna have Labine throw a fast one in there and let him hit it out of the park?" he said. "Hell, no. If Labine doesn't get it over, one run is better than four."

As the game went on its dreary way—for Giant fans, that is— my father-in-law became increasingly distraught. His opinions about Jones had already been confirmed, as he would have been the first to tell you.

When Fred finally bolted from his seat along about the sixth inning, the skies suddenly darkened and a bone-chilling rain fell on the proceedings, causing a brief suspension of play. During Fred's absence a man who had been sitting behind our party tapped me on the shoulder.

"Would you please tell me who that fellow was?" he asked, not impolitely. Obviously he had never before seen such red-faced, choleric behavior at a ball game.

"He's my father-in-law," I confessed, with a certain measure of embarrassment. "He's really a kind and rational man when he's not at the ballpark."

"You're lucky he's not your mother-in-law," my neighbor concluded.

Labine was inclined to be modest about his achievement. "I was lucky with my curve all day," he said. "My sinker was working pretty good, too. But it's not so much what you throw but what you can get over the plate."

But Clem had no right to be so modest. His pitching for the moment had ended the Giants' stream of successes and given the Dodgers one more chance for a comeback.

"I was surprised Durocher picked me," said Jones about his own ill-fated nomination to pitch. "I'd had enough rest. But everything seemed to go sour. The ball that Robinson hit was a curve that hung high. I just couldn't seem to get the ball down low. I was lousy, that's all."

Refusing to play Hamlet over the setback, Durocher behaved in exemplary style. When reporters clustered around him in the clubhouse after the game—some even suggesting that he'd been at fault for giving the ball to Jones—the manager was unexpectedly forthcoming.

"We didn't blow anything," he said. "There wasn't any one play that broke the game open. Nothing like that. We just got the pants kicked off us."

For the first time in a month Dressen broke open a smile for the photographers. The front page of the *Times* had him standing there with Labine, Pafko, Hodges, and Walker, grinning like Halloween pumpkins, in a triumphant group photo.

Hey, somebody asked, why wasn't Robinson included in that happy little family shot?

Jackie was quick to set the facts straight. "That was my own choice," he said. "I've had enough of the limelight."

Now there was only one more tomorrow. It would all come down to a final test on Wednesday, October 3, 1951.

Could the Giants produce one more miracle to garnish their season? Would the Dodgers, a team that had squandered a 13½-game lead, restore itself in the eyes of its admirers? Did the overwhelming superiority of the Dodgers in that Tuesday game foretell a sickening resolution for the Giants the next day?

17

The Home Run Heard 'Round the World

THERE WERE SOME 150 million people in the United States on Wednesday, October 3, 1951, a four-door Kaiser went for $2,289.99, and sportswriters carted $37.50 portable typewriters to ball games.

No census has ever been taken on just how many of those 150 million rooted for the Giants or for the Dodgers—or how many didn't know or care whether or where they were playing that day. But what was about to transpire at the Polo Grounds on that gray, sixty-degree afternoon appeared to be the primary concern of most New Yorkers as they greeted the day.

Fans began arriving in the early hours of the morning at 155th Street and Eighth Avenue for what most of them guessed would be hard-to-get grandstand and bleacher seats. But a threat of rain and the pasting the Giants had received the day before probably discouraged many from making one last trip to the Polo Grounds, which some felt would become a desperate morgue for the New York team. Only 34,000 paid their way in, leaving at least 15,000 pews without bodies. (Despite the heated pennant race, Giants' attendance for the year was up less than 60,000, while the Dodgers improved by only 84,000. The fact that in the last week of the race both the Dodgers and Giants played on the road certainly didn't help. But baseball in general that year was down over 1,200,000, a dramatic decline from the first post–World War II years.)

On this autumn day the United States revealed that the Soviet Union had set off its second atom blast in two years and the Senate Foreign Relations Committee wrestled with Philip Jessup's nomination as a delegate to the United Nations. *An American in Paris*, with an old Giant fan, Gene Kelly, and Leslie Caron, was at Radio City Music Hall and Josephine Baker was in person at the Roxy.

Everywhere in New York the city was wired to the summit event that was about to take place at the Polo Grounds. On radio, WMCA, the Giants' station, and WMGM, the Dodgers' stronghold, carried play-by-play, Mutual Network had it on national TV, and Channel 11 was televising this last game, as they had the second one. The first play-off game had been on Channel 9.

In the bustling financial district the Dow-Jones tickers were prepared to carry the latest baseball news, along with their usual money coverage. In city prisons inmates would spend their day huddling over radios, while at Belmont Park the track announcer, Fred Caposella, was warming up his progress-of-the-game reports for the lovers of horseflesh. No barber in his right mind could be without a humming radio if he expected to have any customers that day, and General Electric took ads in newspapers promoting its seventeen-inch Black Daylite TV set, for eighty dollars less than usual, as a play-off special. How many played hooky from school or called in sick to their bosses has never been estimated; the number probably could have filled the Polo Grounds several times over.

Though the New York public, with its split camp of supporters, had been aroused by this ultimate confrontation, the players themselves, relatively speaking, were able to take it in stride. Indeed, they were true professionals, and by this late date all of them had given their last ounce of emotion to the struggle. For some, it was almost strangely anticlimactic. After all they had been through during the long season, why should anything bother them now?

Sure, there would be the usual pregame butterflies on that day, but most players slept soundly the night before the game.

Don Mueller, for example, got his normal amount of sleep—nine or ten hours. "I didn't feel much tension because we'd been battling five or six weeks, without letup, so this was nothing new at all. I don't even remember what I had for breakfast and I forget who rode to the park with me that day on the subway."

Maglie, Durocher's inevitable choice to start this game, was dog-tired. "I felt dead," he said, "and didn't expect to last very long." But the frown on his face was meant only to unsettle Dodger batters, for he had long since learned how to cope with the tensions that emanate from the baseball arena. He had iron nerves when he needed them and little trouble sleeping before his final assignment. Hell, he'd beaten this Brooklyn team five times already—why not once more!

Equally as exhausted as Maglie, Newcombe, who would pitch the final game, didn't have to cope with images of Giant hitters in his dreams, for he, too, slept well. Jansen didn't think he'd be called on to pitch, for he'd worked on Sunday, only two days before. The fact that Durocher would probably want him in the bull pen for this one didn't bother him at all.

Durocher wasn't going to hit, pitch, or field on Wednesday, but he was as fully involved as any of his employees. Yet he was calmer than he'd been all year. "It's been tough," he said, "but we've never quit—and we're not about to do that now." The man thrived on such nerve-jostling encounters.

Dressen issued his usual precombat readiness statement and swore out an affidavit that his Dodgers would definitely show up for the game. He swallowed all his clichés along with some good Italian wine at a restaurant and went to sleep hoping his team would equal its previous day's performance.

Thomson was in bed early in his family's home in New Dorp, Staten Island. When he drove to work the next morning, he kept thinking how nice it would be if he could continue to hit the way he had in the latter part of the season. "Three hits would be just fine for the team," he thought. That is, three hits that he'd get himself, an arbitrary figure that somehow stuck in his mind.

Al Dark got lots of sleep, too; he needed it, for he played the game with great intensity. Branca, loser of the first play-off game, figured that Dressen would call on others if Newk needed help and went to sleep in Mount Vernon, New York, after a quick perusal of the newspapers.

Of all the Dodgers, it may have been Pafko who felt the most pressure. He was away from his wife, who lived in Chicago, and he was a true family man. All season long he'd been touted by the press as the pennant insurance that Brooklyn had obtained in the midseason trade with the Cubs. Here it was, October 3, and the Dodgers still didn't have that pennant yet.

As far as pregame pep talks to the troops were concerned,

there was little new that either Dressen or Durocher could add to the verbal stew at this point. Certainly Dressen wasn't a stirring orator of the Knute Rockne mold or, for that matter, even of the Wilbert Robinson genre. Leo hadn't had a meeting since Godknowswhen—the players, led by Dark and Rigney, had done that for him. Now he'd utter a few last words of encouragement, remind Maglie to keep the ball away from the hitters, then issue his last "Let's get 'em" of the year. What more could he say at this juncture to arouse the natives other than to make a plea for divine intervention?

It's been said that exhortations and clubhouse meetings are fine, provided the team wins after they take place. That probably says it all about this practice.

A notoriously slow starter, Maglie gave up walks to Reese and Snider in the first inning. Then the nemesis himself, Robinson, hit one sharply into left field for a first-pitch single. One run scored. Durocher immediately sent word out to the bull pen for Jansen to start heating up. Perhaps the 298 innings Maglie had pitched during the season had caught up with him. This was a day when a manager couldn't wait too long for results. But Maglie worked out of further trouble by getting Pafko to hit into a force-out at third and Hodges to pop to Thomson. In the stands Laraine Day sat next to Mrs. John McGraw. They weren't the only ones breathing easier when the inning ended with only a 1–0 Dodger lead.

With one out in the second inning, the Giants launched their first threat. Lockman cracked a single for the Giants' first hit, and Thomson banged one down the line in left. From the moment he hit the ball, Bobby was thinking "double." So, running hard with his head down, he didn't realize that Pafko's arm, much respected by Lockman, would cause Whitey to stop at second base. At third Cox received Pafko's throw and was surprised to see both Lockman and Thomson vying to occupy second base. It was then just a simple matter to catch Thomson in a rundown, Robinson finally putting the tag on him. Bobby ran off the field, his head resting on his chest in embarrassment. After all the good things he'd accomplished in the last months, now this base-running gaffe! The incipient rally had been thwarted as Mays flied out to end the inning. By the third inning, the lights were turned on as the day became overcast—how could such a transcendent game be played in such gloom!

In the fifth inning Thomson sent a double whistling to left-center. But the Giants failed to bring him around. Each time a Giant managed to get a hit, Dressen would squirm a little more in the Dodger dugout. And each time the manager would communicate with coach Clyde Sukeforth, who was presiding over the Dodgers bull pen in left field.

"Who's ready, who's ready?" Dressen asked anxiously, and Sukeforth would volunteer his wisdom. Sukeforth had managed the Dodgers briefly in 1947, as an interim choice when Durocher had been suspended. ("I managed two games against Boston and won both," recalled Sukeforth, proud of his perfect slate, "but I always preferred being a coach.")

"I kept telling Dressen that Branca looked ready to me," said Sukeforth. "I'd been catching Branca, Labine, and Erskine out there for twenty or thirty minutes at a stretch—and when I wasn't doing that I was sunning myself, except on that afternoon there wasn't much sun."

Sukeforth also told Dressen he didn't think Labine was the right guy to come in because he'd pitched only the day before. "I didn't want him in that spot, with no rest," said Sukeforth, "and I didn't think Erskine was ready, either. Carl had a doubtful arm all his life, and he hadn't shown me his best curve or fastball that day."

Maglie and Newcombe, bone-tired as they were, were also men of great pride and determination. As the innings went by, without further damage, they became convinced that they were getting stronger. It may have been little more than self-hypnosis, but it was working.

As the seventh inning arrived for the Giants, Irvin doubled to left. Again the worried Dressen wanted to know from Sukeforth what was going on in the bull pen. "I kept telling him Branca seemed pretty loose to me," said Sukeforth.

Now Durocher called for a bunt to move Irvin to third. Lockman performed the task to perfection, dropping the ball near the plate, where Rube Walker quickly pounced on it and threw to Cox at third. But Irvin beat the throw. Some imagined that if Campanella, instead of Walker, had been catching that afternoon his throw might have shot down Irvin. Campanella had a damaged thigh muscle, however, and Dressen hadn't been able to start him that day.

With Irvin on third, it was up to Thomson to bring him home. As he had done so often in recent weeks, Bobby came through again. His long fly to center field scored Irvin after the catch with the tying run, bringing a heartfelt roar from Giant fans.

When Newcombe returned to the Dodger bench, he informed Campanella and Robinson that he had nothing left. It made sense, after all the big pitcher had been through in the last week. But Robinson wouldn't hear of it. "Shit," he said, "you keep pitching out there 'til your fuckin' arm falls off!" Robinson had challenged Newcombe many times before in such a harsh way. Usually the strategy had worked. Robinson liked to light fires under people, especially Newcombe. For another inning it seemed to help: Newk's fast one had enough zip on it to retire three more Giants in the seventh.

With the score deadlocked in the eighth at 1–1, the crowd stirred, loudly demanding that the matter be resolved once and for all. It implored the teams—roughly half the people in the park were rooting for the Giants, half for the Dodgers—to settle this grudge.

"It was what the boys in the back room call the moment of truth," said Hodges, doing the play-by-play on radio.

To start the eighth, Furillo made out. But Reese followed with a single and scampered to third on Snider's clean shot to right field. With Robinson at bat, backed by a crescendo of support from Dodger fans, Maglie unleashed a wild pitch that escaped Westrum's mitt. It was only the third time the pitcher had done that all year—but it couldn't have come at a worse moment. Robinson, always Robinson. Reese scored with the go-ahead run, as Snider beat it down to second. Had Maglie lost his sangfroid, if only for a second?

Durocher walked slowly to the mound. When he got there he ordered Maglie to put Robinson on first with an intentional base on balls in order to set up a double play for Pafko, the next batter.

Jansen and Hearn were now throwing increasingly hard in the bull pen. Only the fact that Westrum insisted that Maglie still had enough strength left to get the side out prevented Durocher from peremptorily calling for a reliever.

Pafko hit a tricky bouncer to third, where Thomson, playing in close, tried to backhand it. Bobby wanted to make a force on Snider at third. Instead, the ball got past his glove and wound up in left field as Snider scored and Robinson ran all the way to third. It was a tough play for Thomson to make, and the official scorer was kind enough to recognize this, since Pafko got credit for a hit. Giving support to Westrum's prognosis that he could still retire the side, Maglie bravely fanned Hodges for the second out. But then Cox sent another tough grounder in the direction of Thomson. This time he desperately tried to get some part—any part—of his body in front of the ball. But the ball shot by him into left field. Things happen quickly at third base, as Thomson had learned. Robinson crossed the plate, making the score 4–1.

While the Dodger fans roared with delight, the Giant fans, only a few minutes before so euphoric, were now plunged into Stygian gloom. The improbable was not about to happen after all. Their team of destiny was going to lose because of a ball that got away from a normally dependable pitcher and a couple that got away from a less dependable third baseman. It was a harsh assessment. But now it had to be faced. At long last, the damage had been done, exulted the Dodger devotees, and the National League would have its champion, the same team that should have won in regulation time.

Maglie finally retired Walker for the third out. Applauded loudly and sympathetically as he walked off the field, Maglie's disheartened admirers assumed he had done his work for the year. Due up second in the bottom of the eighth, Maglie would be replaced by a pinch hitter.

With three big runs to work on, Newcombe was infused with new energy—a rush of adrenaline—that would carry him through the eighth. He got Rigney, batting for Westrum, on strikes, got Thompson, pinch-hitting for Maglie, to squibble one back to the mound, and blurred one by Stanky for the third out. Durocher's strident voice still barked out words of encouragement to his men, but now they sounded hollow and hopeless.

With Maglie out of the game, the Giants needed a new pitcher in the ninth. As Jansen marched in from the bull pen, a driblet of fans could be seen moving toward the exits. Were they being disloyal, or were they realists? Whatever the case, the same mood of melancholy had not yet gripped Jansen. If some fans believed the miracle gestating in Coogan's Bluff had come to an abrupt halt, Jansen wasn't thinking that way.

"The Dodgers stood there, at the edge of their dugout, as I

came in to pitch. They were yelling at me, 'Jansen, you can go home now, Jansen you can go home!' But I just kept thinking that all I wanted to do was prevent further scoring," said Jansen. "I wanted to face three guys and get three out. Sure, with the score, 4–1, it didn't look like we could pull it out. But strange things can happen in this game. It was my duty just to keep pitching and hoping."

Jansen got his three ninth-inning outs with dispatch. Now it was up to Newcombe, hurling for the fourth time in eight days, to set the Giants down one last time. The ninth inning can be a mine field—or a mean field—for pitchers. In this case, all Newcombe had to do was dispose of Dark, Mueller, and Irvin and his team would be National League champs.

As the teams changed sides, Mays and Irvin came trotting in from center and left field. They were the last to arrive back in the dugout, since their stations were the furthest from the Giants' bench. Irvin knew he would bat in the last inning but Willie wasn't certain he would, for his team would have to get some men on base if he were to have another shot at it. Normally, Durocher would already have been in his third-base coaching roost by the time Willie and Monte reached the dugout. But this time he waited for them because he wanted all the Giants to be there to hear what he had to say. Turning to face his players, with his right hand on the dugout roof for support, Durocher was composed. If this was a time for a burial speech, the manager wasn't pronouncing it. He hadn't made many speeches all year and wasn't about to do that now.

"Well, we've come a helluva long way," he said, "and you've still got a chance to hit."

Then he turned and walked rapidly to the third-base coaching box, a last-ditch optimist prepared to conduct any late-afternoon traffic that might come his way.

There was frustration, inner rage, resignation, and some tears among the players on that Giant bench—some, perhaps, even had quietly given up. But Durocher knew that Newcombe still had to get three more outs.

Before Dark stepped in to face Newcombe, he swung his black bat back and forth several times. Mueller, up next, did the same with two of his bats. Even at such a lugubrious moment, baseball's rituals went on. Then Dark, in his high-hipped stance from the right side of the plate, stood there, facing the pitcher.

Newcombe got ahead of Dark with two strikes, but on the next pitch the shortstop made contact with the ball, sending it toward the hole on the right side of the infield. Both Robinson, at second, and Hodges, at first, went for it—in sort of a scissors movement—but the ball had eyes, squeaking through for a single. Hodges' mitt deflected it but not enough to prevent it from rolling into right field.

"You don't have to open your mouth to lead," Dark, the team captain, said later. "Look at Pee Wee Reese. I never saw him open his mouth. You lead by example. That single, in the ninth, to start it off, was the best kind of leadership I can think of."

With Dark edging warily off first, Hodges, for some inexplicable reason, played close to the bag. Holding Dark on first at this stage made little sense, for the Giants needed three runs to tie the game. There was no chance that Dark would try to steal—the Giants needed more base runners right now. Some in the press box scratched their heads at Hodges' strategy—or was it Dressen's?—and wondered what the man was doing.

Mueller also noticed Hodges' positioning. He had made a living by being an observant hitter. He knew, along with Willie Keeler, that it's best "to hit 'em where they ain't"—especially if they don't know where the devil they're supposed to be.

"If Hodges had played in his normal position," said Mueller, "I wouldn't have hit the ball where I did. I would have gone down the middle. I was always good at being able to place the ball where I wanted to if I was on equal terms with the pitcher. Durocher had always said that Newcombe was a great pitcher but that if we stayed close we'd have a good chance of beating him."

Mueller's bat directed the ball, almost casually, to the left of first base, wide of Hodges' bare, outstretched hand. If Gil had ignored Dark at first base and played Mueller to pull the ball less, he might have trapped the bounder and started a double play. As it was, the ball skipped past him into right field, sending Dark along to third.

Suddenly the fans stopped shuffling toward the exits. Two men on, no one out. Irvin, the league's best RBI man and the Giants' premier clutch hitter, was coming to bat.

Furious at the developing situation, Dressen growled his discontent at Hodges' failure to come up with the ball. Then he walked to the mound to ask Newcombe how he felt. Curses and roars went up from the Giant fans, while Dodger supporters suffered in silence. What was going on here? Would Dressen go to his bull pen? "Branca's ready," Sukeforth had told his manager at least a half-dozen times. He told him again. But after a few words with his pitcher, Dressen returned to the dugout. Newcombe didn't return with him. He was staying in to face Irvin, a right-handed batter.

Overanxious, Irvin swung mightily at a high, outside delivery that he never could have pulled to the left-field seats. The ball was lofted in the air, a simple foul fly, not far from Hodges. As Hodges camped under it, the Dodger loyalists let out a roar of relief.

"I didn't throw my bat in anger, because I was never a bat-breaker," said Irvin. "But I stood there, frustrated, trying to 'root' the ball into the stands and away from Hodges' glove. I kept urging it with my shoulder and heart. But it didn't help."

It was one of the few times in his career that Irvin violated his own precious sense of privacy to show emotion on a ball field.

At this moment the journalists in the press box were informed over the loudspeaker, rather prematurely as it turned out, that World Series credentials for Ebbets Field "could be picked up at six o'clock tonight at the Biltmore Hotel." That information would soon become as obsolete as the score of the second play-off game.

As Giant fans implored him to connect safely, Lockman, the next hitter, ground his spikes in at the plate. Breathing hard, sweat rolling down his long-jawed face, Newcombe looked down at the left-handed batter. Lockman could hit bad pitches about as well as any batter in memory. The Cards' Ducky Medwick, whose career had ended only a few years before, sometimes swung at balls over his head. Lockman didn't do that as often, but when Newcombe's second pitch—a high, outside ball at least six inches away from the plate—came toward him, he stroked it over third base, close to the left-field line.

As Pafko madly chased the ball in the corner, Dark scored. Mueller, facing a potential Pafko throw toward third, managed to reach the base safely, but at a price. Lockman was now perched at second, with his second double of the game, the score was 4–2, and the noise in the park was deafening.

"My one thought when I went up to bat in the ninth was to go all-out for a homer, although I wasn't that much of a homer hitter, especially against Newcombe. I'd had twelve homers all year. When Newcombe threw that ball in to me my instinct and muscle control took over. I knew it was impossible to pull it for a homer, so I sliced it to left," said Lockman.

As Lockman pulled into second, few paid attention to Mueller's plight at third. He had gone into the bag half standing, for he had considered heading for home if Pafko's throw had gone awry.

"It wasn't a slide," said Mueller, "because I was looking over my shoulder at Pafko's throw to the cutoff man. On a bad throw I would have gone for home and would have scored. The ligaments on both sides of my ankle were pulled; so were the tendons. At the end of the game it hurt awfully. The swelling was as big as a softball."

When Durocher, still celebrating Lockman's hit, saw that Mueller was writhing in agony, he motioned for Doc Bowman. Stretcher bearers were summoned as the crowd's tumult ceased for a minute. "The corniest possible Hollywood schmalz," wrote Red Smith, "symbolic of the Giants themselves."

Clint Hartung, the all-but-forgotten would-be wunderkind, was sent in to run for Mueller. "When Leo called me to go in there," said Hartung, "I wasn't thinking much about the game. I was just thinking of how bad Don was hurt."

As Mueller was removed to the Giant clubhouse, Dressen had to mull over the removal of his pitcher. Newcombe was obviously not only distraught about what was happening, he was pooped. There was no other way of putting it—he'd run out of gas. As Dressen walked slowly to the mound, Reese, Robinson, and Walker joined him for the committee meeting.

"Talk to Jackie and Pee Wee," Newcombe said to his manager. "They've been watching my stuff. They know how much I've been pitching in the last week."

Robinson might have gone for the needle once more. It had worked in the past. But one look at Newcombe assured him the man had had enough.

"How do you feel, big fellow?" he asked. But he knew the answer before Newcombe volunteered it.

"I'll give it all I've got," said Newcombe. "But I'm tired."

Dressen listened to the exchange, with the noise of the crowd cracking around his ears. "Ralph's throwing the hardest out here," Sukeforth had told him for the last forty-five minutes. Then, Dressen thought, there was still Labine—and how about Erskine?

Labine had been in the bull pen for the entire game. "I didn't really feel uneasy about the game until late in the day," he said. "Carl and Ralph had been warming up. Then, I started to warm up in the ninth. Funny thing, but I always thought there was an outside chance of my being used again, even after I'd pitched the whole game the day before. I had a history of being able to work after going nine innings. I knew I might be asked."

Erskine, too, was eager to come in if Dressen asked him. "I balked at pitching batting practice because I wanted to get into the game," he said. "Ralph and I were warming up early, then I stopped. Sukey kept a close eye on us. He had seen that I was bouncing my curveball in the dirt, and I guess that's what decided him against me."

At last, Dressen made up his mind. "Okay," he said on the intercom to the bull pen. "Gimme Branca." Nobody else tried to influence Dressen's decision. "They couldn't have," said Reese. "He wouldn't have listened to them."

(Later Sukeforth acknowledged that it was on his own say-so that Dressen decided to bring in Branca, although the manager could have ignored the suggestion and picked Labine or Erskine. "I don't know why people make such a fuss about it. I just told him what I thought.")

As Branca began his long walk in from left field, the Brooklyn doubters in the stands, and elsewhere, were already having a field day. "Get out the crepe," they muttered, pointing out that Branca had pitched and lost only two days before. Hadn't he been giving up homers all year to the Giants? Hadn't Thomson, whom he would now face, cracked two off him? As a matter of fact, hadn't 25 percent of Bobby's homers during the season been hit against Dodger pitching? Two off Erskine, one each off Roe, Newk, Phil Haugstad, and the two off Branca? Wouldn't Labine's sinking curveball be more effective against Thomson, who generally ate up fastball pitching? Hadn't Thomson struck out the day before against Clem with the bases loaded?

By the time Branca, sober-faced and heavy-limbed, had reached the mound, excitement had reached a peak not only in the Polo Grounds but also in the outside world. New York cabbies were turning down fares so they could give their undivided attention to the game on the radio. People in the "most unfriendly city in the world" were stopping total strangers to inquire, "What's the score?" and the clattering of play-by-play descriptions could be heard throbbing through open windows. The whole town seemed to be tuned in to Dressen's last-second strategy and had a pipeline to Thomson's bat and Branca's right arm.

Waiting at the mound for Branca, Dressen handed him the ball. "Get this guy out," he said. Then he turned on his heel and walked back to the dugout, where every Dodger was perched anxiously on the front of the steps. Baseball is not a game that should be played with clenched teeth—but there were plenty of clenched teeth among those Dodgers.

Reese and Robinson stood alongside Branca to give their encouragement. "Anyone here have butterflies?" the pitcher asked, wryly.

Not a word had passed between Dressen and Branca about the possibility of intentionally walking Thomson to load the bases in order to face the first-year man Mays, scheduled to follow Bobby to the plate. One had to suppose that Dressen was paying homage to traditionalists by refusing to put the winning run on base.

While Branca took his eight warm-up pitches, looking loose and strong, Thomson's eyes scanned his movements, then followed the ball as it thundered into Walker's mitt. If either man felt strangled by tension they didn't show it.

Mays, anticipating that he might yet come to bat, was down on one knee in the on-deck circle. If Bobby got a hit or made an out, he would come to the plate.

"With two men on and first base open," said Willie, "I was sure they were gonna pass Bobby. I figured it that way even if it meant putting the winning run on. You see, I hadn't been hitting much in the last three weeks of the season and my average had gone down almost twenty points. Besides, I thought they'd rather take a chance on a kid like me. To tell you the truth, I really didn't look forward to coming to bat because the way I'd been going I didn't think I'd help much."

Soon Willie would know whether he'd face his own test, for Thomson was getting set to bat. Here is how Thomson remembers those last few frenetic moments of the 1951 race:

"When I was in the dugout during that last inning, I thought we were dead. I felt dejected. I'm sure some of the other guys felt that way, too. I didn't think I'd get to face Newcombe, either, because I was too far down in the order. Then suddenly things began to happen and Mueller got hurt. That upset all of us. But oddly you can rationalize that that may have helped me because it took my mind away from the game for a little while.

"I walked down to third base, where Don was on the ground. All of us liked him so much and were so sorry that it had happened. Then it was time to go back to work.

"Even if Newk was overpowering, I didn't lack self-confidence. I was a competitive guy. When I started to walk back to home plate from third base, I was hardly aware that the Dodgers had made a pitching change until I saw Branca standing out there. How often does a batter get to walk back from third to home in order to bat? But this wasn't a normal day, was it?

"Before I settled in to bat, Leo said to me, 'Bobby, if you ever hit one, hit one now.' I didn't say anything, but in my mind I was thinking base hit, not homer.

"Usually, I never tried to psych myself up. That just wasn't my way. A man does the best he can. But when I made that ninety-foot walk from third base, I kept calling myself all sorts of names: 'You son of a bitch, do a good job, get a hit, wait for the ball, you son of a bitch, wait and watch!'

"Then I realized Branca was ready to pitch. I took the first one down the middle, a ball I should have swung at. I waited again. Branca's pitch came in high and inside and I got a fleeting glimpse of it. [Bobby laughs at this point]. I guess I saw it better than that! I was quick with my hands. After I hit it, I watched it go. At first I was sure it was a home run, then I saw the ball start to sink when I got halfway to first. A look again, and I realized it was disappearing into the stands. Then I knew we were all right. I jumped and skipped around those bases like I was half nuts. Gee whiz, I kept saying, gee whiz! I guess you could call me an 'accidental hero.' "

The stunned Pafko, in left field, could only gaze heavenward. "It was a hard shot, right down the line," he said. "I wasn't aware at first that it was going in for a homer. But when it passed over my head, the whole thing became a terrible blur. I had the best view of it of anyone in the house—and wish I hadn't."

Reluctant to concede that it was all over, Robinson stood his ground near second, peering at Thomson's crazy gavotte around the bases. Jackie wanted to make sure that Bobby touched all the bases. When he saw that he did, Robinson slowly started his trek to the clubhouse in center field, a melancholy promenade if ever there was one.

Representing the tying run at second, Lockman had had a clear view of Walker's signals to Branca. "That first pitch had been perfect for Bobby," he said, "the kind he could knock out of the park. But when he took it for a strike, my heart sank. Then I watched Walker cup his hand for the next pitch and motion upward and to his left. That meant it would be a high, inside pitch, Bobby's *weakness*. When it came in that way, he tomahawked it, anyway."

At the moment of truth—3:58 P.M.—Erskine turned to Labine in the bull pen, his handsome face masked in pain. "That's the first time in my life," he said, "that I've ever seen a fat wallet flying into the stands." (The next day the papers reported that Labine angrily bit off a chunk of the bull pen bench. "Baloney," said Clem. "I would never have taken such a chance with my teeth. That was only a figure of speech—but I sure felt like doing it!")

Rube Walker, the catcher who some insisted should have been replaced by Campanella, sidelined with the only charley horse in his career, was willing to accept the blame for the pitch that Thomson hit.

"It's probably my fault," he said, crustily. "But I wouldn't change a damn thing, no sir. I called it, and the pitcher threw it. I'm not going to blame anyone for something I called."

But he wouldn't accept the responsibility for the choice of Branca. "I wasn't asked by Dressen," Walker said. "He never bothered talking to me about it. He had his mind made up—and that was it!"

In the Giant clubhouse, nursing his ninth-inning wound on the dressing table, Mueller said he wasn't sure how to interpret the great roar from the crowd. "I couldn't be certain that it wasn't something good for the Dodgers because there were plenty of Brooklyn fans in that park. There was no radio in the clubhouse, so I couldn't have figured that Bobby had hit a game-winner. But I knew pretty quickly what had happened once the players got back to the clubhouse and started to pour champagne over my injured ankle."

Finally, there was the tormented Branca to be heard from, the pitcher who had gone one-on-one with Thomson—and failed. It became the game's classic confrontation—an echo of Fletcher Christian facing Captain Bligh on the high seas, Dempsey going against Tunney, Burr dueling Hamilton at Weehawken Heights.

"When I came in to relieve Newcombe, I just kept thinking, 'Get these two guys out and we're in the Series,' " said Branca. "I didn't give any thought to some of the other home runs that Thomson had hit off me. There were no specific instructions from Sukeforth or Dressen on how to pitch to Thomson. Rube gave me the signals on each pitch. Since it's against baseball percentage to walk the winning run on base, that strategy wasn't used. I got a fastball over the inside corner between the belt and the knees for the first strike on Thomson, but I still didn't think I was going to get him on strikes. The ball that Bobby hit for a homer was a fastball, chin high and inside. Though the ball was hit in the air, it had overspin or topspin and was sinking. I didn't think it was going to go in until I realized it was down the foul line. Then I kept praying for it to sink and hit the wall. Frankly, I was glad I was chosen to face Thomson because I knew Erskine was having trouble getting loosened up and Clem was tired from the shutout the day before. I felt fine and had good stuff out there, and I didn't have any doubts I was going to get the next two guys out . . ."

On TV Ernie Harwell, thinking at first that Pafko might catch Thomson's drive, told his audience, *"It's gone!"*

From his WMCA radio booth, Russ Hodges, screaming in triplicate, while the Polo Grounds became an instant madhouse, said: *"The Giants win the pennant, the Giants win the pennant, the Giants win the pennant . . . I don't believe it, I don't believe it, I don't believe it . . ."*

On WMGM radio Red Barber, with possibly an even larger audience than Hodges, announced *"It's in there for the pennant!"* Then the engineer, Joe Chambers, told Barber to keep quiet and he did. "I had learned never to talk against a crowd," said Barber, "and I didn't now."

So it ended, a 5–4 victory for the Giants. Finishing one game ahead of the Dodgers, the Giants had ninety-eight victories and fifty-nine losses. The Brooklyn record was ninety-seven and sixty.

The next day Red Smith entitled his column "Miracle of Coogan's Bluff," which was hardly hyperbole.

"Now it is done, now the story ends. And there is no way to tell it," Smith wrote. "The art of fiction is dead. Reality has strangled invention. Only the utterly impossible, the inexpressibly fantastic can ever be plausible again . . ."

18

The Aftermath

THE CHAIN REACTION was incredible.

Seconds after Stanky galloped down the third-base line to engage Durocher in a joyous wrestling match, Thomson jumped on home plate to be met by a mob of hysterical teammates. As he did, an entire city erupted. In the Polo Grounds, the crowd, stunned for a moment, unleashed a scene of collective jubilation that rivaled the mass reaction in Times Square at the end of World War II.

Work in a city of 8 million was something only telephone operators performed, as they placed calls for people having little more to impart than incoherent babblings. So busy were phones in Manhattan and Brooklyn that some businesses were cut off from the outside world. Harlem, still a neighborhood where baseball was appreciated, celebrated minutes after Pafko backed his behind against the left-field wall. There had been nothing like it there since Joe Louis revenged himself on Max Schmeling.

Many Jews in synagogues for the Jewish holy days followed the progress of the game and exclaimed out loud when Thomson's homer fell into the lower left-field grandstand. Auto horns blew a medley; taverns were loaded with people who nursed beers for hours; heart attacks felled two people in the Polo Grounds; a coffee cup hurled by a disgruntled Dodger fan in a Mamaroneck, New York, diner hit an innocent bystander in the head; customers snake-danced around barber chairs on West 44th Street; bartenders forgot to serve drinks in the Astor Bar; a florist carried a wreath labeled "Sympathy for the Dodgers"; people donating blood at a Brooklyn Red Cross Center were so enraged at the presence of a gloating Giant fan that they shrieked for a nurse to drain all of his blood.

Thomson's girlfriend, Elaine, was working in a New Jersey hospital that afternoon. Her friends had sneaked her upstairs into an office, where she could watch the last innings on television. When Bobby came to bat in the ninth she promised to buy champagne for the house if Bobby got a hit. He did, and she did. In Staten Island, the natives exulted over their greatest hero since Giovanni da Verrazano discovered the island in 1524. Ferry boats halted and whistles set up a din at the charmed hour of four o'clock.

Once "brooding over his sins of the afternoon," as *Daily Mirror* columnist Dan Parker described it, Thomson was now busy in the Giant clubhouse, sawing off his horns for good. Known as a third baseman of spectacular immobility, Thomson could now blow triumphant notes on his Scotch bagpipes. Outside, screaming like children, thousands of fans clamored for their hero. Cashing in their chips on their baseball emotions, they demanded to see Thomson's glowing face.

When he finally appeared, Thomson was like a paternal, smiling dictator, waving happily at the fans from the clubhouse verandah. He had transcended the cold statistics of the game's record books to enter the realm of folklore. A mighty roar of approval assailed his ears. It was the most pleasant sound of his life, even more agreeable than the soft scratching of a fountain pen that would soon write an extra $5,000 of World Series money into his bank account.

The same crowd of hero-worshipers (Ralph Waldo Emerson wrote that "heroism feels and never reasons, and therefore is always right") only hours before could have committed bodily harm to the strapping third baseman. Instead, he was now canonized, having performed a valorous feat in battle.

While a delighted city was ignited by one swipe of Thomson's bat, the Giants' clubhouse resembled Grand Central Station. Shoving his way to Thomson's side, a representative of Perry Como's CBS TV show shouted an offer of $500 for him to appear that night.

Bobby answered that he preferred spending the evening with his family, celebrating the events of the day with them, instead of millions of Americans. The rep upped the offer to $1,000.

"For one thousand dollars I guess the family can wait," said Thomson, sensible even in the midst of such tumult. Those were not the days of $2,000,000 ball players.

When Red Barber inched his microphone close to Thomson, Stanky grabbed it and screeched: "This is Red Barber, signing off for 1951!"

"None of us Giants liked Red," said Bobby. "We didn't like any of those guys from Brooklyn."

Over and over, Thomson would relate his story of that last inning, the walk to the plate, the striking of the ball, the prayerful look at its flight, the kangaroo romp around the bases, the emotional overkill that followed.

"While circling the bases Leo tried to grab me as I ran by him," Thomson said. "I kept fending him off because I wanted to make sure that I touched the plate. While chasing after me Leo stepped on the back of my spikes and tore the shoe off before I took my one last leap. The next thing I knew everyone was swarming all over me. My brother Jim kept repeating, 'Bobby, do you realize what you did? It may never happen again.' I finally did realize it."

The other part of the world—the Dodger dressing room—was like a crypt; it could have been a dormitory for the deaf. His head bowed, Branca sat, weeping and disconsolate, on the steps of the Dodger clubhouse. Cookie Lavagetto, once a Brooklyn hero, sat alongside him, not uttering a word.

After several minutes the press was permitted in but only after Barney Stein, a veteran photographer for the New York *Post*, pleaded with the Dodger batboy, Charlie Di Giovanna, to go to Dressen and ask him to open the doors. Not as down-in-the-mouth as the others, the manager finally obliged. "I was a true-blue Dodger fan all my life," said Stein. "This hurt me almost as much as it hurt Branca."

Stein started to snap away with his camera. Branca noticed Stein working but didn't try to stop him. As Ken Smith of the *Daily Mirror* watched, Stein's camera caught Branca brooding on the steps. Smith knew at once that the tableau Stein captured was a great shot. "That's a prizewinner, if I've ever seen one," Smith said.

He was right. The photo, freezing Branca forever in a posture of grinding distress, won the New York Press Photographers Award, and the *Post* presented Stein with $100.

Trying to break the gloom, Dodgers general manager Buzzy Bavasi walked from one player to another, assuring them, "It can happen to anyone."

"Yeah, but we hope it happens only once to us," a couple of Dodgers wailed.

On the way home in his Oldsmobile, where his fiancée, Ann Mulvey, was waiting to provide solace, Branca wanted to know why it had happened to him.

"I don't smoke, I don't drink, I don't run around," he said. "Baseball is my whole life. Why me?" Father Frank Rowley of Fordham thought he had an answer: "God chose you because he knew you had faith and strength enough to bear this cross."

Just seventeen days after the blast that destroyed the Dodgers, Branca married Ann, whose mother, the daughter of Judge Steve McKeever, owned 25 percent of the Dodgers' stock. Thomson married Elaine a year after his homer.

That winter Thomson and Branca, now inexorably entwined in the game's history, were invited to appear as featured performers at the annual New York Writers Dinner in the grand ballroom of the Waldorf-Astoria Hotel. They would play themselves in an encore of the melodrama that had taken place at the Polo Grounds.

First it was Bobby's turn. He stepped out onto the stage, where a huge portrait of himself stared him in the face. Taking a deep breath, as he did on October 3, he started to sing to the same tune as "Because of You," a popular song that year:

> Because of you, there's a song in my heart.
> Because of you, my technique is an art.
> Because of you, a fastball high
> Became a dinky, chinky fly.
> Now Leo and me-o won't part.
> My fame is sure, thanks to your Sunday pitch,
> Up high or low, I don't know which is which.
> But come next spring, keep throwing that thing,
> And I will swing, because of you.

When he finished, Thomson received a rousing round of applause. The audience was much taken with this modest fellow, who was enjoying the limelight and good-naturedly playing along with his stage managers.

Next came Branca's turn to sing. In a pleasant, clear baritone, he sang words that could have stuck in his throat:

> Because of you, I should never have been born.
> Because of you, Dodger fans are forlorn.
> Because of you, they yell drop dead,
> And several millions want my head.
> To sever, forever, in scorn
> One lonely bird had a word for my ear.
> The only girl, what a pearl, of good cheer.
> I lost the game, but wound up with the dame
> She took my name
> In spite of you.

Branca's parody took the gathering of 1,200 by storm. Time and again they called for him to come back, as they cheered him to the echo. As the walls shook with applause, the two ball players threw their arms around each other's shoulders. It was a stirring demonstration of good sportsmanship, too often lost in the heat and anger of battle. At one table, a writer, with tears welling in his eyes, said to Harold Rosenthal, who had covered the Dodgers till the bitter end in 1951: "I don't like the Dodgers, I never have, I probably never will. But Branca I'll buy. What a man and what guts!"

As the years went by, Thomson and Branca were always bracketed together and constantly reminded of the roles they had played. The fans and the press wouldn't ever let them forget, not that Thomson cared to forget. Why should he?

Branca, however, reacted to the continued assault on his privacy with a mixture of annoyance and acceptance. An intelligent and sensitive man, he was sometimes cooperative when reporters badgered him with never-ending queries about the last pitch of the play-off. At other times he gruffly rebuffed all efforts on the part of his inquisitors.

For example, during the preparation of this book, I sent Branca letters and phoned him, and intermediaries were used to encourage him to talk to the author. He was insistent that he had nothing more to add on the subject, having said enough in the past. He wanted no more to do with the matter. He was aware that his most infamous pitch had forever caused his name to be remembered by baseball fans. But notoriety gained in such a manner was something he had never cared or bargained for. "You know, if you kill somebody," Branca said, "they sentence you to life. You serve twenty years and you get paroled. I've never been paroled." He thought he deserved to be remembered more as a twenty-game winner for Brooklyn at the age of twenty-one than as the unwitting architect of perhaps the most painful episode in Dodger history.

But Thomson accepted, with a measure of pleasure, gratitude, and bemusement, the everlasting fame that came his way with one swing of his bat.

"People remember me because of it," he said. "I don't think anyone would have paid much attention to me if it hadn't happened."

The day after Bobby's homer, the balls started to roll in—that is, the ball that was supposed to have been the one he hit. One man, claiming to have been exactly in the right place when the homer landed, asked him to autograph the ball. But when other fans made the same claim, it became clear that "the ball" never could be certified.

"I don't have *the* ball," Thomson said, "because if I did have it, I'd always wonder whether that was really *the* ball."

When fans wrote to Thomson years after the event, he responded faithfully. A paper products salesman, Thomson had no secretary, but he tried to answer every letter or card. When reporters kept asking him the same questions he answered patiently, even suggesting that he now be called Bob. "I'm no longer a young ballplayer," he said. "My son Robert should be called Bobby, not me." Invited to appear at autograph-signing sessions, he usually went.

In 1989, thirty-eight years after he heard the 1951 game on the radio, Albert Engelken, a Washington, D.C., transit association official, was preparing to celebrate his fiftieth birthday. His wife, Betsy, knowing her husband's feelings about Thomson (Engelken's license plate was ENG-23, which was Thomson's baseball number), secretly arranged with Bobby to have him meet Engelken just off Exit 10 of the New Jersey turnpike. Betsy kept the rendezvous details from Albert, pretending she had to pick up some papers for a neighbor.

When the Engelkens parked their car, Thomson suddenly appeared. He then spent an hour talking with Engelken, putting the man on cloud nine.

"There he was, the hero of my youth, the one person in history I'd like to meet. Keep Jefferson, Saint Augustine, or Michelangelo," said Engelken. "I'll take The Flying Scot!"

When *Wall Street Journal* reporter Albert Karr asked Thomson why he bothered to take time off from work to meet a man he didn't know, Bobby replied: "If you have the chance in life to make somebody this happy, you have an obligation to do it."

Branca lost some of his luster as a counterhero by chafing somewhat under the continual questioning. When photographers constantly asked him to pose with Thomson, he often begged off, citing that he was "only human." Both Thomson and Branca suggested that they were never close friends, just old acquaintances, by way of an extraordinary event.

Trying to live down the hurt, Branca once told a cameraman that if he wanted a picture he should "take one of the guy with binoculars, who stole our signs that day. There's your picture!"

Indeed, following Thomson's homer, there had been some talk that the Giants had swiped Rube Walker's signals to Branca via an electrical apparatus in the center-field clubhouse. The message was then supposedly dispatched to the Giant dugout, as the operator pressed once for a fastball, twice for a breaking pitch, and so forth.

Thomson always angrily denied that he knew what pitch was coming. He challenged the man (presumably an ex-Giant) to "show some character and come out in the open and reveal yourself . . . there are always malcontents who want to kick up a fuss . . ."

If there was anything to this story, added Thomson, "Why didn't I hit the first one?" Durocher said that "if we had such signals Bobby would have murdered the first pitch, since it was right down the pipe."

When Durocher wasn't restlessly pacing back and forth in the third-base coach's box, thirty-seven-year-old Herman Franks, an ex-catcher with the Dodgers and Giants, was in charge there. (Franks later managed the Giants when they moved to San Francisco.)

Franks acknowledges that "everyone was out to steal signals if they could, and they usually did it from second base. Some guys were better at it than others." But he rejects the notion that there was a spy-in-the-sky in the Polo Grounds.

"Thomson himself always denied it," said Franks. "I don't know why they keep bringing it up, but if we were doing it, I didn't know a darn thing about it. You'd think I would have known because I always had a close relationship with Leo. I always told him just what I thought and he liked that, even when I disagreed with him. I don't remember discussing this stuff with him."

But some corroboration for Branca's original comment came years later from Sal Yvars. "We really shouldn't have won that thing," said the Giants' substitute catcher, "but we were helped for a month or more by knowing almost every pitch that was coming in. We stole signs pretty good, with the help of a telescope in center field. Leo had a reputation for that sort of thing and knew how to work it. Sometimes our guys even purposely looked bad on certain pitches, so they wouldn't give away the fact that we were getting the signs . . . but, hell, the Dodgers were getting our signs, too, to the point we had to change our signs almost every three innings. Dressen was pretty good at it, like Leo. It sort of balanced things out. It was no big deal."

Yvars never insisted that the sign-stealing actually went on during the last play-off game or when Thomson hit his homer, thus reducing the issue to an intriguing footnote in baseball history.

Whatever the truth, most of the Dodgers refused to blame the purloined signals or Branca for their grievous defeat. The generous Carl Erskine tried to put it in his own perspective. "Maybe you could say," he said with a laugh, "that when I was beaten in the season opener, there went the pennant! After all, we lost it by only one game, so that opener made all the difference."

Today Branca's license plate reads RB-13, which happily indicates that he isn't still haunted by the number he wore on October 3, 1951. He is a successful insurance salesman and the devoted chairman of BAT, which originally stood for Baseball Alumni Team but has recently been changed to Baseball Assistance Team. The organization, which includes Joe Garagiola, Joe Black, Larry Doby, and Rusty Staub, all former players, on its board, and non-player Frank Slocum, as its executive director, provides help to ball players who have fallen on hard times or have become ill and disabled. To date, BAT has aided over 150 players.

19

Where Were You When Thomson Connected?

THERE WERE SOME 34,000 people at the Polo Grounds on the afternoon of October 3, 1951. But since that day virtually millions have claimed they were there, choosing to park themselves at a point of history. It is natural that many people fantasize about this because they wish they had been there. And it is not surprising that so many *feel* they were there, for many identified, in those years, with the Dodgers of Robinson and Reese and the Giants of Mays and Durocher.

I feel I was there, too. But, as I have noted, I made the mistake of attending the *wrong* game the day before.

There are millions of others who recall that day and that game with such clarity and fondness (if they were Giant fans) and with such dismay (if they were Dodger fans) that it's as if they were talking about something that happened only yesterday.

Some of those with vivid memories were young at the time, some were old, some were famous—or would become famous. Some were in their homes, some in the streets of New York, others were in bars, others were working or were out of the country. But the common denominator among them is that they remember precisely where they were when Thomson's home run disappeared under the overhanging grandstand at 3:58 P.M.

Writer George Plimpton was a student at Cambridge University in England. He was playing bridge and keeping half an ear tuned to the game on Armed Forces Network, for he was an avid Giants fan.

"I literally went berserk when Thomson hit the homer," Plimpton said. "I threw the cards in the air, kicked the table, and kept yelling, 'He did it, he did it!' From that moment on, I was considered the American eccentric on campus. At the time my mother was passing through Grand Central Station in New York and noticed men jumping up and down. She always cited that incident to Russians as an example of American character, of the camaraderie of sports fans."

TV documentary producer Alvin Yudkoff, then an army lieutenant serving in Korea, was on his way to Supreme Military Headquarters in Tokyo.

"During the flight and on the jeep ride to the Dai Ichi building, Armed Forces Radio kept us up to date on the game. But at Headquarters no radio listening was allowed—after all, a war was going on. However, a signal detachment GI walked the hallways, Telex strip in hand, giving the update on the score. As a Giant fan, I had just about given up, when all of a sudden the GI started screaming about Thomson's home run," said Yudkoff.

"Everyone went nuts—soldiers, sailors, marines charging out of offices . . . somebody pushed open a window and shouted at GI's down below. Horns sounded, drivers and passengers pounded on each other. Military vehicles came to a halt. Suddenly, everyone was a Giant fan. I spoke some Japanese, so a few local-hires surrounded me. *Gomen nasai. Senso no awari?* Pardon me, is the war over? *Zannen*, I told them, it's a pity, but no. They nodded slightly, but didn't have the faintest idea of what was going on."

On that fateful fall day of 1951 Giant fan Knox Burger, who later became a literary agent, had the radio on full blast as he drove along a deserted road that traversed an expanse of marshy moor near Sparta, New Jersey. His wife and two-year-old daughter were passengers.

Suddenly, one of his tires went flat and he got out of the car to fix it. There wasn't a person, a house, even a tree in sight, in that eerie setting. But there were birds circling overhead.

"As I brandished my jack-handle in the air," Burger recalls, "Russ Hodges went into his 'home run call' and I began to scream along with him, causing every one of the red-winged blackbirds and herons to take immediate flight."

Stephen Jay Gould, professor of geology at Harvard, was a ten-year-old New Yorker and a devoted Giant fan in 1951. When Thomson hit the most famous home run in history, Professor Gould was home alone in his family's garden apartment in Fresh Meadows, Queens, after school, "glued to the tiny TV screen that my folks had just purchased, a family first." He says that he "was never so purely and deliriously happy in my life. . . . I think Bobby was pretty pleased, too, for he later said that he'd be a liar if he didn't admit that he'd cherish that moment 'til the day he died."

In Bogotá, Colombia, twenty-six-year-old Julie Adler, on the road selling ads for the *New York Times,* repeatedly called the U.S. Embassy to get the latest score. When someone informed him of the Giants' victory, he wasn't convinced they'd given him the correct information. "As a lifelong Giant fan," he said, "I couldn't believe such a wonderful thing had happened." (Today Adler owns the Canterbury Book Shop on Manhattan's Upper East Side.)

Bobby Thomson's fifty-seven-year-old mother had been watching the first few innings on television. But she turned it off when the strain became too much for her. When she went into the kitchen to prepare a Scotch dumpling, she heard excited shouting coming from carpenters working on a house nearby. When she heard them yell, "Bobby did it," she broke down and cried.

Jim Bouton, who became a big-league pitcher with the Yankees ten years later, had raced home from school in Rochelle Park, New Jersey, to watch the game on TV. He got his mother, who was ironing, to switch to the game. A few seconds later, Thomson connected. "The minute Stanky jumped on Durocher's back I ran fifteen blocks to a friend's house," said Bouton. "He was a Dodger fan, I was a Giant fan. I kept throwing pebbles at his window, but he never came out."

For Giant fans living in the enemy lair it was positively scary. One such person was Woody Allen, who was from Flatbush but secretly rooted for the Giants.

"I was delivering stationery on Wall Street," Allen remembers, "and I stopped to listen to the game at a newsstand. Everyone went bananas, handing out cigars to friends. I won about thirty dollars from a close cousin of mine, and I made him pay every nickel of it."

A former big-league shortstop, the late George "Specs" Toporcer, had become blind by 1951, but he listened to the game with great enthusiasm. "Yes, I *heard* Thomson's home run," he said, and there was no need for added emphasis on the verb to fully comprehend his message.

David Dinkins, now the mayor of New York City, was a young lawyer in 1951, living in Harlem, not far from the Polo Grounds. But he was a dyed-in-the-wool Dodger supporter, mainly "because of Jackie." He wasn't listening to the game, but the news reached him within minutes. "I figured everyone in New York knew about it," said Dinkins, "and some, like myself, were very sad."

The author and feminist Susan Brownmiller had parents who thought baseball was as bad an influence as comic books, so they forbade her to listen to the game. Her minor rebellion was to walk into the streets of Brooklyn, where radios blared from every window and storefront. "You could hear it everywhere you walked," she said. "Finally, came the crusher. I don't think I've paid attention to baseball since!"

Pete Hamill, the columnist and novelist, was a high school dropout working in a bank in Manhattan, where he sorted coins. "A guy in the bank had a small radio, which we listened to, even if we weren't supposed to. When Bobby hit it I was in shock because I'd been a Brooklyn fan since I was two. When I got home to Brooklyn I went to Rattigan's Bar, where big, grown men were in tears, getting wrecked, drunk. You'd have thought the roof had just blown off their house," he said.

Before he authored thirty-five books on baseball, Donald Honig lived near Jackson Heights, where most of his neighbors were insane Dodger fans, like himself. But there were a few Giant fans, too, and Honig expected they would needle him to death. So he decided to spread the phony word that he'd bet fifty bucks on the Giants "because I had a hunch that Newk couldn't beat Maglie. There I was going around telling these Giant fans I'd won dough betting on their team. But in my heart I was dying."

Another bettor on the game, actor Walter Matthau, put his money on the Dodgers. "I must have heard that maniac scream three hundred and fifty times on the radio that the Giants had won the pennant. That was forty years ago and I haven't listened to a game since!" he said.

Former President of the United States Richard M. Nixon was

then a United States senator from California. "I vividly recall it," he said. "In those days I was a Washington Senators fan, when they invariably wound up in the cellar. But when Thomson hit the homer, it almost made me a Giant fan."

When Frank Sinatra was given four choice seats for the October 3 game by his old buddy Durocher, he asked Jackie Gleason to join him. Also rounding out the party were FBI chief J. Edgar Hoover and restaurateur Toots Shor.

The four men drank heavily on the way to the Polo Grounds and continued to belt down beer during the game. "Comes the last of the ninth," Sinatra recalled, "the fans are going wild and Thomson comes to bat. Then Gleason throws up all over me! Here's one of the all-time games and I don't even get to see Bobby hit that homer. Only Gleason, a Brooklyn fan, would get sick at a time like that!"

But the real kicker to the story was that on the way home Gleason kept muttering that Sinatra should be thrown out of the car.

"The goddamn bum's smelling up the car," growled Gleason.

Far above Cayuga's waters, in Cornell's Phi Sigma Delta fraternity, Evan Janovic, a freshman, was pinned to the radio with several of his fraternity brothers. When Hodges started to scream about Thomson's homer, all of the young men—except a few Dodger fans—started screaming, too.

"You'd have thought everyone in the fraternity had just gotten A's on their final exams," said Janovic, now a paint-store entrepreneur in New York.

Dodger fan Gerald Green later wrote a novel entitled *To Brooklyn with Love,* but in 1951 he was working on NBC's "Today" show at 106th Street in Harlem. "There was a black-and-white TV set in a corner," he said, "and when Branca replaced Newcombe I turned to Reuven Frank, who became president of NBC News, and whispered conspiratorially, 'This guy throws home run balls.' A minute later I was proven right, unfortunately."

A Brooklyn boy who grew up to become Governor Nelson Rockefeller's press secretary, Leslie Slote, was at police headquarters on Centre Street, working as a reporter for the chief. "I walked down the street to a bar—what was a nice Jewish boy doing in such a place—and when Thomson lowered the boom, I aggravated in my heart. It was the worst day I had since Owen let Casey's pitch get away in 1941."

Writer Sidney Zion was a Yankee fan, really a DiMaggio fan, living in Passaic, New Jersey. A student at Penn, he was listening to the game with a group in Houston Hall. "In those days the Giants seemed to have lost some of their cachet—it used to be that all Jewish cab drivers rooted for them, as well as unemployed Broadway actors. Willie brought some of them back to the Giants. When Thomson hit it, I went crazy because I had a cousin, a Dodger fan, who I knew was going to throw up."

Larry King, now one of television and radio's most popular interviewers, remembers October 3 as "the second saddest day of my life." The saddest was the death of his father.

As an 18-year-old, he was listening in his Brooklyn apartment at 83rd Street in Bensonhurst (where Sandy Koufax also grew up) to Red Barber's radio account. When Barber's fateful words were pronounced over the airwaves, King felt "as if I had just died."

But King also remembers that Barber tried to put the episode into perspective by reminding people about how many young men were killed that same day in Korea. Branca will get over it, so will Dodger fans, said Barber.

"I knew that was all true," says King. "But it was still painful—and every time I looked at Danny Fried, a local Giant fan, I hated the sight of him!"

The National League's home run king that year, Ralph Kiner, was on his way to California to obtain a wedding license to marry Nancy Chaffee, the tennis player. "I watched Thomson do it on TV," he said, "and I knew it was one homer nobody would ever forget."

Jack Newfield, the newspaper columnist, was thirteen in 1951 and had just been bar mitzvahed. "When Dressen took out Newcombe, I put on my Hebrew prayer shawl and yarmulke and started reading my prayer book," he said. "But when Thomson hit it, I concluded that God may be good for long relief but not for short relief."

For those who were present at the Polo Grounds and didn't have to trust to TV or radio to certify that Thomson had, indeed, crushed the life out of the Dodgers, it was an unforgettable experience. In a masterpiece of poor timing, Charles Rollins, an advertising executive and Giants fan, left the game in the eighth inning.

"I sneaked off from work to go to the game," he said, "but with the Giants losing, I was disgusted. So I took the subway back to my office, where I'd left some work undone. When I saw all those screaming people watching TV sets in stores, I knew I'd done something horrible. I was angry at myself for my lack of faith. I was ashamed to admit I had left the game; to this day I feel guilty!"

Several of the New York Yankees, including Yogi Berra, Vic Raschi, and Allie Reynolds, went to the game together. Since the Yankees had already won the American League pennant, they were there on a busman's holiday, or, better yet, a holiday from Casey Stengel. They knew it would mean more money for them if the Giants took it, since the Polo Grounds seated more people than Ebbets Field. They left after the eighth inning to beat the crowd. It wasn't until they were on the road across the George Washington Bridge that they heard Thomson had banged a homer.

"All I remember is Russ Hodges going crazy," said Yogi.

Marvin Davis, now an oil multimillionaire, was sitting in a first-base box with his father, who was a friend of Durocher. "I remember standing there yelling and hollering," Davis said. "I couldn't believe it, and I couldn't stop screaming. For years I've watched replays of the homer—and it gets better each time I see it."

Jackie Robinson had left his house in St. Albans early that day for the ballpark. Rachel, his wife, left a bit later. During the season she saw almost all of the Dodger games at Ebbets Field. She had seen the first two play-off games and was eager to see the last one.

"Although the Dodgers had once been classified as perennial underdogs, it wasn't a label that Jackie and I liked because neither of us felt like victims. On that October day I had the feeling we'd transcend everything," she said. "When Thomson hit the homer, I was absolutely stunned. I felt so alone, while almost everyone around us went crazy. While Jackie watched to make sure that Thomson touched each base, I never saw him do it, since I was crying too hard. I couldn't see the field through my tears."

The former editor of *Manhattan Inc.*, Clay Felker, in 1951 was a statistician working in the press box with Russ Hodges. He had dined out a couple of times with Thomson for hamburgers and "felt in my bones" that Bobby was going to hit a homer. Just out of Duke, Felker wanted to get a job with *Life* magazine but hadn't been able to land there yet.

As soon as Thomson was elevated to herohood, *Life*'s editor asked Felker if he could get hold of the secret scouting report that

Andy High of the Dodgers had put together on the Yankees in anticipation of a Brooklyn win. Since the Dodgers were no longer in it, High didn't think it made any difference if Felker saw the report.

"The report really had only one newsworthy thing in it," said Felker. "It said that DiMaggio's arm was shot and that he could only make one good throw a game with it. The Yankees hated me for what I'd done and DiMaggio was so humiliated, he quit. Maybe you could say that Thomson's homer got me my job with *Life!*"

Charles Einstein, reporting on the game for International News Service from the upper grandstand press section directly behind home plate, had as good a seat as anyone in the park.

"I put some fresh paper into my typewriter, as did Bob Considine beside me, and we both began to work out our stories on the *Dodger* victory," he said. When the Giants staged their rally, Einstein and Considine stopped typing.

"I turned to Benny-the-puncher, our teletype operator, and said, 'If Thomson hits a homer, we'll flash and dictate.' There was no prescience in what I said. The flat fact was that the winning run was at the plate and there'd be no time to roll new paper into the typewriter and confect a new lead," Einstein said. "When Thomson hit it, I had no feel for how fast I reacted, for the fact was that in losing track of the ball, I had trained on Pafko instead and he knew it was gone before anybody . . ."

While so many people remembered so many facets, personal and otherwise, about October 3, 1951, ironically the two leading players of the drama came up short on one important detail.

Years after the event, Thomson was asked the name of the umpire who worked behind the plate that day.

"I don't recall," he said.

Branca was asked the same question. He didn't recall, either.

The umpire's name was Lou Jorda, obviously the forgotten man in baseball's most priceless moment.